CW00411417

booksonline

Read SAP PRESS online also

With booksonline we offer you online access to leading SAP experts'
knowledge. Whether you use it as a beneficial supplement or as an
alternative to the printed book – with booksonline you can:

- Access any book at any time
- Quickly look up and find what you need
- Compile your own SAP library

Your advantage as the reader of this book

Register your book on our website and obtain an exclusive and free test
access to its online version. You're convinced you like the online book?
Then you can purchase it at a preferential price!

And here's how to make use of your advantage

1. Visit www.sap-press.com
2. Click on the link for SAP PRESS booksonline
3. Enter your free trial license key
4. Test-drive your online book with full access for a limited time!

Your personal **license key** for your test
access including the preferential offer

sbja-ngk5-fv6z-hx38

Surviving an SAP® Audit

 **PRESS**

SAP PRESS is a joint initiative of SAP and Galileo Press. The know-how offered by SAP specialists combined with the expertise of the Galileo Press publishing house offers the reader expert books in the field. SAP PRESS features first-hand information and expert advice, and provides useful skills for professional decision-making.

SAP PRESS offers a variety of books on technical and business related topics for the SAP user. For further information, please visit our website: *www.sap-press.com*.

Arjun Krishnan and Balaji Kumar Alamanda
SOX Compliance with SAP Treasury and Risk Management
2009, 437 pp.
978-1-59229-200-4

Sabine Schöler and Olaf Zink
SAP Governance, Risk and Compliance
2009, 312 pp.
978-1-59229-191-5

Raj Behera
Cross-Enterprise Integration with SAP GRC Access Control
2009, 138 pp.
978-1-59229-250-9

Martin Ullmann
Maximizing SAP ERP Financials Accounts Payable
2009, 496 pp.
978-1-59229-198-4

Steve Biskie

Surviving an SAP® Audit

Bonn • Boston

Galileo Press is named after the Italian physicist, mathematician and philosopher Galileo Galilei (1564–1642). He is known as one of the founders of modern science and an advocate of our contemporary, heliocentric worldview. His words *Eppur se muove* (And yet it moves) have become legendary. The Galileo Press logo depicts Jupiter orbited by the four Galilean moons, which were discovered by Galileo in 1610.

Editor Stephen Solomon
Developmental Editor Kelly Grace Harris
Copyeditor Lori Newhouse
Cover Design Jill Winitzer
Photo Credit iStockphoto.com/mevens
Layout Design Vera Brauner
Production Editor Kelly O'Callaghan
Assistant Production Editor Graham Geary
Typesetting Publishers' Design and Production Services, Inc.
Printed and bound in Canada

ISBN 978-1-59229-253-0

© 2010 by Galileo Press Inc., Boston (MA)

1st Edition 2010

Library of Congress Cataloging-in-Publication Data
Biskie, Steve.
  Surviving an SAP audit / Steve Biskie.
    p. cm.
  Includes bibliographical references and index.
  ISBN-13: 978-1-59229-253-0 (alk. paper)
  ISBN-10: 1-59229-253-4 (alk. paper)
  1. SAP R/3. 2. Auditing — Computer programs. I. Title.
  HF5667.12.B57 2010
  657'.45028553 — dc22   2009045222

All rights reserved. Neither this publication nor any part of it may be copied or reproduced in any form or by any means or translated into another language, without the prior consent of Galileo Press GmbH, Rheinwerkallee 4, 53227 Bonn, Germany.

Galileo Press makes no warranties or representations with respect to the content hereof and specifically disclaims any implied warranties of merchantability or fitness for any particular purpose. Galileo Press assumes no responsibility for any errors that may appear in this publication.

"Galileo Press" and the Galileo Press logo are registered trademarks of Galileo Press GmbH, Bonn, Germany. SAP PRESS is an imprint of Galileo Press.

All of the screenshots and graphics reproduced in this book are subject to copyright © SAP AG, Dietmar-Hopp-Allee 16, 69190 Walldorf, Germany.

SAP, the SAP-Logo, mySAP, mySAP.com, mySAP Business Suite, SAP NetWeaver, SAP R/3, SAP R/2, SAP B2B, SAPtronic, SAPscript, SAP BW, SAP CRM, SAP Early Watch, SAP ArchiveLink, SAP GUI, SAP Business Workflow, SAP Business Engineer, SAP Business Navigator, SAP Business Framework, SAP Business Information Warehouse, SAP inter-enterprise solutions, SAP APO, AcceleratedSAP, InterSAP, SAPoffice, SAPfind, SAPfile, SAPtime, SAPmail, SAPaccess, SAP-EDI, R/3 Retail, Accelerated HR, Accelerated HiTech, Accelerated Consumer Products, ABAP, ABAP/4, ALE/WEB, Alloy, BAPI, Business Framework, BW Explorer, Duet, Enjoy-SAP, mySAP.com e-business platform, mySAP Enterprise Portals, RIVA, SAPPHIRE, TeamSAP, Webflow and SAP PRESS are registered or unregistered trademarks of SAP AG, Walldorf, Germany.

All other products mentioned in this book are registered or unregistered trademarks of their respective companies.

Contents at a Glance

Contents

"The art of war teaches us to rely not on the likelihood of the enemy's not coming, but on our own readiness to receive him; not on the chance of his not attacking, but rather on the fact that we have made our position unassailable." — Sun Tsu

Preface

Everybody hates audits. Audits consume valuable time and scarce resources, distract employees from critical tasks, and often occur when you have neither time nor energy to spare. Audits can breed a sense of mistrust, create an environment of conflict, and cause a high degree of stress. Individuals may feel they have let their teams down if they expose a potential problem when responding honestly to an auditor's inquiry. Managers may feel they have lost credibility in the eyes of senior management if decisions they made (or did not make) become audit concerns. Entire departments may feel like they have failed the company if a reportable condition results from a process for which they are responsible. And few audits have the potential to be more painful than an audit of your company's SAP system.

Fortunately, your experience can be different. Many common audit issues can be avoided. Knowing where these issues are and understanding common ways to deal with them can eliminate countless headaches. Being familiar with ways to think of and manage risk, whether in aggregate or specific to your area of responsibility, can help your business decisions pass audit scrutiny. Capturing certain information throughout the normal course of business and having it available for your auditor can save significant time during the audit. This book will share these insights and more.

This book is designed to help SAP project managers, administrators, and users understand typical audit requirements related to SAP and ultimately be better prepared for their next SAP-related audits. The early chapters will provide an overview of how auditors approach an SAP audit, discuss typical audit techniques, describe the common elements required for a well-controlled SAP infrastructure, and set the foundation for ensuring success in any type of SAP audit. The middle chapters will look at specific SAP components and related business processes in detail, outlining the most common audit objectives specific to those components. These chapters will go into more detail on specific SAP configuration elements, key reports and queries, and common mistakes. The final chapters will discuss audit issues when dealing with an SAP implementation or upgrade, and also take a look at the future of SAP auditing — examining in detail the use of automated audit tools, emerging "tricks" used by auditors to uncover problems, and the impact of continuous monitoring.

Why This Book is Important

A common statement among many auditors is that 90% of all audit findings can be applied to any organization. While the actual percentage may be arguable, the essence of this statement is true — organizations, regardless of location or industry, continue to make the same types of mistakes that lead to audit issues. In the fifteen years that I've been in audit and compliance-related positions, my own audit experience supports this statement as well. Very rarely did I encounter an issue at one organization that I had not already seen or heard about at another.

Why do organizations continue to make the same mistakes? I've come to believe that it's not the result of laziness, as I thought early in my career, but rather due to poor education and understanding. Organizations don't want to have the types of conditions that result in audit findings; in many cases, they simply don't know any better. These conditions exist because those being audited have never been trained on how to survive an audit.

Individuals who have chosen to be auditors can attest that learning to be an effective auditor can be time consuming. Most auditors, particularly those who begin their careers in professional accounting firms, will accumulate months of training hours in their first few years, combined with a tremendous amount of ongoing coaching and mentoring. They will immerse themselves in the concepts of risk, risk management, and control. Reaching an advanced level of competence requires years of formal development, often on top of advanced college degrees.

By contrast, a typical individual under audit scrutiny (also known as the *auditee*), has no formal audit, risk, or control training. His sole understanding of audit concerns comes from his limited experience in prior audits. It's no wonder that audit concerns are common across organizations. Auditors have been trained to look for specific things, while auditees are operating blindly — having never been educated on what areas can raise audit red flags, nor how these items can be best managed.

In an SAP environment, this knowledge gap has the potential to be disastrous. Some audit findings related to an SAP system may result in configuration changes that consume precious time and resources. Other audit findings might require costly re-work.

More challenging, however, is the fact that certain issues become increasingly difficult to correct the longer they go undetected — and some can be nearly impossible to resolve without a re-implementation. And while guidance exists for auditors on how to review SAP, little guidance exists for those being audited. Audit findings are common; and unfortunately, many could have been avoided.

This book is written for you: the SAP user, project manager, administrator, and other non-audit personnel. Rather than being written for auditors, this book is designed for those on the receiving end of an SAP audit. The goal of this book is to help you avoid many common audit findings and allow you to have better, more productive discussions with your auditors. As an outcome of this increased knowledge and understanding, you will hopefully foster better relationships with your auditors, experience a smoother audit process, have fewer audit findings, and maybe even surprise management with reduced audit costs. We can't promise that you will ever enjoy being audited, but if you happen to work for an organization where a portion of your bonus is tied to audit results (or lack thereof), perhaps this book can help you be rewarded for your efforts.

How to Use This Book

Like many books of this type, you will probably not need to read this book from cover to cover. Chapters 1 and 2 discuss typical audit techniques, review how auditors approach an SAP audit, describe the common elements required for a well-controlled SAP infrastructure, and set the foundation for ensuring success in any type of SAP audit. These chapters are likely to be beneficial for every non-audit reader of this text.

Chapter 3, while focused specifically on implementations and upgrades, provides an overall framework for considering risk, documenting decisions, and determining appropriate controls applicable to any component of SAP. This chapter provides a framework for thinking through potential audit issues and ensuring nothing significant gets missed when process decisions are being made.

Chapters 4 through 7 go into more detail on specific components of an SAP audit, and are most relevant to users of those components or staff involved in managing the relevant SAP component. These chapters walk through component-specific details that are likely to be important from an audit perspective, and can serve as a useful reference as processes related to these components are being considered for change.

While there are many possible ways to use this book, the specific way you progress through it's largely dependent on your role within your organization, and your specific involvement with your organization's SAP system.

SAP Project Managers

SAP project managers, or anyone responsible for managing the implementation or ongoing operation of an SAP system or component, should pay particular attention to Chapter 2, Overview of the Typical SAP Audit, to understand the areas of the SAP system that will likely be under the greatest scrutiny. Making sure that someone is assigned responsibility for, and understands the typical audit concerns within, each of the areas discussed in this chapter will greatly enhance audit success.

Chapter 3, SAP Implementations and Upgrades, will also be beneficial to SAP project managers, even if they are not currently experiencing either of these events. Application of thought processes and techniques discussed in this chapter can help any organization gain more confidence in the ability of their SAP system to withstand changing risks and business conditions. Incorporating these techniques into the daily decisions that accompany successful management of an SAP system should also have a positive operational impact — reducing the impact of user errors and ensuring management is aware of and has accepted any risk associated with key decisions.

An SAP project manager should also benefit from Chapter 9, Final Audit Preparations. By ensuring that the information outlined in this chapter is captured and documented in advance of an audit, an SAP project manager can minimize the time commitment required by his team once an audit starts. Additionally, this chapter can help reduce the impact of working with new auditors — ensuring that each audit is as efficient as possible.

SAP Basis, SAP Security, or other Technical SAP Administrators

Technical administrators, such as SAP Basis, SAP security, and similar functions should pay particular attention to Chapter 4 on SAP General Computer Controls. This chapter will review in detail the security and infrastructure-related issues that could be part of an SAP audit. This chapter will also review some of the more common audit issues in these areas and provide ways to avoid these common audit findings.

Those administrators who feel confident that they've addressed the basics may also find value in Chapter 8, SAP Audit Tricks and Tools. This chapter will review more advanced audit techniques and discuss how findings can be discovered in areas where SAP appears to be configured appropriately. This chapter will also outline specific queries that can be performed in SAP using tools within the application, as well as discuss specialized audit tools that could also prove valuable to an SAP administrator.

Business Analyst

A business analyst, often serving as the liaison between business users and those responsible for configuring and managing an SAP system, identifies and manages risks in an SAP system. Particular attention should be paid to Chapter 3, SAP Implementations and Upgrades, even if such an event is not in-process. Like an SAP project manager, a business analyst will find the concepts and techniques for thinking through risks and designing appropriate controls readily applicable to his daily decision-making activities.

Business analysts, depending on the functions they support, may also want to review Chapters 5 through 7, which explore the financial reporting, order-to-cash, and purchase-to-pay business cycles in detail. These chapters discuss specific process risks, SAP configuration parameters, and reports that support a well-managed process.

Chapter 8, SAP Audit Tricks and Tools, may also prove to be valuable, because some of the techniques shared can also be used by a business analyst to ensure processes are working as designed. Too often, business analysts fail to look beyond SAP system settings to validate that processes are working appropriately, and the techniques and tools discussed in this chapter can help them do just that.

SAP User

General SAP users will be primarily interested in Chapters 1 and 2 to obtain an overview of the audit function and typical SAP audit. During an audit, SAP users will often find themselves describing their interactions with SAP, answering questions posed by the auditor, and preparing information for the audit. Understanding the audit function, and specifically the typical SAP audit process, will help SAP users feel better prepared for this interaction. These chapters will also discuss how best to interact with the auditor to ensure responses are not misunderstood or results are not misinterpreted.

An SAP user may also be interested in Chapter 9, Final Audit Preparations. While not entirely relevant to an SAP user, information in this chapter can also shed some light on ways the user can prepare in advance for the audit, and ensure an efficient process.

Functional Business Manager

A functional business manager overseeing a process enabled by an SAP system will want to have a basic understanding of Chapters 2 and 3 to ensure that his staff is asking appropriate questions to design effective, auditable processes. If the manager oversees the financial reporting, order-to-cash, or purchase-to-pay processes, he will also find value in the detailed analyses of Chapters 5 through 7. Before an audit, a functional business manager should ensure that his team has addressed all of the considerations in Chapter 9, Final Audit Preparations.

Senior Management

A senior manager of a company running an SAP system should, at a minimum, have an understanding of the chapters in this book and ensure someone on his team is taking responsibility for the considerations identified therein. By understanding at a high level the primary activities involved in surviving an SAP audit and the preparations that can be taken in advance to prepare for the audit, senior management should hold their teams accountable for critical processes.

SAP Consultants

SAP consultants, particularly those involved in SAP implementations and upgrades, should understand in detail the processes described in Chapter 3, SAP Implementations and Upgrades. The best time to address potential audit issues is before an SAP system goes live; considering risks and controls during the implementation process are key parts of making this happen. Working through a structured process that will withstand even the most rigorous audit scrutiny is important when competing for clients.

Auditors

While this book is not explicitly intended for auditors, many auditors will likely find it valuable. Auditors new to reviewing SAP will get value from Chapter 2, Overview of the Typical SAP Audit, because it provides a comprehensive SAP review. Auditors who are dealing with a new SAP implementation or upgrade should review Chapter 3, SAP Implementations and Upgrades. For an auditor who has never been through an implementation process before, this chapter provides a good foundation for not only auditing a new SAP system but for dealing with implementations of any of the major enterprise resource planning (ERP) systems.

Auditors who are already comfortable working in an SAP environment may pick up some new ideas in Chapter 8, SAP Audit Tricks and Tools. While some of these may be second-hand, most auditors will likely find some useful tidbits in this section.

All auditors may also like Chapter 9, Final Audit Preparations. While this chapter is unlikely to provide new insights to their own activities, auditors may be interested in sharing certain concepts found in this section with their auditees to make the audit process more efficient.

Disclaimer

While I am an auditor, I am not your auditor. Opinions vary widely (even within the same audit firm) as to which areas of SAP are most critical from an audit perspective, and how to test them. Additionally, little comprehensive guidance exists in the public domain about SAP audits, risks, and controls. Large, external audit firms have internal guides that they are sometimes willing to share with their auditees; however, much of the focus of your SAP audit will depend on the specific auditor (and his management) responsible for the review.

Throughout the course of this book, I'll attempt to present a balanced, comprehensive overview of key audit issues in and around an SAP environment. Given the complexity of SAP and the number of configuration and customization options available, however, it will not be possible to discuss every potential audit concern. Entire books have been written just on SAP security, and security is only one part of a comprehensive SAP audit. As such, rather than attempt to be an all-inclusive reference, this book is intended to provide a good understanding of basic audit objectives, and allow you to apply this understanding to specific issues within your organization. Using this understanding as a starting point, determine with your auditor if the steps and techniques you plan to apply will also meet your auditor's objectives.

International Issues

While there are many similarities in audit practices worldwide, this book was written with primary emphasis on audit standards endorsed by the Institute of Internal Auditors and ISACA (formerly known as the Information Systems Audit and Control Association). While these are two of the more prevalent standard-setting bodies internationally, depending on the country in which you do business, the standards identified by these organizations may or may not be recognized.

If you operate in a country where the audit standards set by these two organizations are not recognized, the concepts outlined in the first two chapters of this book, which also carry through to the considerations described in later chapters, are largely universal. While specific audit practices may vary, the general principles that support these practices are fairly common. When you meet with your auditor to discuss what you've learned from this text, discuss where the standards in the countries your organization operates differ from the standards described in this book. While specific details may differ, the general concepts remain the same.

Not surprisingly, companies that operate in multiple countries or regions will likely find differences in regulatory requirements. When it comes to the approach for complying with these regulations (which is typically reviewed as part of an audit), organizations typically have multiple options. Understanding your own organization's strategy for dealing with multiple international regulations will help ensure the effort you spend on compliance is appropriate. Consider the following:

▶ **Most-restrictive approach**: Organizations taking the *most-restrictive* approach prefer that all operations comply with a single standard, the one associated with the most restrictive regulation. Even if a specific location is not within the jurisdiction of the regulation and, as such, does not technically need to comply, organizational policy dictates that if the regulation is applicable to one business unit, then all must comply. This is the most conservative approach, and helps to ensure that surprises do not occur by mandating a single, uniform policy across the organization. While this approach can be straightforward to manage, it can result in unnecessary costs.

▶ **As-required approach**: Organizations taking the *as-required* approach follow, in essence, the opposite practice of those following the most-restrictive approach. These organizations choose to mandate compliance only where local regulations demand. As such, processes in one location may differ from those in another. This approach is the most liberal, and is often seen as the least costly — incurring additional compliance costs only in those regions where required by law. The management effort associated with needing to be intimately familiar with — and construct separate processes for — local regulations, however, can chip away at the potential benefit.

▶ **Blended approach**: The *blended* approach is probably the most common for organizations operating in multiple regulatory jurisdictions. As the name implies, this approach to regulatory compliance combines elements of the most-restrictive approach with elements of the as-required approach. In essence, organizations using a blended approach determine on a regulation-by-regulation basis whether they will standardize compliance across the organization, or apply specific procedures to a limited entity.

For international organizations, the compliance effort is generally proportionate to the number of countries for which you operate. Regardless of the regulatory complexity, however, the principles outlined in this book will provide an appropriate foundation for compliance.

"You can discover what your enemy fears most by observing the means he uses to frighten you." — *Eric Hoffer*

1   Introduction

To survive an SAP audit, you must first understand the rules. Despite occasional appearances to the contrary, there is actually sound logic to the way auditors work. Once you understand the audit approach, and recognize what the audit is intended to achieve, you can be better prepared for audit success.

This chapter is the linchpin for everything we will discuss in this book — helping you understand the basic audit concepts that ultimately affect the nature, scope, timing, and requirements associated with an SAP audit. We provide an overview of the different types of auditors as well as different types of audits, both of which directly impact the nature and scope of your audit. We explain why auditors do what they do, and review techniques they may use during the course of their reviews. We also discuss ways of working with your auditor, including the types of discussions and negotiations that can influence the final content of the audit report. By the end of this chapter, you should have the knowledge required to work effectively with your auditor toward a positive audit outcome.

1.1   Audit Overview

We often think of audits, and auditors, with negative connotations. It may be hard to find the positive in certain types of audits, such as a personal tax audit, where the outcome may be discovering that an inaccurate calculation has resulted in an underpayment (and loads of penalties and interest). Sure, you may walk away with the knowledge required to avoid similar mistakes in the future, but the fines associated with the audit finding, however, cloud the benefits received. Jokes about auditors abound, and in many cases for good reason.

In a business context, however, audits can have tremendous value. We work hard in our organizations to ensure the accuracy and integrity of information and our business processes. We are proud of the increased efficiencies and control that SAP can provide, and an audit can turn skeptics into believers by independently demonstrating that we've met that objective. An audit can support the diligence and quality that we've put into our work as much as it can be an indictment of poor work. And if done well, an audit can provide valuable feedback and commentary that allows us to continuously improve our operations.

In their *International Professional Practices Framework*, the Institute of Internal Auditors (IIA), defines internal auditing as:

> *Internal auditing is an independent, objective assurance and consulting activity to add value and improve an organization's operations. It helps an organization accomplish its objectives by bringing a systematic, disciplined approach to evaluate and improve the effectiveness of risk management, control, and governance processes.*

While this definition is focused on internal auditing (a concept we'll discuss in the next section), it can broadly be applied to audits in general. Audits are fundamentally designed to improve processes. They do this by taking a fresh look at operations, and providing insight that may not be readily apparent to those who are close to the process. Audits are not about finding problems; they are about identifying opportunities for improvement. These opportunities may result from identified problems, but what drives the audit ultimately is the desire to make processes better.

Examples of High-Value Audit Findings

Depending on the area under review, a good audit can have measurable value. This value may come indirectly through process efficiencies or cost savings identified during the audit process. In other cases, an audit can have a direct and positive impact on the bottom line — finding revenue leakage or recoverable overpayments, for example. Because audit results can be sensitive and politically charged, results such as these often go unnoticed outside the audit community.

1.2　Types of Auditors

The common thread to any audit is the auditor. Auditors are bound by a set of rules, and those rules govern how an audit is conducted. To be effective at an SAP audit, therefore, you must first understand the characteristics that define those who are doing the auditing.

As discussed in the preceding section, the goal of the auditor is not to cause problems. Conversely, the goal of the auditor is to identify where potential problems *might occur* or *have occurred,* and communicate sufficient information to interested parties so that informed decisions can be made. Each of these interested parties may have different concerns relative to the process or system being audited. Thus, the nature and extent of the audit may take on different characteristics depending on the type of auditor involved. At a high level, auditors generally fall into one of two categories: *internal auditors* and *external auditors*. Both internal and external auditors may also be categorized into specific audit specialties, or disciplines. In this section, we discuss not only the category of auditor, but more importantly, the impact a specific type of auditor may have on your audit.

1.2.1　Internal Auditors

Internal audit is a function within an organization, and the goal of the internal auditor is to protect management and the board of directors. Internal audit departments may exist as the result of regulation in specific industries or market segments, or from desire by management to have an independent set of eyes within the organization. Most internal audit functions report to the audit committee of the company's board of directors, although many also have an administrative reporting relationship to the CFO. Internal auditors provide the board with valuable information about the company's operations that the board may not receive directly from management due to biases, lack of objectivity, or merely a desire by management to look good in the eyes of the board. As a result, the internal audit function provides a system of checks and balances so the board of directors can better assure that its directives and objectives are being carried out appropriately.

Internal auditors are employed by the organization; however, they may not always be part of the company's payroll. Smaller organizations in particular may choose to outsource the internal audit function to a third-party provider. Even larger organizations may choose to supplement an existing internal audit department's knowledge and skills, particularly in specialty areas like SAP auditing, through the use of outside resources — often called *co-sourcing*. Regardless of who ultimately pays a specific auditor's salary, an internal auditor is ultimately employed full time or on a contract basis by your organization.

Because an internal auditor reports to the board, internal audit reports are primarily viewed inside an organization. They are rarely distributed to external parties. This is an important distinction between internal auditors and the external auditors we'll discuss next.

1.2.2　External Auditors

When most people think of external auditors, they think of financial statement auditors, typically employed by large accounting firms that opine on the integrity of a public company's financial statements as part of the year-end financial reporting process. For purposes of this text, we'll refer to external auditors in the broader, more inclusive sense, consisting of the various types of auditors an organization may encounter who are not ultimately employed by an organization.

The most common type of external auditor is the financial statement auditor. In the United States, an accounting firm is paid by an organization being audited (creating a lack of pure independence, which arguably has resulted in some of the accounting scandals seen in recent years); however, the external auditor officially represents the interests of investors (e.g., company stockholders). External auditors may also represent banks and report on issues such as compliance with loan covenants. They may represent governmental agencies such as tax authorities and report on compliance with specific laws and regulations (these auditors are sometimes called *governmental auditors*). Certain industries, such as financial services, pharmaceuticals/chemicals, and utilities (to name a few) also have industry-specific auditors that report on compliance to a governing entity.

Depending on the nature of your business, you may also have external auditors who report to your customers. Customers may include right-to-audit clause in contracts, particularly related to services such as outsourced IT or HR/payroll functions. In this case, depending on the specifics of your contract with the customer, they may periodically send a team of their own auditors into your organization to review a specified function. For organizations that perform services-related functions for many companies, the customers' desire to periodically audit these service-related processes can become particularly burdensome (imagine if every one of your customers decided to send their own audit teams to audit your SAP processing). As a result, some companies may choose to hire independent audit firms to issue what is known as a *service audit report* (also known as a *SAS-70 report* in the United States). Depending on circumstances, this report may be used by customers to gain assurance as to the effectiveness of operations in lieu of having to send their own audit teams to perform independent audits.

While at times the external auditor's fees may be paid by the organization being audited (as in audits governed by certain regulatory agencies), the ultimate goal of an external auditor is to protect investors, customers, or other interested external parties. Similar to how an internal auditor provides the board with objective information that may not be received directly from management, external auditors provide these external parties with information and insights that may not be received directly from your organization.

During the audit, the external auditor may at times make observations that he reports to management as additional value-added services (e.g., suggestions for improving SAP observed while performing other audit procedures but not relevant to the context of the audit being performed). These recommendations, sometimes included in a document called a *management comment letter*, are typically for your organization only. Be aware, however, that no matter what type of external auditor is working with your organization, or what type of audit he is performing, one important fact remains constant: Reports from external auditors (when serving in an external audit capacity) are issued outside the walls of your organization.

External Auditor Providing Internal Audit Services

Organizations looking to outsource or co-source all or part of the internal audit department often look to firms that provide external audit services. An organization is typically restricted from outsourcing its internal audit function to the same firm it uses for the external financial statement audit; however, it's possible from such an arrangement that the co-sourced internal auditor working in an organization's internal audit department is also an external auditor for another organization. When this is the case, the reporting relationship and report distribution procedures follow the function that the auditor is performing, independent of the type of auditing the auditor in question typically performs. If the auditor is operating in an internal audit capacity, his report is for internal use even if that same auditor performs external audits for another organization.

Knowing the type of auditor you're working with, and how the resulting audit report will be distributed, is important whenever you're going through an audit. Audit findings are never desired, but audit findings from an external auditor can be particularly problematic. In the case of a financial statement audit, the final report may be issued to the public as a whole, and is thus accessible to anyone with access to public records (including your competitors). Financial statement audit findings can have an almost immediate negative effect on stock prices, and depending on the finding, can turn into a public relations disaster.

In the case of certain types of audits (such as those conducted by your financial institution or by a customer), the distribution of the audit report may be limited to specific organizations. Negative external audit findings can be problematic even if the final report is not issued for public consumption. Failure to comply with financial covenants could result in credit lines being dissolved. Failure to conform to customer service level agreements could result in the loss of a key customer. In essence, certain audit findings can haunt an organization for years.

While it's always important to work with your auditor to ensure that the issued report is relevant, factual, and fairly stated, the nature of the distribution of external audit reports makes this an even greater concern. Many auditees don't realize that they can work with an auditor to negotiate the specific wording and even the severity rating for audit findings. We'll discuss the process of negotiating with your auditor in Section 1.6.3, Negotiating Issues.

1.2.3 Specialty Auditors

In the same way that individuals within many organizations become specialists in certain functions, both internal and external auditors often specialize in different audit disciplines. A typical internal audit department, for example, may contain multiple specialists. Some auditors may focus on financials statements and specialized reporting (e.g., tax reporting). Other auditors may focus on operational efficiency. Some auditors may specialize in technology, whether from a general technology management viewpoint or a specific application or hardware viewpoint. Other auditors may focus on areas such as internal investigations and fraud.

Depending on how audits are conducted within your organization, you may be subject to multiple audits with different focuses. Many audit departments are moving toward more integrated audits, where multiple disciplines are combined into the same audit. This helps to save time and may reduce the "pain factor" of the auditee as well.

Some auditors, typically *IT auditors*, specialize in auditing technology. IT auditors may specialize in a subset of technology, such as networks or firewalls, although many IT auditors are technology generalists. Of course, there are also auditors who specialize in auditing specific computer-based applications such as SAP. In general, the more specialized the auditor, the higher the internal/external cost, and thus the more likely your organization may not be able to afford their services full time. For this reason, organizations seeking a thorough audit of their SAP systems often turn to outside organizations or individuals for assistance.

Are They Capable of Auditing SAP?

If you've ever been through an SAP audit, you've probably at some point been frustrated by how little your auditor actually knows about SAP. You may be convinced that you know more about the system than he ever will. The reality is that you probably should. You know how SAP is being used in your organization, you probably have an understanding of how it was configured during the implementation, and you very likely use SAP more frequently than your auditor.

If you're lucky, you may find yourself with an auditor who at least understands the basics of SAP. In many situations, however, you may find that your auditor has little to no SAP experience at all. Perhaps he is merely following a standard SAP audit checklist, and, as such, try to apply questions and tests to your organization that are, in your mind, clearly irrelevant. Maybe his SAP experience is in a different component and he has only cursory knowledge of configuration options of the component you work with. The sad truth is that those auditing SAP typically have limited SAP audit experience.

This situation is unlikely to change in the near future. Given the complexity of SAP, the number of configurable variations, the differences between components and industry-specific functions, and even the ongoing improvements released by SAP, expecting any auditor to be an SAP expert in all aspects of your system is unrealistic. Even if an "expert" team of auditors could be brought together, few organizations are willing to make the financial investment it would take bring them in

Fortunately, any good auditor (even one with limited exposure to SAP or other ERP systems) can lead an effective assessment of SAP. The key lies in the auditor understanding how SAP works in a general sense, and in learning to apply traditional audit techniques to the SAP system and related processes. A good auditor is like a good private investigator — he knows what questions to ask! A good auditor learns to ask key questions from the SAP experts already housed within your organization, and adapt the audit appropriately based on their responses and independent validation of data within your SAP system.

1.3   Categories of Audit Objectives

Not only are there many different types of auditors and audits, there are also many different types of audit objectives. A commonly used internal control framework known as *COSO* (Based on a 1992 report from the Committee of Sponsoring Organizations of the Treadway Committee, www.coso.org), classifies an organization's objectives as falling into one of four categories:

▶ Strategic: High-level goals, aligned with and supporting the company's mission.

▶ Operational: Effective and efficient use of resources including safeguarding of assets.

▶ Reporting: Reliability of public reporting.

  Compliance: Compliance with applicable laws and regulations.

Using this same categorization for audit objectives, Table 1.1 presents a small sampling of audit objectives that may involve an assessment of SAP.

Category	Example Audit Type	Example Audit Objective	Typical Audience
Strategic	Software Selection	Verify that the software selection process follows standard practices and is conducted in a well-controlled manner	Board
	Organizational Planning	Assess the effectiveness of processes for ensuring the SAP system will continue to meet the organization's objectives over time	Management
Operational	Implementation Review	Review the SAP implementation process and ensure project status reports and other communications are an appropriate reflection of reality	Management
	SAP Processing	Ensure SAP administration and operational processes effectively support service level agreements	Customers
	Maintenance and Change Control	Verify that all changes to SAP are appropriately designed, approved, configured, tested, and reviewed prior to movement into the production instance	Management Customers Regulators
Reporting	Financial Reporting	Assess the reliability of SAP data used to generate financial reports	Investors
	Tax	Assess the ability of SAP tax calculations and reporting sufficiently for accurately represent tax liabilities	Management Regulators
Compliance	Sarbanes-Oxley	Ensure SAP and related manual controls and processes effectively support Sarbanes-Oxley compliance	Investors
	Privacy	Review compliance with HIPAA, GLBA, and other privacy-related regulations and ensure access to key SAP transactions and data is appropriately restricted	Management Regulators

Table 1.1 Audit Objectives

Clearly, the sheer possibilities related to what an SAP audit could be looking to achieve are countless. Because the audience of various reviews is different, the auditor performing the review may also be different. Considering the number of different types of auditors and the wide variety of potential audit objectives, is it any wonder that some audits of SAP look different from others?

Every SAP audit has the potential to be different, and, as such, you must prepare comprehensively in advance of an audit. Depending on the context of the specific review, something considered important for one audit may be completely ignored in another. For example, consider an audit of SAP security. For Sarbanes-Oxley purposes, the security assessment will likely focus on segregation of duties, and also examine a few basic SAP security administration and management controls. If the SAP security review is part of a HIPAA privacy audit, however, heavy emphasis will be placed on the ability to users to see sensitive information, the encryption of that data both in SAP and in transit between SAP and other systems, and the processes for identifying protected information. Two different audits, two different approaches and concerns relative to SAP security.

Key Observation
Success (or failure) in a prior SAP audit has little bearing on success or failure in a future SAP audit, particularly if those audits serve different purposes.

1.4   Auditing Principles and Considerations

Before we discuss the SAP audit, understand some key audit principles. These principles often require auditors to behave in ways that seem foreign to those new to the audit process. Understanding these principles will better prepare you for and react to the audit.

1.4.1   Independence

Professional standards require that the audit function be independent. Audit independence generally refers to reporting relationships and communication channels, and grants the auditor department (through the chief audit executive) unrestricted access to the board via direct communication channels. Given that an auditor performs an important and sometimes sensitive function on behalf of the board, audit independence is intended to ensure that the auditor is free from interference in all aspects of his work.

The concept of audit independence can sometimes come up during an audit. For example, the internal audit department may determine that an SAP audit is warranted. In particular, he may wish to review new functionality currently being configured, and he may wish to conduct this review just before a critical deadline. The SAP project manager may object to the time or the scope of the review, even to the extent of escalating the concern all the way up to the CIO. Even in an organization where the CIO has a higher title than the head of the audit group, the CIO dictates neither when the audit occurs nor what information the auditors have access to. Most auditors would be reasonable with such a request, and if the request did not affect the ability to meet the audit objectives, the auditor would likely change at least the timing of the review. If the auditor, for whatever reason (perhaps because of a time-sensitive confidential analysis at the request of the board), does not want to change the audit, he is in no means obligated to do what the CIO requests — or even what the CEO requests, for that matter. Audit independence grants them that right, and professional audit standards require that they disclose formally in writing if that right has ever been violated.

Another common issue that can raise concerns about audit independence relates to system and data access. An organization's SAP system can house a lot of sensitive data, and companies spend significant effort securing that data. Because of the nature of audit work, normal data access restrictions do not apply to the audit function. Most auditors are allowed access to any data they request (although the head of the audit department may put restrictions on who in his department can request what type of data), and preventing that access can raise scope restriction concerns that have to be reported to the board. Internal audit departments operate in different ways, however, so it's always good to understand the way that yours works.

The actual specifics detailing the work that your internal audit department is charged with performing, the nature of the information they have access to, and other similar information can be found in what is known as the *audit charter*. This formal document, approved by the board and mandated by the IIA's International Professional Practices Framework, will describe the purpose, responsibility, and authority of your organization's internal audit department. If you're interested in learning more about the internal audit function in your organization, most auditors are happy to share the audit charter with you, and in many organizations, it's even posted on the company's website for investors and other interested parties to see.

1.4.2 Objectivity

Professional standards also require each auditor to be objective. Objectivity is different from independence in that, whereas independence is associated with the audit function in general, objectivity is applied to the individual auditor. An auditor working objectively is free from bias, and is impartial in fact and appearance to the outcome. His professional judgment is not influenced or impaired, and he is not in a position where his judgment could be influenced or impaired. This last point is important, because a conflict of interest can arise even if no unethical or improper behavior occurs, and conflicts of interest that could affect objectivity must be fully disclosed.

Seeking auditor advice during an SAP system implementation or upgrade is common practice, and can benefit the implementation team by helping ensure audit concerns are addressed before the system goes live. Auditor involvement as part of an implementation has the potential to impair the auditor's objectivity, however, so auditors are often cautious as to their specific levels of involvement. As an example, an auditor who was involved in designing or configuring the SAP ERP Financials solution of SAP would be prohibited from later auditing that solution (because his involvement in the implementation would make it appear as if he was not objective, even if he attempted to audit in an objective and unbiased way).

> **The Institute of Internal Auditors, Practice Advisory 1120-1**
>
> "The internal auditor's objectivity is not adversely affected when the auditor recommends standards of control for systems or reviews procedures before they are implemented. The auditor's objectivity is considered to be impaired if the auditor designs, installs, drafts procedures for, or operates such systems."

If you're looking for advice or assistance and your auditor is hesitant to provide it over concerns related to objectivity, work to an acceptable scenario. What you may be specifically asking for may compromise the auditor's objectivity if he provided it; however, often, you can work to a compromise where you still gain insight but not in a manner that compromises objectivity. Coming to such a compromise can be a win for your organization. Rather than asking the auditor to give you the answer, consider using him as a coach or a mentor — providing you with structure and tips on considerations for your decision-making process but not making the decision for you.

1.4.3 Professional Skepticism

Have you ever felt that, no matter how many years you've worked with an auditor and how forthcoming you've been in previous audits, you just can't seem to get the auditor to trust what you're saying? The reality is, per audit standards, he cannot trust you without additional evidence. Auditors are required to operate in a mode of professional skepticism, which is a manner of operating objectively. Professional skepticism suggests that an auditor cannot merely trust what someone says, and must gather additional evidence to support (or potentially refute) what he has been told. Specifically, auditors must operate in a neutral position on a scale where trust is at one end and distrust is at another (Figure 1.1). As such, the auditor's beliefs (or the beliefs of the individuals who the auditor is working with) should not influence the outcome. Audit evidence must stand on its own and support the conclusions of the audit.

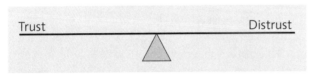

Figure 1.1 Professional Skepticism Requires Being Neutral

This standard may initially seem harsh, but we've seen first-hand how lack of professional skepticism can have a serious impact on an organization. A number of years ago, there was a company that practically revered one particular employee for his ability to reconcile SAP General Ledger accounts during period-end. This individual typically had the fewest number of outstanding reconciling items and comparatively very few dollars outstanding at any given point in time. In fact, management began looking to this person to coach others in how to effectively reconcile SAP. It wasn't until after an audit, however, that this person's true success mechanism was revealed — once the reconciliation was "close enough" (relative to the overall account balance, which was a very sizeable number), he merely created a journal entry to clear out the remaining items. In essence, this "SAP reconciling superstar" only appeared good on the surface.

You may wonder from this example how professional skepticism is relevant, because the problem was caught during an audit. In this case, professional skepticism was used during the audit, which is why the individual's actions were detected. Where professional skepticism failed was as part of the management's review processes. The issue persisted for years, despite processes that should have detected the problem. Managers were supposed to review every reconciliation to ensure completeness and accuracy. Unfortunately, this individual's manager was not operating in a neutral position on the professional skepticism scale — in essence, trusting the integrity of the employee's ongoing work based on results that appeared reasonable in the past. As a result of this lapse, the organization lost a sizeable amount of money, a large effort was required to go back through history and clean up the mess, and management was left looking foolish. We encourage every manager (not just those in audit) to apply professional skepticism in his work as well. Review the work of your SAP developers, periodically assess the accuracy of your SAP security setup and maintenance processes, determine whether those reviewing SAP exception reports are following through on identified items appropriately — whatever the role, spend some time validating your own assumptions about performance.

If We Can't Trust Our Employees, Who Can We Trust?

We're not suggesting that you completely distrust every employee. Professional skepticism is not about distrust — it's about neutrality. Clearly, you should be spending more effort reviewing the work of those employees who have proven to be inaccurate, incomplete, or otherwise problematic. Newly trained employees may also warrant more attention than seasoned employees. We are merely suggesting that you do not wholly ignore your most trusted staff and rely on faith in their continued performance. While you may choose not to review everything they do, you may consider periodically, for a selection of their work, examining what they have done to ensure that your trust in their performance is still based on reality and not on a historic perception that is no longer accurate.

1.4.4 Evidence

The concept of evidence proves to be problematic in many organizations. For audit purposes, evidence must stand on its own — meaning that a second independent auditor looking at the same information would come to similar conclusions regarding the test results. To some extent, evidence requirements are part of the topic of professional skepticism discussed previously.

In the early years following the U.S. Sarbanes-Oxley Act, some companies were shocked when their external auditors issued significant deficiencies (a type of statement that appeared in public reports) merely because the companies were unable to show evidence of signed documents — even though they performed related reviews. Some auditors went a step further by declaring "if you can't prove it, it didn't happen." Obviously, this is a little extreme, but the reality is this: If you don't have sufficient evidence to prove it, an auditor cannot independently attest that it happened. Thus, "lack of sufficient evidence" during an SAP audit becomes an audit issue itself. Beyond resulting in the auditor being unable to attest to the adequacy of audit results, lack of evidence also begs the question of how management can be assured that processes are working as intended. If, as in the example from the section above, management is merely relying on employees to perform as expected, this can raise broader audit concerns around the effectiveness of the control environment that management has established. In short, evidence should exist that processes are operating as management intends — both for audit as well as for management.

Electronic Evidence

Many people, particularly those in IT, dislike the "paperwork factor" often associated with evidence. The reality is that evidence can also take the form of electronic evidence. The key with effective electronic evidence is in having appropriate controls, assuring that (1) the "who" (e.g, originator, approver) is the person we believe; (2) the evidence hasn't been changed or modified in any way from its original state; (3) the data contained cannot be wholly or partially removed; and (4) the evidence can be appropriately associated with what it is being used to prove. Of course, the other key to effective evidence is being able to find and retrieve it when you need to — hence, sometimes it may be easier to maintain hardcopy documents in readily-accessible files unless strong electronic document management procedures are in place.

1.5 Understanding the Audit

Now that you understand some of the common audit principles, it's time to look at several common audit techniques and processes.

1.5.1 Risk-Based Auditing

The scope of many audits is often determined by applying a *risk-based* approach. There are many different approaches and techniques of risk-based auditing, but fundamentally it's a technique for focusing more attention on organization-specific risks with a higher likelihood and/or impact than other risks (Figure 1.2). Using an SAP example, an insurance company using SAP Treasury and Risk Management applicationas well as SAP Project Management services may find that significantly more attention is placed on SAP Treasury and Risk Management, with potentially little-to-no attention on SAP Project Management. This makes sense, because the risks in an insurance company typically center more on cash and the tracing and flow of money than on projects. Conversely, a company whose primary business is construction may find their SAP audit having the exact opposite focus.

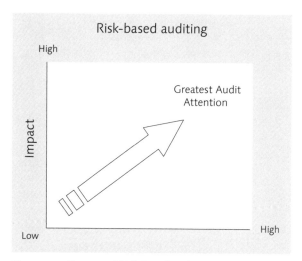

Figure 1.2 Essence of Risk-Based Auditing

1.5.2 Internal Controls

A concept related to risk is that of control. When dealing with an audit, or, even more broadly, the entire field of governance, risk, and compliance, the words *internal control* or simply *control* are used frequently. We've used the term several times in this chapter already. There are a number of different definitions for this term.

COSO, a framework mentioned in Section 1.3, Categories of Audit Objectives, suggests that: *"Internal control is broadly defined as a process, effected by an entity's board of directors, management and other personnel, designed to provide reasonable assurance regarding the achievement of objectives in the following categories: 1. Effectiveness and efficiency of operations, 2. Reliability of financial reporting, and 3. Compliance with applicable laws and regulations."*

The Institute of Internal Auditors defines a control as: *"Any action taken by management, the board, and other parties to manage risk and increase the likelihood that established objectives and goals will be achieved. Management plans, organizes, and directs the performance of sufficient actions to provide reasonable assurance that objectives and goals will be achieved."*

ISACA defines internal control as: *"The policies, plans and procedures, and organisational structures designed to provide reasonable assurance that business objectives will be achieved and undesired events will be prevented or detected and corrected."*

> **A Simpler Definition of Internal Control**
>
> A control is a process or activity designed to prevent "bad things" from happening, or to detect these things within a sufficient time to stop unacceptable damage from happening.

While this definition is concise, the specific words are important. Understanding the concept of internal controls is absolutely essential to understanding the audit process, and preparing yourself for an eventual audit. Let's look at each component of this definition separately.

"A Process or Activity"

A control is active, not passive. Something specific is occurring, and that something may be as simple as a single action, or as complex as a multi-step *process*. The focus on the action in this definition is important — without action, a control does not exist.

Let's look at a specific example. SAP contains numerous exception reports that allow users to review the results of processing and follow up on potential issues, such as the report showing goods invoiced but not yet received (RM07MSAL). The mere existence of this report is not a control. The control comes when someone reviews the report and determines what type of action to take on the information in it.

By this same definition, policies and procedures are not controls (despite being referenced in many texts, and even one of the definitions above, as being such). It's the *communication* of those policies and procedures in a way that the recipient understands their responsibilities and can take appropriate action, and the *enforcement* of the policies and procedures that are the controls. The evidence as to the effectiveness of these controls (in this case, the communication and enforcement separately) is indirectly demonstrated by the right action being taken when that policy or procedure needs to be applied.

"Designed"

A control must be intentional. Because it's intentional, a control is *designed* with a specific purpose in mind. Accident does not make a control. The control, rather, comes from thoughtful consideration of the processes or activities needed to mitigate a risk, and the effective construct of those processes and activities to do just that.

Imagine that a purchasing clerk is entering contract details (for a contract that has already been initiated) into SAP and mis-keys the price on one of the line items. If the vendor associated with this particular purchase order (PO) is set up in SAP as an ERS (Evaluated Receipts Settlement) vendor, the vendor invoice will not be compared to the PO and thus the common three-way match control will not detect this mistake. Now imagine that another employee catches the mistake before the organization pays the vendor. Obviously, the fact that the mistake has been caught and corrected is a good thing. But is this the result of a control?

If the employee who found the mistake in this case did so by accident, perhaps inadvertently finding the pricing difference while he was looking into something else, then the activity that exposed the problem would likely not be considered a control. If, however, the employee who detected the issue did so as part of his designated responsibilities (perhaps he was part of a quality assurance function), then it would be the result of a control.

"Prevent or Detect"

Controls tend to fall into two categories: those that stop a potential problem from occurring, and those that allow problems to be identified if they have occurred. These are often known as *preventive* and *detective* controls, respectively. Some auditors may also refer to a class of controls known as *corrective controls*, which fix an identified error after it has occurred and before it results in harm. Corrective controls typically rely on detective procedures, however, so for the sake of this text, we will consider detective and corrective controls to be the same.

SAP security is an example of a preventive control. Thinking of this in terms of the action required for a control to exist, the fact that "Upon login, SAP verifies that the user ID is valid and that an appropriate password has been entered for that user ID before the user is granted access to the system" is a preventive control. SAP security prevents a user who does not have a valid ID/password combination from logging into an SAP system, which is designed to ensure that only authorized individuals can process transactions using SAP.

A manager reviewing the RM07MSAL report (where an invoice has been received but corresponding goods have not been received) and investigating outstanding items is an example of a detective control. If the review occurs when it's scheduled, it's likely to detect payments that have been made or are about to be made when contract terms have not been fulfilled.

"Bad Things"

Controls are not intended to, nor could they ever, prevent (or detect) every possible unintended situation. Effective control design balances the cost of the control with the benefit of that control. A situation can be less than perfect but still not be *bad*. Controls in the context of this definition are those controls that are designed well — focused not on every condition that is less than perfect but on those where the impact has the potential to be harmful in a magnitude that is not desired. The definition of this exact point is a judgment call.

Using one of the examples used earlier, let's say that the purchasing clerk who mis-keyed a price on the PO was off by $1. Is that "bad," and should a control be designed to prevent or detect this type of occurrence? It all depends on the organization. If the purchasing clerk is a buyer for the retailer Dollar Tree, and the PO is for a large quantity of goods being purchased for ultimate sale for under $1, then the situation is clearly "bad" and one for which a control should be in place. If, however, they are the buyer for an aircraft manufacturer and the item in question is a multi-million dollar part, then it makes little sense (unless required by contract or regulation) to design a control to detect an amount so miniscule when compared to the overall purchase.

"Sufficient Time to Stop"

Detective controls occur after-the-fact, and thus it's important to understand the time frame at which the detection is likely to occur. The value of detection is limited if by the time the problem is identified, significant harm has occurred to the business. For a detective control to be effective, problems identified from the process must be both stopped from future recurrence, and fundamentally resolved. The specific time frame associated with the phrase *sufficient time* depends on your organization and the specific risk being addressed.

Continuing on with our example of a mis-keyed price on a PO, the ideal timing on the quality assurance process would ensure that the incorrect payment amount is not paid against that PO. In the previous example, the contract had already been executed and thus what was keyed into SAP would not affect what we legally owe the vendor, so some organizations may also allow the detection window to extend beyond payment but within sufficient time reasonable to still expect to recover the funds from the vendor. In a more typical situation where the issuance of the PO to the vendor may create a contractual obligation, we'd likely want the detective control to occur in time to stop the incorrect PO from being sent.

"Unacceptable Damage"

The notion of damage or harm caused to the organization is also tied in to the analysis of the timeframe before which detective controls should catch a problem. Damage could be direct (such as payments exceeding contracted rates where an employee chose to make a purchase outside the normal purchasing process), or indirect (such as loss of customer goodwill, which could eventually result in future revenue loss). Like the discussion regarding "bad things," *unacceptable damage* recognizes that there is a level of harm that may not be desired but which still has not reached the level of being unacceptable. Detective controls do not need to stop all damage, but they should certainly be designed to ensure that if the organization is harmed that the level of harm does not exceed a reasonable threshold.

Internal Controls are Everywhere

Every organization has internal controls, and you deal with these controls frequently (even if you don't recognize them as such). Edit checks configured within SAP to prevent erroneous input are one example of internal controls. Other examples of internal controls include processes designed to prevent duplicate payments, procedures to ensure the confidentiality of pricing/purchasing arrangements, management reviews of SAP exception reports that facilitate the identification and investigation of potential problems, and training and education programs designed to reduce the likelihood of user error.

1.5.3 Thinking Like an Auditor

Learning to *think like an auditor* is actually one of the best things you can do to prepare for, and ultimately survive, an SAP audit. You may think your auditor is cynical and pessimistic, but in reality there is simple logic behind most audit concerns. The key lies in continuously asking "What could go wrong?," taking that answer, and asking, "And then what could go wrong?" Considering risk-based auditing, you would then gauge the impact/likelihood of the event/issue to determine whether this warrants attention and investigation (not every audit is risk-based, however, so at times your SAP auditor may be concerned with issues that do not seem likely or impactful). For the items deemed important enough to warrant further consideration, you would then think through "Given that this could go wrong, what do we do to prevent it from happening, or detect it in a timely fashion if it does?"

The issues that can cause problems in an organization fall into several common buckets, so you may see audit objectives centered on themes such as validity, accuracy, completeness, timeliness, relevance, and recording. Asking your "What could go wrong" questions in the context of these categories can be particularly helpful in ensuring you've appropriately addressed all the risks in your SAP system.

▶ What could result in a payroll adjustment in SAP being invalid?

▶ What could result in checks cut from SAP having inaccurate amounts?

▶ What could result in the information we use to calculate liabilities being incomplete?

▶ What could cause goods receipts to not be entered into SAP and processed in a timely fashion?

▶ What could result in the information used to determine write-offs being irrelevant?

▶ What could result in sales being recorded in the wrong period?

As mentioned above, for each of these questions, you would then list possible causes and the impact/likelihood of occurrence for your organization. Taking the question "What could cause goods receipts to not be entered into SAP and processed in a timely fashion?," a partial list of potential causes and their impact might include:

1. Goods were received in the warehouse but not entered into SAP within the 24-hour corporate policy standard (high likelihood, low impact for parts; moderate likelihood, high impact for equipment).

2. The receipts file transmitted nightly from warehouses not running SAP was not received (low likelihood, moderate impact).

3. The receipts file transmitted nightly from warehouses not running SAP was not processed in SAP (low likelihood, moderate impact).

4. Third parties who receive and store goods on behalf of the company to not submit file for processing within corporate guidelines (high likelihood, low impact).

Lastly, you should have sufficient processes to ensure these potential causes are either prevented, or detected in a timely fashion if they occur. These processes may differ by type or category. Taking the first potential cause, you might have:

▶ For goods of type X: RFID tags automatically update SAP inventory records upon receipt into the warehouse (preventative).

▶ For all goods (both type X and not-X): All employees whose job responsibilities include entering or transmitting goods receipt information are required to periodically (at least once per year) sign off on compliance with receiving policies, which dictate that all receipts must be entered into SAP within 24 hours.

▶ For all goods (both type X and not-X): Every week, managers review reports of invoiced items that have not been received, and investigate items that have been outstanding for more than "Z" days (detective).

▶ For all goods (both type X and not-X): Physical inventories are performed quarterly and inventory adjustments are made in SAP based on actual physical count (detective).

Of course, just being able to list processes that detect/prevent is not enough. Show that these processes would prevent errors above a cumulative magnitude that would cause key stakeholder (management, supplier, investor, etc.) concern, or detect such problems in sufficient time to correct them before uncorrected errors would cause stakeholder concern. In the example above, you primarily rely upon detective controls for goods receipts that are not of type-X (although there is a preventative control listed, it's fairly weak — all organizations have periodic employee performance problems). Determine whether these controls are sufficient to reduce the level of overall risk to one that is acceptable. Upon evaluation, you may need to increase the frequency of certain controls, or add additional controls. We'll discuss the principles of designing effective controls in SAP in Chapter 3.

1.5.4 Applying Audit Investigative Techniques

The audit process can be compared, in some ways, to the scientific process. In science, you have a theory that you work to prove. The audit investigative process is similar. The controls (each of the items identified that could prevent or detect the potential problem from occurring) can be considered management's theories. The auditor attempts to gather evidence to prove (or in many cases, disprove) management's view as to the effectiveness and reliability of these controls.

Related to these controls, the auditor looks both at the design (if it's operating as intended, would it sufficiently mitigate risk to the desired level), and subsequently the operation (now that he's comfortable with the design of the control, can he determine whether it's performing as intended) of the control. Throughout the process, the auditor is gathering evidence to support the conclusion.

> **Note**
>
> Different from the scientific process, the auditor is not looking to prove absolutely. Most audits operate in a way to statistically target a 95% confidence level.

There are generally four different types of evidence that auditors gather during the course of their SAP reviews. In order of reliance, the first is *corroborative inquiry*, which ensures that the people interviewed (formally or in casual conversation) during the audit share the same belief. The second is *observation*, in which the auditor observes whether the intended process is occurring consistently based on how he sees people or systems performing their required actions. The third is *direct examination of evidence*, in which the auditor looks for other indications (such as paper trails or details within electronic transaction records) to further validate the consistency and integrity of the process. The final type of evidence is *re-performance*, in which the auditor independently performs all or part of the action (review, calculation, data extraction, etc.) and compares their result of evidence to what actually occurred. Auditors often perform a combination of these techniques to increase the level of assurance.

Knowing these evidence-gathering techniques can be useful as you prepare for your own SAP audit. We discussed how auditors are attempting to prove or disprove management's theories, and there is certainly no reason why you can't (or shouldn't) do the same in advance of your own audit. Let's talk about how each of these techniques could be applied to investigate one of the controls we identified in the example earlier — that every week, managers review reports of invoiced items that have not been received and investigate items that have been outstanding for more than "Z" days.

Corroborative Inquiry Example Tests

Discuss the process with the managers who are responsible for reviewing the invoiced-not-received report in SAP. Determine how frequently they are reviewing the report. Determine whether actions taken as a result of the review are appropriate, and who else (e.g., receiving dock employees, vendors, etc.) are involved in those actions. Assess based on their description of the process and the report whether they are following company policy.

Have discussions with the "who else" involved in the actions above to determine how frequently they have been contacted, and assess whether this is appropriate given the frequency of items appearing on the report.

Observation Example Tests

Ask to watch the manager review the report. Observe that he selects appropriate items for follow-up. Also, observe how readily he navigates to the correct report in SAP, and that he appears familiar with the report's contents.

If possible during the course of the review, observe other instances where the manager is reviewing the report (when he is not aware that you're observing).

Direct Examination of Evidence Example Tests

Review for report sign-off, tickmarks, or other evidence of review on any available hard copies of the report. Review emails sent to other parties for follow-up or meeting minutes with issues resulting from the review. If security settings allow, review in SAP the last date the manager executed the SAP transaction that calls the report, and determine whether it's consistent with how frequently he should be reviewing the report (e.g., using RBE – Reverse Business Engineering in versions prior to 4.6).

Re-Performance Example Tests

At various dates, review the SAP report of goods invoiced but not received and determine which items, based on policy guidelines, should have follow-up. For these items, follow these same evidence-gathering techniques to determine if appropriate follow-up occurred (e.g., discuss with receiving dock employees, look for supporting emails, etc.).

Be objective and use professional skepticism when performing these and similar tests in your own SAP environment. If you can get in the habit of thinking like an auditor and applying audit techniques to your everyday processes, you can significantly reduce the pain and duration of your SAP audits.

1.6   Audit Reporting

The result of the audit is, of course, the *audit report*. The audit report is the culmination of the entire audit process. Interestingly enough, while the audit report is typically discussed singularly, the final audit documentation typically includes numerous reports. We'll discuss these in this section.

The audit reporting process can be specific to the type of audit or the category of auditor preparing the report. Talk to your auditor about the nature of the report and the reporting process that will be used in your SAP audit.

> **The Tone of the Typical Audit Report**
>
> As discussed earlier in this chapter, a common audit objective is to find opportunities for improvement. The report from such an audit is likely to appear negative. To recommend opportunities for improvement, the auditor must identify real or potential problems in the current system, and present them so the need for change is obvious to the reader. While some auditors may do so out of courtesy, it's typically not the auditors job to identify those things that are going well.

1.6.1   Reporting Process

The audit report typically goes through a series of stages before release. The auditor often draws some preliminary conclusions early in the audit process, and, depending on your role in the audit, may share those with you in advance of report creation. Once the auditor begins to document findings, preliminary findings and issues are often shared with management over the area being audited. At this point, you can influence, to a limited extent, the content of the report.

1.6.2 Responding to Preliminary Audit Issues

If an auditor has made you aware of preliminary issues or concerns that may appear in the report, you've been offered an opportunity. Your auditor will typically solicit your feedback. Depending on the time spent on report development, there could be several iterations of report drafts. You auditor will (almost always) adjust facts or representations if they are inaccurate or misleading. The auditor will typically also add commentary, if you've provided it, on what is being done with the issue. As such, it's useful to understand how your feedback will be used and when the final report will be issued. If you know, for example, that the auditor discovered a configuration problem with an SAP setting, let the auditor know it's been fixed so that he can include that information in the report as well. You'll also typically be asked to respond to each of the issues with information about what will be done to resolve the problem.

1.6.3 Negotiating Issues

The audit reporting process can at times be contentious, but it's important for you to be diligent as the report is being drafted. In Sections 1.4.1, Independence, and 1.4.2, Objectivity, we discussed how the auditor must express his professional opinion without undue influence. Many auditees believe that, as a result, little can be done if there is disagreement on issues. In reality, there are at least three items you may be able to influence.

▶ **Facts**. These are the most straightforward part of an audit report. If you find yourself in disagreement with your auditor, separate facts from opinion and make sure the facts are accurate. Provide the auditor with details related to the facts you believe to be accurate — it's possible the auditor received outdated or incomplete information.

▶ **Risks**. The risk related to the audit issue is one of the most common points of disagreement. The auditor may believe that the issue exposes the organization to a large amount of risk, and you may believe it to be otherwise. While the assessment of risk is a very subjective process and entails a great deal of professional judgment, the basis of risk should be a set of facts. If you have facts to support your differing assessment of risk, show the factual evidence to the auditor and discuss why you believe it impacts the risk. The auditor may not have been provided with all the information you have, and as such may be basing his opinion of risk on an incomplete set of facts.

▸ **Cause**. Depending on the nature of the audit in question, the auditor may also be asked to document the cause of the issue identified. Usually, the auditor will work with you or your team to understand what happened, but if the audit process was rushed, it's possible the analysis was not as thorough as it could have been. Similar to what we discuss with risks above, provide the auditor with facts that support your conclusion about the cause. Auditors are allowed, and encouraged, to adjust their reports if new facts emerge — it's only when opinions are cited as the basis for adjustment that auditor independence and objectivity can be compromised.

Sometimes, even after negotiation and presentation of your side of the issue, you and your auditor may not reach a consensus. If this is the case, you can request that your auditor document your position in his report. The auditor is not obligated to do so, but many will take this step to ensure the final report is balanced and the reader has sufficient information to draw his own conclusions.

1.6.4   Report Distribution

The final report is typically a combination of multiple reports. You as the auditee will usually get a copy of the report, as well as the specific detail supporting the audit findings. For example, if the report indicates that the auditor found 25 terminated employees who still had access to SAP, you would typically be provided with the names of those 25 employees so you can clean up the issue with user access.

In addition to your report, a copy of the report will also typically be presented to the head of the department or division, sometimes in a summarized fashion. Given the scope of most organization's usage of SAP, it's not uncommon for an SAP audit report to make it up to your CIO and the CFO. This is why it's important, as previously discussed, to work closely with your auditor to ensure all facts are correct.

> **Reporting to the Board**
>
> Internal audit departments, as previously mentioned, typically report to the audit committee of the board of directors. Depending on the desire of the board, however, the audit committee may not see every detail of every audit report. In many organizations, the head of the internal audit department will summarize the audits performed during the period and report to the board only those audit issues corresponding to the highest organizational risk.

1.6.5 Management Response and Follow-Up

If the audit report for your SAP audit contained findings, you'll typically be charged with making sure the corresponding issues have been resolved. When finalizing the audit report, you likely provided your auditor with a *management response*, describing how and when each of the issues will be addressed. Follow through on what you've indicated as the result. Depending on the nature of the audit and the audit findings, your auditor may periodically check in with you, and may even perform some additional focused testing to independently verify that the issue has been resolved. If for some reason you determine after audit report issuance that the way you intended to resolve the issue is no longer practical, keeping your auditor informed of your new plans and rationale will make the post-audit process easier for everyone.

It's Not My Responsibility!

Often after an SAP audit, certain employees, such as SAP project managers or administrators, may feel they've been blamed for things that are not their responsibility. The audit report is not about blame, nor is it about you. The audit report is about issues and opportunities for improvement, and likely covers the entire SAP system, which includes areas that are end-user and manager responsibilities.

1.7 Rules of Engagement

Now that you understand the audit process better, a few additional tips will help you get through your SAP audit smoothly.

1.7.1 Understanding the Audit Objective

By now, you recognize that your upcoming SAP audit could be different from your last, and both of these could be different from those at another organization. As soon as you learn that your SAP system is being audited, determine the objectives, scope, and timing of the audit. Many auditors will provide an audit kickoff memo that will detail this information, although, like everything we discussed, this depends on your specific audit. Talk to your auditor well before he comes on-site, so you have a clear understanding of what will be required and when you'll be required to provide it.

1.7.2 Working with the Auditor

Auditors sometimes get a bad rap. Some of it's deserved, and some is not. Just remember that your auditor is a person, he has a job to do, and the quicker he gets it done, the sooner he will be out of your hair. Treat your auditor with respect, and you'll typically get respect in return. Make his life and the completion of his tasks easy. Provide him with what he needs when he requests it, and eliminate any road-blocks that could get in the way of his progress. The sooner he completes his audit, the earlier you'll be able to get back to focusing on your own work.

1.7.3 Establishing the Audit Environment

Have an audit-ready environment set up and ready for your auditor when he arrives. This may include having space available near the SAP team where the auditor can work, enable IDs within SAP that the auditor may use for the review, update and reconcile a non-production environment for certain types of audit testing, and other similar activities.

1.7.4 Do's and Don'ts

In addition to making sure your SAP system is ready for the audit, prepare your own employees for the audit as well. Your interest in this book is a great start, and provides you with some great ideas and tips for your employees. We recommend, at a minimum, that you provide your employees with a list of do's and don'ts for working with the auditor.

▶ Do answer all auditor questions openly and honestly.

▶ Don't speculate on the answer to a question if you do not know the answer.

▶ Do direct the auditor to the right team member if you're not in the best position to answer a question.

▶ Don't joke about things that may not be happening.

▶ Do take time to research and provide the right information.

▶ Don't provide more information than the auditor asks.

▶ Do clarify what the auditor is looking for if you do not understand.

▶ Don't take pointed audit questions as an indication you've done anything wrong.

At a minimum, having such a list can help spark a valuable discussion within your team, and ensure that everyone understands and is prepared for the upcoming review.

1.8 Summary

In this chapter, we discussed auditors and the audit process. We shared some of the principals that an auditor must follow, and provided a few tips on ways to think like an auditor that can help you ready your SAP system well in advance of any audit.

We also walked through the audit reporting process, and suggested ways to ensure the accuracy of reported audit findings. You should have a better understanding of why auditors do what they do, and the things you can do to make the audit process easier.

In the next chapter, we'll look at the SAP audit process, including the primary areas typically reviewed. We'll also share a few common problems that exist in many organizations, and the things you can do to alleviate audit concerns.

A person who never made a mistake never tried anything new.
— Albert Einstein

2   Overview of the Typical SAP Audit

Now that you've learned some key auditing fundamentals from Chapter 1, it's time to talk about the typical SAP audit. This chapter will give you a sense of the structure, in broad terms, of how an auditor constructs a review of SAP. We'll also detail the first area an auditor will often examine (primarily applicable to companies going through an SAP implementation or major upgrade). We'll touch briefly on each of the remaining components of an SAP audit (covering these in more detail in subsequent chapters). Lastly, we'll describe some of the high-level issues that are often common findings from an SAP audit, and what you can do to avoid them. By the end of this chapter, you should understand the fundamental building blocks of an SAP audit, and be prepared to begin structuring your readiness appropriately.

2.1   Timing for the SAP Audit

An SAP audit can occur at a variety of intervals, and both when it occurs and how much time passes between audits are often subject to a number of factors. Audit budget and resource availability is one constraint, particularly for internal audit departments, and can heavily influence when and how much time the auditor will be able to spend and at what points during the SAP life cycle the audit will occur. Management's relationship with an audit can also play a part, because often management wishes to avoid potential issues down-the-road, and thus desires to include audit as a consultant to the implementation, to provide advice and guidance. Probably the biggest factor, however, will be how well your own internal audit department has evolved over the years as systems have become a more important part of your business.

> ### A Brief History of SAP Auditing
>
> As recently as a decade ago, it was common for many auditors to "audit around the system." An auditor would, in essence, treat the application system as a "black box." Rather than audit the system, they would reconcile what came out of the system (through reports or other data feeds) to what went into the system (based on data entry documents). General theory was that if the outputs could be reconciled to the inputs, then the system must be working as intended.
>
> The introduction and rapid adoption of SAP and other ERP systems by organizations has resulted in a fundamental change to the audit process. While many auditors are still adjusting to the process, it's no longer acceptable (or in many cases even possible) to audit around the system. SAP has eliminated the need for data entry clerks to process paper. Organizations can now conduct their entire business electronically. Additionally, improved management reporting and dashboarding has reduced, if not eliminated, the massive print centers that many organizations required to produce the hardcopy reports that management used to run daily operations.
>
> As auditors began recognizing the need to audit within the system, the next question became one of timing. Auditors have historically only been concerned with business operations as they exist in practice, and because the work involved in implementing SAP did not affect the daily operations of the organization until it cut over from its old system, many audit shops chose to continue reviewing existing processes and ignore SAP until after go-live. Even those audit departments that recognized the value of assessing a system before go-live were challenged — early adopters of the major ERP packages often found themselves dealing with three- to four-year implementations, and many auditors chose not to insert themselves and potentially slow down an already protracted process.
>
> Today, more so than ever before, auditors involve themselves with the SAP team early and build an ongoing relationship. SAP audits typically start before the implementation, and audits then become an ongoing part of the SAP-enabled business.

An SAP audit typically occurs in at least one of three distinct time frames. If the audit occurs prior to SAP (or a specific SAP component under review) going live in your production environment, that audit is typically termed a *pre-implementation review*. An audit occurring after go-live is often termed a *post-implementation review*. And after SAP has been in running in production for a period of time and become stable, ongoing SAP *operational reviews* are common. Each of these three reviews provide unique value to management, and thus in a well-run organization you'd typically be subject to all of them.

2.1.1 Pre-Implementation Review

The *pre-implementation review* is a proactive audit, and is often more of a consulting effort than a traditional audit. The goal of the pre-implementation review is to ensure that before your organization goes live with SAP, appropriate controls and procedures mitigate the most relevant and impactful risks. A pre-implementation review can be extremely valuable, because problems and potential issues after go-live can be time consuming and costly to fix.

Historically, this type of review has been uncommon, but over the last decade, it has become more common. Pre-implementation reviews allow decisions to be changed and corrected before the related process design has been completed, and often in advance of SAP configuration. Our own experience has taught us that an SAP pre-implementation review can provide some of the most valuable recommendations that an organization will receive.

2.1.2 Post-Implementation Review

An auditor will typically perform a *post-implementation review* shortly after SAP go-live, and often before business processes have stabilized. The goal of the post-implementation review is to identify issues that are affecting the business and allow them to be corrected before they snowball. The integrated nature of ERP systems makes this type of assessment important, because undetected mistakes or errors related to SAP configuration or master data can affect every transaction that SAP processes.

Post-implementation reviews are fairly common in the audit community. Auditing after the implementation is easy compared to the pre-implementation review, because the latter must account for the numerous moving parts and changing decisions that are typical of most implementation processes. If not also paired with a pre-implementation review, however, the post-implementation review is convenient only to the auditor, not the organization. While it may at first seem nice to not have to deal with audit distractions during the implementation, a significant audit finding requiring re-work of a component just deployed can quickly turn a short-term benefit into a headache.

2.1.3 Ongoing SAP Operations Review

After the SAP system has operated in production for awhile, and the organization has adapted to the change, further audits become part of traditional, *ongoing* operations audits. The goal of the ongoing SAP operations review is to ensure that processes and controls remain sound over time. Most organizations go through significant amounts of change as time passes, whether as the result of management and employee turnover, changes to the business environment, or just natural business evolution. Over time, processes and configuration settings that were once sound begin to diminish in value. For example, the tolerance levels and settings configured within SAP become outdated — applicable to what the business was then, instead of what the business is now. As a result, periodic ongoing audits of SAP help ensure that the business adapts to changing conditions and risks.

The time after an implementation at which an audit transforms from a post-implementation review to an ongoing SAP operations review is difficult to pinpoint. For some organizations, the post-implementation review may be within a few weeks of go-live. For others, it may be months after the implementation. Given the natural adjustment period that organizations face when going through major change initiatives, the difference in the value of findings can be dramatic. By the time an operational review finds a potential issue, assuming it's the type of issue that has been ongoing and could have been detected earlier, the organization is likely to incur significant costs and effort to resolve it. Habits become hard to break, and once new processes have been ingrained into the way employees naturally work with SAP, they become hard to change. If you have recently completed an SAP implementation and have had neither a pre-implementation review nor a post-implementation review, request an audit shortly so you have the opportunity to resolve potential issues.

2.2 The Building Blocks of an SAP Audit

You can probably speculate that, given the different types of auditors and different types of audits that we discussed in Chapter 1, the concept of a "typical SAP audit" is a misnomer. There are at least as many different approaches to auditing SAP as there are audit firms, and even individual auditors within the major audit firms often have different ways of approaching a review. As such, coming up with a single depiction of an SAP audit valid across all scenarios can be challenging.

We discussed in Chapter 1 that, despite differences in auditors and the types of reviews they perform, there are some fundamental characteristics common to the audit process. Most audits focus on risk, with a general sense that those areas of risk have the greatest likelihood and the potential for the highest impact are more critical to assess than those with a low likelihood/impact assessment. Auditors use this concept of risk when planning an audit. Areas of a process that can have a more pervasive or damaging impact on the end-result are prioritized above those that are not. Given this and other areas of commonality, we can now begin to sketch a structure for a "typical" SAP audit.

Broadly, a robust SAP audit will generally touch on four main categories of processes, and a fifth category if implementation or major upgrade is underway or has recently occurred. These are:

- SAP-enabled business processes
- Component-specific configuration

- ▶ SAP Basis settings and security
- ▶ General computer controls (GCC)
- ▶ Project management (of the implementation process, for organizations where this is applicable)

Figure 2.1: Building Blocks of an SAP Audit, represents these categories pictorially.

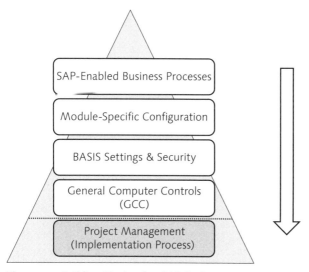

Figure 2.1 Building Blocks of an SAP Audit

The diagram above is shaped like a pyramid, and there is an arrow pointing from the top of the pyramid to the bottom. This representation illustrates another core reality of auditing — control dependence. We discussed the concept of internal control in Chapter 1. Control dependence recognizes that in order for a control to be reliable, we must also ensure that other processes that support that control are also reliable. For example, the control that states, "upon login, SAP ensures that the user enters a valid user ID and password combination before they can proceed," is a common preventive control in SAP. To rely on that control, there are other processes that must also be well controlled. The processes for both approving initial access and for terminating access when a user leaves the organization, for example, must be deemed reliable before we can even consider the role of SAP. The pyramid shape shows that the strength of the controls at the lower level of the pyramid provides the foundation for reliance at higher levels of the pyramid. The arrow depicts the order upon which the auditor will typically base their reliance.

The pyramid also prioritizes audit work when time and other resources are scarce. In a perfect world, your auditor could fully validate every control setting and process within SAP. Given the complexity of SAP and the number of possible settings, however, this is a practical impossibility. As such, an auditor charged with assessing a business process supported by SAP may actually spend more time examining the process areas that provide the foundation for this business process than he does within the specific process. If evidence can show that the right people are involved in SAP-related decisions, sufficient testing occurs over all changes, an overall control mindset pervades the organization, and similar control foundation-related elements exist, then the auditor can have greater comfort that the specific details of the process are also done well without examining each of them exhaustively.

Applying the Pyramid to SAP Authorization Limits

Let's apply the concept illustrated by the pyramid in Figure 2.1: Building Blocks of an SAP Audit to a real-life scenario. Consider a control within the financial reporting process that involves CFO review of large-dollar transactions before posting. Let's assume that SAP authorization limits combined with workflow is used to enable this control. Accounting staff are assigned authorization limits related to the transactions they can post in SAP, and any journal entry exceeding that limit is sent via workflow to the CFO for approval and posting.

To assess the reliability of this control, the auditor must consider whether configuration settings within the Financial Accounting component support the process as defined. If, for example, authorization limits have been configured but these limits are outdated based on current company policy, then the auditor questions the reliability of the primary control.

Assuming that Financial Accounting configuration settings are deemed appropriate to support the control, the auditor must next consider SAP Basis settings and security. If SAP security settings have been ineffectively configured to allow weak passwords and authentication processes (e.g., low number of characters required for passwords, no forced password changes, no automatic account locking from invalid password attempts, etc.), the auditor may question the integrity of the authorization process. While SAP may require that the user ID associated with the CFO approves these high-value postings, weak security controls can cause questions to be raised as to whether it was the CFO actually logged into the ID when the approval occurred.

If the auditor is comfortable with SAP Basis settings and SAP security, they would then look to the general computer controls surrounding SAP. If the process for making system changes to SAP is weak, perhaps allowing changes to go through without sufficient testing or authorization, then the auditor could become concerned that the settings reviewed may not be reliable — exposing the risk that those settings were changed right before the review, or may be changed immediately after.

The auditor would continue this logic if the organization were going through an implementation.

As we've mentioned before, however, the scope of your audit may vary based on the specific audit objectives. Additionally, it's common that components of this pyramid are assessed at separate items, and thus the effort during your specific audit may appear out of skew.

Thinking of the components of an SAP audit as building blocks of a pyramid is an oversimplification. The audit process is complex, and a lot goes into planning appropriate audit procedures. The depiction does, however, generally represent how an auditor may think of the process for auditing SAP. In general, the auditor must consider the reliability of controls that the primary control depends, and adjusts the scope and depth of the SAP audit accordingly based on his findings. It's also possible that the auditor may discover that the foundation for reliance is so weak that controls assurance at higher levels simply cannot be provided. To use a simple analogy, there's no point for the auditor to spend time checking the deadbolt on the door if the back door is wide open.

Let's look at each of these areas in more detail.

2.2.1 Project Management (Implementations and Upgrades)

The *project management* category is concerned broadly with ensuring that SAP meetsing the needs of your business, and includes the selection, implementation, and upgrading of SAP and related components. This category does not include ongoing maintenance and development (which is part of the general computer control category), and focuses exclusively on SAP implementations and upgrades.

> **Note**
>
> For ease of reference, we'll subsequently refer to both implementations and upgrades as "implementations," unless a specific difference exists.

Because the actual implementation for most organizations is an infrequent event, this category is shaded in the diagram in Figure 2.1. Project management as part of a comprehensive SAP audit typically only occurs during, or shortly after, the implementation.

The project management category is primarily concerned with your *process* for managing the implementation and making decisions related to how to configure SAP and how to construct your business processes around SAP. This category is more about strategy, management, and execution than about SAP or IT specifically. While your final decisions are important, the more critical concern with a project management review is how you arrive at these decisions. A few examples of audit questions related to project management include:

▶ Who are you including in the decision-making process?

▶ Is appropriate information available and sufficient time spent understanding issues and their potential implications before decisions are made?

▶ How are open issues (where decisions have yet to be made) being tracked and managed?

▶ Is upper management receiving appropriate information, and is it in sufficient time to make effective decisions?

▶ How are you determining appropriate tolerance levels for SAP configured controls, and after such decisions, how do you ensure these make it into the final SAP configuration?

▶ How will you determine whether you are ready to go live with SAP or the new SAP component?

While these questions are a small subset of the questions that an auditor concerned with project management will ask, you can begin to see a pattern. These questions are less tactical and more strategic in nature. They focus on process over outcome. Another way to think about this category is that it's concerned with the things you do to ensure that SAP works well for your organization, both today and in the future. The reason this is important to the auditor is simple. If the auditor can gain comfort in the way that decisions are made and that the process for managing the overall SAP implementation is sound, then the auditor has more assurance that the actual outcome of those decisions is also appropriate.

Taking a specific example, SAP contains literally thousands of potential configuration settings. These configuration settings all support effective business processes, and may either be component-specific or SAP Basis and security-related on the SAP audit building blocks pyramid. While it's possible that an auditor could look at each of these settings and ensure that your organization has configured them appropriately for your business situation, such an audit is highly impractical. An audit like this could take months, if not years, to complete. A more effective audit would likely gain assurance that the process for determining configuration settings is sound, and also examine some of the more high-risk settings to determine if they are appropriate (and support the auditor's conclusions on the project management process). If so, the auditor might likely conclude that the combination of a sound project management process combined with the effective configuration of higher-risk configuration settings make the risk of SAP configuration problems low. Of course, in this same example, if the auditor concluded that the project management process was ineffective, he may need to do more thorough testing of specific configuration settings to draw an effective conclusion on the reliability of SAP (and in some cases could even conclude that the project management process is so unreliable that examining specific settings is unnecessary and that the SAP system in question is fundamentally unreliable).

We'll examine the project management audit category in more detail later in this chapter.

Project Management vs. General Computer Controls

Some auditors consider the project management audit as we've described it to be part of the general computer controls (GCC) audit, and the IT audit frameworks, which reference GCCs, support this. Our experience suggests, however, that it's easier to explain the two separately when discussing SAP audits. Project management in this vein is primarily an infrequent event. After the initial SAP implementation, an organization typically does not undergo another for several years. The administration, maintenance, and development processes that are part of GCCs, however, are ongoing processes and become ingrained within the daily operations of an organization. Thinking of these two categories separately allows the auditor, and the auditee, to recognize the different nature of these two functions and their relative risks.

2.2.2 General Computer Controls

General computer controls GCCs refer to a category of controls common to the information systems auditing profession, and reflects a standard set of higher-level controls that should be in place to support the effective operation of any system (SAP included). While this category of controls is not specific to SAP, these controls ultimately support the SAP application and are thus relevant to the context of an SAP audit. GCCs are applicable to *any* organization using computers and computer software to run core business processes. Thus, every organization using SAP is subject to the GCCs category.

Similar to the way that project management controls provide the foundation for audit reliance, GCCs also set the stage for relying on SAP and SAP-supported business processes. Whereas the project management category is focused on the decisions during the initial implementation, GCCs are focused on ongoing management processes and business procedures that support SAP once it operates in the production environment. The controls included within general controls apply to categories of hardware and software applications (or sometimes every system managed by IT), and are generally not specific to SAP. During a GCCs review, the auditor is asking questions such as:

▸ Does the information systems department have sufficient skills and resources to effectively accomplish their duties?

▸ How is access to systems (in general) granted and controlled?

▸ Where systems pass information to each other, how does the organization ensure the complete and accurate transfer of information?

▸ How are processing problems and system errors detected and resolved?

▸ Who has the ability to update information within key databases directly, and how are these capabilities controlled and monitored?

▸ What processes and procedures ensure that users are effectively authenticated to systems?

▸ What prevents unauthorized changes from being made to applications?

▸ If system processing is interrupted for any reason, would the organization be able to effectively recover in a reasonable time frame?

Consistent with our description, none of these questions are concerned with SAP specifically. During an SAP audit, these questions would identify controls that ultimately support SAP processing. If the answer to a question depends on a category of applications within the organization that does not include SAP, the auditor would primarily be interested in the answers related to the SAP system.

To understand the importance of GCCs, consider an instance where SAP receives information from another system for processing. Perhaps this is a check clearing file from your bank fed to SAP for automatic bank reconciliation. In this example, we'll consider the situation where, for whatever reason, SAP is not interfacing directly with your banking system data. Rather, check clearing information is downloaded from the bank and placed in an area on your network to be later picked up by SAP during nightly processing. At the point that this file is picked up by SAP, processing integrity results from controls within SAP. Prior to it being picked up by SAP, however, GCCs regulate the integrity of the information. For example, if the process for downloading the file from the bank is not well controlled, then it's possible that SAP picks up an incomplete set of information (and then completely processes that incomplete information). Additionally, if network security is not sufficient to regulate access to the file before it's loaded by SAP, it's possible that changes could be made (perhaps as the result of someone trying to hide a fraud), and thus inaccurate information would be fed to SAP. While SAP would accurately process the information it receives, because the data was inaccurate or incomplete, the results of SAP processing would be inaccurate or incomplete. Thus, these GCCs, fully outside the auspices of the SAP application, directly affect the results of SAP processing.

GCCs in Practice

IT auditors have focused on GCCs as a core part of their audit procedures. Drawing a direct link to how a weakness in GCCs results in a significant risk to the organization, however, can be somewhat challenging. Regulations like the Sarbanes-Oxley Act in the United States have forced more focus on quantifying potential risk, and as a result, the primary governing bodies for auditors have issued more guidance as to the effect that GCCs have on organizational risk and the impact that specific audit findings have on the organization. General consensus suggests that a single weakness in GCCs can certainly be problematic, but when combined with other weaknesses, an auditor may discover during the course of a review, the combination of shortcomings can have serious consequences.

You may be thinking at this point that the controls in this category are outside of your responsibility, and that they're generally outside of the control of anyone in the "SAP department." Given the effect that these controls and related processes have on the reliability of SAP processing, however, the auditor cannot overlook this category. As such, your effectiveness at surviving an SAP audit will be dependent on processes for which others in your organization are responsible. We'll discuss GCCs in more detail in Chapter 4.

2.2.3 SAP Basis Settings and Security

As we explore the building blocks of an SAP audit, we now get to the first category of processes and controls that are SAP specific. Once an auditor has determined that project management controls are sufficient (where relevant as part of an implementation) and that the GCCs supporting SAP are also appropriate, he is then ready to tackle SAP. The first area of interest involves SAP Basis settings, which broadly affect component-independent processes, as well as SAP security settings and administration. The *SAP Basis settings and security* portion of the audit is important for the auditor to understand how the overall setup and administration of SAP may affect ongoing processing integrity.

A Useful Correlation

SAP Basis settings and security is to SAP components and related business processes as GCCs are to the SAP application. Whereas GCCs are not specific to the SAP application and yet critical to its effective process, SAP Basis settings and security are independent of specific SAP components or business processes and yet fundamental to the processing within these components and processes.

Different from the other categories of audit procedures that we've discussed thus far, an auditor working on evaluating SAP Basis settings and security will be interested in specific SAP configuration settings in addition to supporting processes. Additionally, due to the complexity of the SAP Basis system and the SAP security model, auditors spending more than a nominal amount of time in these areas are likely experts in one or both of them. Given the power of SAP and the way in which the system has been designed, effectively auditing SAP Basis and security is arguably more challenging and requires more technical knowledge to do well than any other ERP application.

We discussed in Chapter 1 how the scope of the SAP audit can differ dramatically depending on the nature and type of audit being performed. This statement is true related to SAP Basis settings and security. An audit concerned with the integrity of financial reporting may only be interested in a handful of SAP Basis and security settings. An operational audit focused on system efficiency and performance, however, may dive deeply into specific configuration settings. As such, the types of questions encountered during this part of the review can vary widely.

▶ How are changes to the Implementation Guide (IMG) managed and controlled?

▶ What clients are enabled within the SAP system, and how are each of these clients used?

▶ What is the process for running changes through the SAP transport system?

▶ How well does the enterprise structure configured within the IMG map to the business structure, and, if changes exist, why?

▶ Is the SAP production client restricted from change through the "no changes allowed" flag in the client setup screen?

▶ Where are remote function calls (RFCs) used and how are these managed and controlled?

▶ Are password and security settings identified in report RSPARAM appropriate for the organization and consistent with company-wide security policies?

▶ Are password restriction lists being used, and if so, how are they being maintained?

These questions cast a wide net, with some focusing on general administration processes, and others focused on specific technical settings. You'll quickly learn how technically proficient your auditor is when he conducts this portion of the review, and if you're not already aware, you should come away with a better understanding of the nature of the audit based on how much time your auditor spends testing SAP Basis settings and security.

Extent of Audit Guidance

While the breadth and depth of their functionality have changed, the SAP Basis system and the SAP security model have been the underpinnings of the SAP system since the early days of the application. Unlike other areas of the application that have changed dramatically with the introduction of SAP NetWeaver and the SAP ERP platform, from an audit perspective the relevant issues and concerns associated with SAP Basis and security remain largely unchanged. As a result, there is perhaps more audit-specific guidance on these areas than any other part of the SAP system. This is a double-edged sword. On one hand, it means there is less ambiguity around audit expectations for these areas. On the other hand, it increases the risk that auditors applying standard checklists find their way into your audit. In our experience, the technical nature of this section of the audit is often one of the areas where less technical SAP auditors using checklists report findings over issues they don't fully understand. If you find yourself in this situation, review the information on negotiating with your auditors discussed in Chapter 1.

Consider the relevance of SAP Basis settings and security on specific controls within a business process. Assume for a moment that the auditor is most interested in senior management review of key information contained on custom reports that have been created to manage the business. The auditor will likely test the accuracy and completeness of these reports, and also spend time ensuring that the management review is sufficient and that the follow-up actions are taken as a result of that review. The problem with most audits, however, is that the auditor is looking at only a point-in-time. To gain further assurance as to the completeness and accuracy of the reports that the auditor just reviewed, he must look to SAP Basis settings and security to support their assessments. An IMG setting that allows changes directly to the production client could result in document types being added or removed, and if the design of the reports being relied upon is affected by the existence (or nonexistence) of certain document types, then the completeness of the report could be compromised. If user security is not sufficient to prevent unauthorized updates to the ABAP code that generates the report, then the accuracy of the report could be impacted. Thus, while the auditor verified the accuracy and integrity of the report at the time of his review, a potential risk suggests that the report could have been different before the assessment, or could be changed shortly after the assessment. The auditor needs to look at these factors and determine the implications that SAP Basis settings and security has on his ultimate conclusions related to the management review in question.

The SAP Basis settings and security category of the SAP audit process is generally focused on SAP settings and processes that are not component specific. In addition to specific configuration settings, the review also considers powerful administrative functions such as backups, archiving, and mass-maintenance. Within security, significant emphasis is placed on global security settings, such as minimum password lengths, passwords for default SAP accounts, logout and locking parameters, and other settings that provide the foundation for SAP's powerful security model. We'll discuss these issues in more detail later in this chapter; however, because so much guidance already exists on these issues (entire books have been written, for example, on SAP security), the majority of our discussion is intended to highlight some of the most important considerations and provide tips for success.

2.2.4 SAP Component-specific Technical Settings

As we move up the layers of audit areas common within an SAP audit, *SAP component-specific technical settings* addresses those settings that are specific to a given SAP component, such as PP, Financial Accounting, or SD. Within any given component, the specifics important for audit assurance are often variable. However, even between components, the auditor is often concerned with issues that fall into a set of standard categories. Thus, while the specifics are different, a set of common audit questions can generally apply to component-specific technical settings.

▶ How are changes, additions, and deletions to master data tables controlled?

▶ How do you prevent duplicates, outdated information, and other situations from affecting the integrity of your master data?

▶ Are SAP role and profile assignments sufficient to ensure appropriate segregation of duties within the process?

▶ What configurable tolerance levels are used, and how did you determine what those tolerance levels would be?

▶ Is it appropriate that this parameter is still set at the default setting supplied by SAP?

▶ Who has the ability to perform powerful or sensitive transactions (such as changing a bank account number)?

▶ How do you monitor the usage of non-standard transactions?

▶ What reports are available for management monitoring?

▶ What additional customizations (transactions, reports, and other similar changes) have been added or modified to the SAP system?

You may wonder why segregation of duties is included in this section vs. the SAP Basis settings and security section. Different auditors may treat segregation of duties in many ways. However, in our view, segregation of duties is more closely associated with a specific component than SAP security in general. The SAP Basis settings and security portion of the review would consider the process for managing security within SAP, including how segregation of duties is considered when security is being enacted, but the actual audit review for segregation, or separation, of duties (SOD) violations typically occurs at the component level (recognizing that a few violations result from the interaction between multiple components).

Segregation of Duties (SOD)

SOD is a key part of almost every audit. The principal behind SOD is that certain functions should be performed by separate individuals in an organization, and no individual should be able to both perpetuate and conceal errors or fraud in the normal course of duty. Improper SOD increases the potential for fraud and abuse, while at the same time decreasing the likelihood that problems, including innocent errors, are detected.

For proper segregation of duties within a business cycle, no single individual should be able to perform two or more of the following general classifications of functions for a single process or class of transaction:

► Authorize

► Record or report

► Maintain custody of or control over assets

► Reconcile or verify

In accounts payable, for example, the employee who records payments in SAP should not also approve those payments, manage or distribute checks related to those payments, or reconcile bank statements containing those payments. SOD concepts also apply to SAP administration and development functions. SAP developers, for example, should not be able to initiate or approve their own development (authorize), should not have access to production (custody of or control over assets), or QA their own changes (reconcile or verify).

Unlike the previous audit categories that we've discussed in this chapter (project management, GCCs, and SAP Basis settings and security), the relevance of the auditor's review is typically very apparent when he's looking at component-specific technical settings. Understanding how the issue tracking process, the administration of network security, or the maintenance of global SAP settings is relevant to vendor management, for example, is sometimes difficult for those who have not been introduced to the building blocks we provided in Figure 2.1: Building Blocks of an SAP Audit, and the explanation in this chapter. The auditor working in component-specific technical configuration, however, is asking questions close to and obviously relevant to the process under review. It's clear to see how SAP settings related to evaluated receipts settlement (ERS) vendors, for example, are relevant to the vendor management function.

Digging further into a specific example of an audit scenario for this area, consider the purchasing process. Depending on the type of audit, the release strategy and related authorization limits configured into SAP likely forms the basis of a control that the auditor may wish to test. Part of the auditor's review would seek to understand how the release strategy works, and probably observe purchase requests being sent for approval and processing within SAP. A more technical audit would also investigate this information further, and look at the specific configuration settings in SAP supporting the release strategy, and verify that they are appropriate for the business. Additionally, the auditor would likely look at security to understand who is authorized to approve and process transactions at each point during the release cycle. The auditor would also look to understand if any customizations, such as creation of new purchasing transactions, have been implemented in SAP that could affect the behavior of or entirely bypass the configured release strategy. The ultimate goal of the review is to validate that SAP is appropriately configured to support the process as defined and approved.

Depending on the extent of the SAP audit, the depth of testing related to component-specific configuration settings could be very detailed or very high level. In Chapters 5 to 8, we'll take a closer look at specific SAP components and the typical audit considerations associated with those components.

2.2.5 Business Processes Enabled by SAP

The final category in a comprehensive SAP audit deals with the *business processes enabled by SAP*. To a large extent, this set of audit procedures deals less with how SAP is administered and configured, and more with how employees use SAP in practice. The extent of audit effort in this area will depend on your auditor. Many auditors spend a lot of time reviewing technical issues in each of the other categories we've described in this chapter, but in our opinion, it's in this last building block of an SAP audit where the most significant and impactful findings can occur.

> **Note**
>
> We are not implying that concrete findings and actual business impact are unlikely from the other SAP audit areas, merely that they are much more common in this area.

In earlier categories of the SAP review, the auditor's findings often relate to issues that pose increased risk to your organization. A common statement in one of these categories is that a situation or problem is possible based on how SAP is configured or managed. Audit findings within the business processes related by SAP, however, are typically much more tangible. Rather than the auditor discussing possibilities or risks that may impact the business, he has likely found something that impacts the business and that impact can be quantified.

> **Blame It on the Users!**
>
> Those involved in managing SAP may find it frustrating when audit findings occur at the business process level, thus preventing a clean audit report. Many people don't realize that an SAP audit can actually result in audit issues even when SAP is configured correctly. SAP audit issues of this type are commonly the result of employees misusing functionality, often due to one or more of the following factors:
>
> ▶ Lack of understanding — poor training or failure to treat employee education as development processes
>
> ▶ Lack of defined process — unclear or poorly communicated policies and procedures
>
> ▶ Insufficient management monitoring — failure to look for or detect situations where a process is not working as intended
>
> ▶ Conscious misuse — intentional circumvention of procedures to perpetrate fraud or abuse
>
> Despite a tremendous amount of both built-in and configurable controls within SAP, it's typically not possible or practical to implement SAP in a way that prevents each of the above situations from occurring. As a result, processes such as management monitoring (and even audits) are typically required to detect these types of situations before they negatively impact the business.
>
> It's for this reason that I have refused to perform SAP audit services for companies where I have not also been involved in an integrated review, which includes the business processes for which SAP supports. In my opinion, it's impossible to merely look at configuration settings and tell an organization that SAP is configured correctly. SAP is only configured correctly if it effectively supports a high-integrity business process in the context of how the business is actually working.
>
> If you are in an organization where your compensation or other incentives are in any way tied to getting through an SAP audit with no significant audit issues, work with your boss and separate those issues that you have the ability to influence from those you do not.

At the business process level, an SAP auditor is often looking to answer questions such as:

▶ What policies and procedures define how users are intended to work with SAP?

▶ What type of training has been provided to users, and how was the training received?

▶ How are you actually using SAP, both in general and for processing specific transactions?

▶ How do you ensure that users working with non-standard transactions, those which they do not encounter frequently, enter those transactions accurately?

▶ How often is this key exception report being reviewed, and what is being done to follow up on suspicious items?

Fundamentally, the auditor at this stage is looking to validate that SAP and the related business process are harmonized — where there's an optimal mix of SAP supporting the business processes, and SAP users leveraging SAP for more efficient and effective operations. The auditor is also looking to learn whether users are working with SAP in the way intended when SAP was configured, and also whether SAP was configured to consider the way that users work.

If it's still not obvious how SAP could be configured correctly and yet the business is not working with SAP properly, consider the following. A typical vendor payment process consists of what is known as a *three-way-match*. SAP matches the information on the PO to what was received, and also compares the quantities and pricing detailed in these documents to the vendor invoice before SAP allows a payment to be processed. SAP has exceptional three-way-match controls, and the process can be highly automated with almost no manual interaction if so configured. While the three-way match is a strength of SAP, not every payment can go through a three-way match process. Some payments, such as utilities, are not received, and to accommodate these types of payments, SAP has functionality called *sundry invoice processing*. While controls can be implemented over sundry invoice processing, by nature of the process, these controls can never be as effective (at least in a preventive sense) as controls in the three-way-match process. We've seen numerous situations where accounts payable clerks, for various reasons, have entered invoices through the sundry invoice process that should have gone through the three-way-match process — thereby bypassing the additional controls in the intended process.

While findings in this area may not be the fault of your employees who support, SAP, your SAP support function can provide a valuable management service. Often, these employees have tools within the SAP suite that can help management proactively identify process issues, and over time turn into additional monitoring routines management can integrate to make their processes more efficient.

2.3 Common Problems and Solutions

In the preface to this book, we shared how many audit issues related to SAP are common across organizations and could be avoided. Now that you've learned more about the typical SAP audit process, it's time to explore some of these issues in more detail. We'll explore some broad categories of issues that consistently cause problems for organizations, independent of stage on the SAP audit pyramid. While this list is by no means exhaustive, at the end of this section, you should have a good understanding of the processes that commonly cause problems, and things you can do to avoid related audit issues. Later in this book, we'll look at issues specific to each slice of the pyramid.

2.3.1 Risk Assessment and Internal Control Design

In our discussion on internal controls in Chapter 1, we shared how internal controls must consciously be designed — accidental control does not qualify. Unfortunately, many organizations still fail to consciously consider their business risks and design effective controls to mitigate those risks. Some organizations fail to realize that while the SAP system has strong capabilities for establishing effective controls, many of these controls must be turned on during implementation. But just enabling the controls within SAP is not enough — often, the default settings provided within the system are inappropriate and need to be further configured to better match the risks of the organization. Even those that do a good job at considering current risks and controls during the SAP implementation process, and configuring SAP accordingly with the right level of preventive and detective controls, often fail to make adjustments as business conditions change. The large majority of SAP audit findings are actually symptoms of ineffective risk assessment and internal control design.

Fortunately, there are some simple things you can do to avoid problems in this area:

▶ *Educate your team about risks and controls.* Most non-auditors have never been trained on the basics of risk and control, and thus lack the foundation for making effective decisions related to risk and control. Most individuals find that there's a "common sense" approach to risks and controls, once they know what to look for — they don't need to attain an advanced degree in auditing to be risk and control savvy.

▶ *Develop a consistent process for designing and documenting your SAP controls.* Having an agreed-on structure and process for designing and maintaining controls can go a long way to ensuring that risks have been effectively mitigated. It's not enough to simply talk about the process you've developed — it must be documented (preferably in an electronic format that key employees can easily access and view) and kept up to date in a timely manner.

▶ *Ensure every SAP configurable control setting is appropriate for your organization.* Enabling controls in SAP is a good first step; however, rarely do the default settings apply to your organization's risks.

> **Finding and Validating Default Parameters**
>
> If you're not familiar with the SAP settings and parameters that contain default values, and you don't feel like reading detailed technical guides and digging through the IMG, a good start is to search SAP's online help for terms like "tolerance" and "default." While this technique won't get you to every relevant default setting, it will help you get started. If you find that many of your own SAP settings have not been changed from their defaults, then you can initiate a more comprehensive review.

▶ *Periodically review your SAP environment* for both business and process changes, and update your controls appropriately. Organizations that have been running SAP for awhile sometimes forget that configuration, particularly around SAP configurable controls, need to continuously evolve and should optimize over time. Also, update any process documentation that discusses these configuration decisions.

2.3.2 Process Inconsistency

Most auditors have a view of the organization that few possess — their work allows them to see organizations in their entirety, and view the complex interrelationships between processes. A common SAP audit finding is the result of *process inconsistencies*, typically in one of two categories: (1) inconsistencies within a single defined process, and (2) inconsistencies in similar processes between locations, divisions, and others. Process differences can certainly be justified — perhaps local regulatory requirements or nuances associated with a particular product make such inconsistencies a necessity. In our experience, however, many process inconsistencies are the result of insufficient business oversight and should be avoided.

> **A Word of Caution about Control Variations**
>
> As discussed in Chapter 1, the right level of internal control strikes a balance between benefit (from reduced risk) and cost. As a result, organizations commonly define a robust set of controls for complex processes, and a more streamlined set of controls for lower-risk areas. When such a situation occurs within the same process (e.g., a QA process where the level of testing is commiserate with the risk and complexity of the change), make sure the decision-making criteria to determine what level of control to apply is reflective of the desired outcome. We've seen some organizations apply QA processes based on the level of coding effort required to make the SAP system change — under 40 hours gets a streamlined set of testing procedures, while over 40 goes through the traditional change control and QA process. The use of hours, in this case, is fundamentally wrong. It's possible that a complex and high risk change can be coded in a short period of time. The right metric in this situation would be based on a complexity and risk-raking rather than number of coding hours or lines of code.

A few simple things can help you avoid additional audit effort resulting from process inconsistency:

- *Self-audit your own process.* Inconsistencies within a single defined process are easy to detect and correct, typically through additional staff coaching and education.

- *Document approved variations to processes, along with the rationale for the variation.* Whether within a single process or across instances of similar processes, maintaining a list of known and approved variations will help the auditor understand and independently determine whether the variations are appropriate based on his knowledge of the business. Lack of recognition for approved process variations is almost a surefire way to receive a negative audit finding.

- *Periodically review these process variations with management in light of current business conditions and technology capabilities.* Often, the rationale for specific process exceptions was valid at the time it was made but no longer holds true over time (perhaps as the result of better SAP functionality for dealing with the cause of the variation).

2.3.3 Documentation

Also in Chapter 1, we discussed the importance of evidence, and the auditor's requirements related to gathering sufficient evidence to support his conclusions. Many organizations fail to retain sufficient evidence, electronic or otherwise, and as a result put themselves in a difficult audit situation. Sometimes, the problem is the result of unclear expectations around the extent and quality of *documentation.* In other cases, employees followed sufficient procedures, but the evidence was not maintained long enough to be available for the audit. More so than simply maintaining evidence and other documentation, however, is to do it consistently. Often, organizations feel that if they do it most of the time, then it's good enough. Failure to show consistent application of procedures during an audit, however, can significantly increase audit testing time and ultimately result in audit findings.

Cascading Effect of Mistakes

If your organization is like most, you likely have a redundant set of controls — providing greater assurance that if one control fails, another control will prevent or detect the mistake before it impacts the business. For example, if a mistake is made when entering a receiving quantity, the discrepancy detected during SAP's three-way-match process is likely to trigger a review that may result in the mistake being found and corrected. It's easy to believe that because of this control redundancy, mistakes in documentation or the application of a single control may not be important — one can just rely on other controls. Such a belief can cause significant grief during an audit, however, as failure of one control can have an exponential effect on the audit testing required (depending on the type of audit).

Auditors using sampling techniques often base their testing procedures on a statistically valid sample. Prior to selecting the sample of items (transactions, system changes, vendor records, etc.) to test, the auditor will determine the number of allowable errors in the sample. The more errors allowed in the sample, the greater the sample size must be. If errors found exceed the number of expected errors, the auditor may need to take a significantly greater sample to test. If the auditor deems the control unreliable, he may need to perform similar testing procedures on any mitigating controls (again, depending on the type of audit), and assess whether these mitigating controls are at the same level as the original control. For some mitigating controls, such as budget-to-actual reviews, the type of error that the control is likely to detect is usually significantly larger than the errors that earlier controls are intended to catch.

Documentation problems are typically easy to address by a few simple things:

▶ *Clearly communicate documentation requirements to your staff.* Often, documentation or process steps are skipped when they become inconvenient, so being clear about the things that need to be completed at all times is critical.

▶ *Maintain a closing checklist for key activities.* A great way to ensure that a complete package of documentation and evidence is maintained according to policy is to include a review of the information as part of your normal quality assurance process.

▶ *Develop standards and consistent processes for maintaining documentation and other evidence.* Email authorizations, manual signoffs, and other non-SAP information likely exist outside of SAP, and having a centralized repository of this information and these images will facilitate easy retrieval if the original recipient is no longer with your organization.

▶ *Use key identifiers to track documentation and allow easier reconciliation back to SAP.* Being able to tie your documentation together to show a complete process is key. An auditor performing an SAP change control audit, for example may want to see the authorizations and test steps used for the objects in a specific SAP transport. If your authorizations are organized by approver, and your test steps are organized by project number, it may be difficult to quickly associate specific approvers and project numbers to the transport reference number in which the auditor is interested.

2.3.4 Periodic SAP User Reviews

Many organizations have a process whereby managers overseeing specific SAP-enabled functions receive a listing of users with the ability to execute SAP transactions specific to the manager's function. Often, this listing will show the manager the name of the user and the SAP role or profile they have been assigned. While this type of review can be effective for getting the "John doesn't work here anymore" response, it's highly ineffective as a segregation of duties control. Most managers don't have the depth of understanding of SAP transactions and security to truly validate whether the "Purchase Order Manager" role contains only appropriate transactions and authorizations. Even when supplemented by transaction and authorization details associated with those roles, managers typically do not have the expertise to truly validate what they are being asked to review.

Maintaining effective segregation of duties in SAP can be challenging and time consuming, particularly for organizations not using SAP BusinessObjects Access Control or a similar security monitoring tool by a third party. Our best advice is that a specialized segregation of duties monitoring tool is essential in any SAP environment. If you are not currently using one, you can put yourself in a better position if you:

▶ *Work with management and your auditors to develop a list of functions within your organization that should be segregated.* Many organizations struggle with SOD because they have not defined what SOD means to them, and a company-wide assessment is a good first step.

▶ *Map these functions to SAP transactions and authorizations that allow a user to perform the respective function.* This step alone helps make an SOD review more effective, allowing you to provide managers with user access by function (typically in terms that management understands), while you have the ability to tie these functions back to SAP transactions and ultimately user roles and profiles.

▶ *Force positive confirmation upon the review of user access.* Some security functions take the approach that if they send an access report to management and they do not hear back, then access must be appropriate. Obviously, this is a big assumption. Only consider access to be appropriate when a knowledgeable reviewer has indicated it's correct.

▶ *Self-audit the review process and re-educate managers who may be cutting corners.* Nothing ensures process compliance like the knowledge that one will likely be caught if he doesn't follow the process.

> **Putting Teeth into User Access Reviews**
>
> Organizations that are serious about security take security seriously. We've seen organizations take user security reviews to the extreme — shutting off access for all employees where positive confirmation has not been received by the date requested by the security team. Obviously, this could result in legitimate access being shut off if management is late in responding to the security review request, but it typically only takes one time being late for a manager to learn the importance of the review process.

2.3.5 Non-Standard Process Monitoring

SAP contains numerous exception processes for dealing with *non-standard* situations. Because of the nature of these processes, many allow certain controls to be bypassed, and organizations that do not closely restrict and monitor their use can be shocked at findings resulting from a comprehensive SAP audit. We've already discussed sundry invoice processing, and how it bypasses three-way match controls. Free-of-charge deliveries allow customers to be compensated for the receipt of damaged goods, but in the hands of a salesperson could be a way to circumvent pricing policies and provide preferred customers with goods for which they are not entitled. Inventory adjustment functionality is also necessary but can compensate for poor receiving processes. While each of these functions has an appropriate use, they can also be used inappropriately.

You can strengthen controls over non-standard and exception processes if you:

▶ *Develop an expected usage benchmark, and monitor against that benchmark.* Knowing that a typical category of transaction occurs only 1% of the time, for example, can allow you to investigate if usage frequency changes significantly from the norm.

▶ *Extend this monitoring to also review by employee, location, day, and similar groupings.* Performing usage trending analysis at a level deeper than a mere corporate aggregate can enable you to highlight individual performance differences that can be indicative of a problem.

2.3.6 User Education and Understanding

As discussed earlier in this chapter, even the most well-configured SAP system is subject to user error and misuse. Some of the most highly publicized implementation disasters have been exacerbated by poor user understanding of new functionality, and lack of recognition of how actions in SAP can affect other system processes. For example, a shipping clerk trying to do right for the customer and quickly get goods shipped in advance of entering the picking, packing, and shipment into SAP is actually doing the organization a disservice. Because SAP is unaware that the goods have left the facility, it loses the ability to effectively manage inventory and additionally is not initiating customer billing or accounting recognition of inventory change.

Potential audit issues associated with user education and understanding can be reduced through additional emphasis in a handful of key areas:

▶ *Develop a means for identifying gaps in user understanding and develop methods to enhance user proficiency in troubled areas.* Simple monitoring routines that can detect issues where users are not using functionality appropriately can greatly enhance an organization's ability to proactively identify performance problem. A clerk processing significantly more reversing entries than his peers, a location that never uses a key document type, or an overall departmental increase in calls to the help desk can all be indicators of performance problems.

▶ *Talk to users about their SAP frustrations.* Often, a fine line exists between something that's frustrating, and something so frustrating that a user chooses to look for workarounds. The areas that users are frustrated with today are often those areas where misuse is detected during an audit.

▶ *Design training to focus on what a user needs to do to complete the process, not just what's available in SAP.* Poorly designed training shows users how to navigate through the SAP system. Well-designed training allows users to understand the entire process from finding relevant information in SAP, to understanding how to interpret it, through to leveraging SAP for further processing based on what they find.

2.3.7 Master Data Control

The integrity of *master data* is paramount to SAP's effective operation. Master data can affect entire categories of transactions or classifications of vendors. Unfortunately, many organizations struggle with keeping master data clean. Duplicate entries begin to appear over time. Outdated information remains active and reduces the ability to find relevant data. Data affected by business conditions, such as customer credit limits, may be set once and never revisited. Auditors often at least one significant problem related to master data, so keeping your data management process strong is essential.

In subsequent chapters, we'll discuss master data considerations for specific SAP processes and components. Until then, the following tips can serve as general guides for audit-proofing your master data:

▶ *Define master data ownership for every type of master data, and establish specific standards and change processes.* Many data problems result from inconsistencies in data usage, and having a single source of control (whether an individual or a committee) can ensure data quality stays high over time.

▶ *Configure appropriate edit checks within SAP to validate data against your standards.* The SAP system contains phenomenal capabilities for validating data at entry; however, many of these features go unused within the typical organization.

▶ *Develop ongoing data quality processes to continuously cleanse data.* Even when master data is entered accurately at input, certain master data can become outdated (credit limits) or irrelevant (unused vendors) over time. Audit findings can result from the continued usage of this data, so ongoing data quality processes can reduce the potential for audit issues.

2.4   The Start of the Audit

Thus far in this chapter, we've discussed the timing of the SAP audit, the building blocks of that audit, and some of the common issues resulting from the audit. In the remainder of this chapter, we'll discuss what you can expect when the audit starts. If you have never been through an audit before, this final section may answer your questions about what will happen when the auditors arrive. If you have already been through an audit before and understand the basics, we might suggest looking through Chapter 9, which provides specific suggestions you can implement when you are preparing for an audit.

Regardless of the nature of the audit, an audit consists of four phases: planning, fieldwork, reporting, and follow-up, as illustrated in Figure 2.2: Stages of the Audit Process. These phases typically occur over a series of months, and given the scope of the typical SAP audit, may extend across a year. During each phase, you have the ability to influence certain parts of the audit.

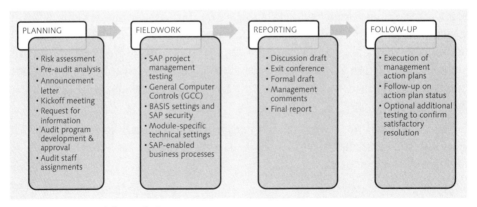

Figure 2.2   Stages of the Audit Process

2.4.1   Planning

In the weeks or months before you first hear of the SAP audit, the auditor is already working on your audit. Auditing requirements specify that the auditor spend sufficient time *planning* the audit in advance of actual testing. This requirement ensures that the audit is well structured and capable of meeting the goals specified by audit management and the board. In many cases, the auditor will likely contact you (or your management team) to confirm the timing of the audit via an announcement letter. The announcement letter informs you of the upcoming audit and solicits additional input into the audit objectives. In some situations, you may have the ability to influence the timing of the audit, although much depends on the audit objectives and the other reviews on the audit schedule.

The SAP audit planning process typically starts with a risk assessment. The auditor examines prior audit reports (if they exist), including SAP evaluations performed by other auditors or consultants in the past few years, and reviews any follow-up procedures designed to ensure that audit issues were effectively resolved. The auditor also reviews specific risks identified during the overall audit risk assessment process (covering the entire organization and typically occurring at least once per year). Depending on when this risk assessment process was performed, the auditor may update the identified risks through additional interviews or management surveys. If any new developments have occurred since the last review, the auditor will likely discuss these with management in advance of preparing the SAP audit test plan.

Depending on the nature of the audit, the auditor may also review SAP reports and other information to gain additional insight into current operations. This information may include relevant financial reports, including budget-to-actual reviews, current policies and procedures, and existing organization charts. Any process flowcharts or process narratives either created during prior audits or available through other means are also reviewed. The goal at this state is for the auditor to gain sufficient information to effectively set the objectives for the audit.

Near the start of the audit, the auditor schedules what is typically known as a *kickoff meeting* with relevant participants. The kickoff meeting is sometimes also referred to as an *entrance conference*. Depending on your role in the organization relative to SAP, you may or may not be included in this meeting. The auditor will share the scope and objectives for the audit, and also confirm the start date and any preliminary materials he will require.

If you are involved, the kickoff meeting is an important chance to influence the scope of the audit. The auditor is looking to validate the audit objectives, confirm that relevant risks are being addressed, and understand any special concerns. While you likely cannot dissuade the auditor from reviewing areas already identified (auditor independence affords the auditor with the ability to test what he thinks is appropriate), if you have concerns not currently included in the scope of the audit, this is your best chance to raise them.

The kickoff meeting is also a good time to share information about your current strategies and objectives, resource constraints, and staff schedules (including vacations, training commitments, or other times where staff will be unavailable). If you'll be going through any significant changes during the course of the audit or shortly thereafter, share the timing and nature of these changes. Depending on the changes being made, the auditor may accelerate or postpone audit fieldwork. The kickoff meeting is also a good time to ask the auditor about the budgeted duration for the audit, so you can get an idea of how much time is being dedicated for the review.

Identifying a Point of Contact

Providing the auditor with a single point of contact can streamline the audit process and ensure effective coordination and resource utilization among your team. Use someone with enough insight into daily operations to effectively direct the auditor to appropriate parties when questions arise.

After the kickoff meeting, the auditor will likely make updates to the SAP audit testing plan based on feedback that you provided during the session. This testing plan will be reviewed and approved by others in the audit organization as part of the audit's quality assurance process. It's unlikely you'll ever see the actual audit plan, but by this point, you should have a sense from your auditor of what the review will entail.

After the auditor has finalized the SAP audit program and received final approval from the head of the audit, the auditor will typically follow up with a scope letter or memorandum. This letter confirms the arrangements of the kickoff meeting, so if the timing or nature of the review differs significantly from what was presented earlier, follow up with the auditor quickly.

The Audit Program

The audit program, also known as the audit workplan, the test plan, or the audit procedures, is a document that describes the test steps that will occur during the SAP audit. The audit program typically describes the audit objectives and outlines in detail the specific audit tests to be performed. As the auditor completes specific test steps contained in the workplan, he typically references the location of testing evidence and signs and dates the test step indicating that it has been completed. As part of a quality assurance process, another auditor will review the test step and relevant evidence and independently verify the auditor's stated conclusions. Auditing standards require that every audit has a workplan.

Sometime before the audit starts, either separately or as part of the scope letter or kickoff meeting, the auditor will also likely request a set of preliminary information. In the context of an SAP audit, this information likely includes:

- ▶ Details on current SAP instances, hardware and software versions supporting those instances, and the SAP clients in use
- ▶ Any process-specific policies and procedures for the area under review
- ▶ High-level flowcharts, process flows, and other information that can help the auditor understand the overall process and flow of information
- ▶ Contact information for key staff
- ▶ Upcoming committee and departmental meeting schedule, along with minutes from a recent set of these meetings

Be aware that despite the fact the real audit testing hasn't yet started, SAP audit issues can be identified even during the planning stages. For example, if the SAP security policy is not in alignment with the organization-wide security policy, an exception could result. Additionally, certain types of analysis that the auditor performs during the planning stage can identify potential problems. In Chapter 8, we'll review audit tips and tricks, and give useful advice for preparing your SAP system for even more advanced auditors.

2.4.2 Fieldwork

In the *fieldwork* stage, also known as *audit testing*, the auditor examines in detail each of the categories we've described earlier in this chapter that are relevant to the audit. As the majority of this book describes activities in the audit fieldwork stage, we won't spend much time discussing it here. The duration of the fieldwork stage can be as short as a week or as long as several months. At this stage, the auditor determines how well the SAP and process risks identified in the planning stage are being managed, and whether the controls designed to address these risks are reliable.

Throughout the course of fieldwork, the auditor maintains various findings. These findings can range from the minor (simple observations the auditor wishes to point out so processes can be improved) to the potentially major. While you may not see the full list of issues that the auditor has prepared, typically he probes into his findings to ask questions to ensure he has all the facts and understands the implications. It's rare that an auditor will report on an issue that hasn't been discussed, at least preliminarily, with you or your team before the report is issued. This is your time to ensure that the auditor possesses all the relevant facts and has sufficiently detailed information to draw his conclusions. While you'll have further opportunity in the reporting phase to correct the auditor if he is off-base or unfairly representing the facts, working with the auditor before the close of fieldwork will go far to ensure that your audit closes smoothly.

2.4.3 Reporting

The outcome of every audit is the audit *report*. The goal of the audit report is to fairly communicate the issues, observations, and recommendations related to the audit objectives. The report ultimately goes through multiple levels of review before it's finally issued. In the case of an SAP audit performed by an internal audit department, the chief audit executive will typically sign off on the contents before distribution to senior management and the audit committee. For an external audit, an audit partner will ultimately sign off on the report before distribution. We discussed in Chapter 1 the distribution differences between internal and external audit reports.

Audit Reporting: The Final Evolution

The audit process is steeped in tradition and is slow to change. Audit reports are a good example of this. Traditionally, audit reports go through a series of formal stages and numerous iterations before final distribution. The goal of these iterations is to ensure that all facts are captured accurately and completely, that issues are presented fairly, and that recommendations are reasonable and achievable. Unfortunately, the back-and-forth nature required to get to the final and approved audit report has historically caused the distribution of the final reports to be months after the completion of fieldwork. In certain government agencies, it's not uncommon for bureaucracy and red tape to result in audit reports being distributed several years after the actual completion of fieldwork.

In an SAP environment, where certain problems can affect entire categories of transactions until corrected, and problems identified well away from initial decision making can be time consuming or impossible to correct, a prolonged reporting cycle is unacceptable. Fortunately, many audit groups are realizing this fact and beginning to change the audit reporting cycle. Many audit reports are now being distributed close to the end of fieldwork, and audit teams are finding ways to communicate potential problems, at least informally, even before fieldwork ends.

Discussion Draft

After the end of fieldwork, the auditor typically prepares a preliminary report, commonly termed a *discussion draft*. The discussion draft shares findings and current causes of those findings. The discussion draft is also typically used as a vehicle to help brainstorm recommendations — both for resolving the specific problem identified, as well as for preventing or detecting similar problems in the future. The discussion draft is typically distributed to SAP management and key personnel, with a formal review following shortly thereafter.

Exit Meeting

During the *exit meeting*, sometimes termed the *exit conference*, audit presents the contents of the discussion draft to management. The exit meeting is typically a collaborative event, seeking to reach agreement on the audit findings. In Chapter 1, we discussed how to negotiate issues with the audit team. If you disagree with your auditors on any point in the report, or believe the facts are presented unfairly, raise your concern and support your belief with specific facts of your own. Be aware, however, that audit is not required to agree with management on every issue reported, and thus some findings with which you disagree may still make the final report.

As the auditor discusses findings with management, issues that are deemed to be minor are typically eliminated from what will become the final report. These issues will often be reported to you in a letter summarizing minor findings but may not be communicated to higher-level management. Depending on the nature of these minor issues, their resolution may or may not be further tracked.

If your SAP audit was conducted by your organization's internal audit department, you'll likely also receive a client satisfaction survey at the exit conference. This is your opportunity to formally comment on the auditor or auditors involved in your audit, and the audit process itself. Audit departments strive to provide an effective, valuable service, and comments and suggestions are typically taken seriously. The head of the internal audit department typically sees every client satisfaction survey, and many organizations also summarize them for the audit committee.

Formal Draft

Based on revisions resulting from the exit conference and other discussions, the auditor updates the discussion draft to create a formal draft. The auditor may also perform additional testing procedures if the exit conference reveals any new information that should be considered, and this additional work is also added to the formal draft. Similar to the discussion draft, the head of audit will typically review the formal draft to ensure it complies with audit standards before issuance.

In addition to specific audit findings, the formal draft also contains specific audit recommendations. These recommendations detail a proposed action plan for resolving the findings and the issues that caused the specific findings in the first place. These recommendations should not come as a surprise — the auditor likely discussed them with you during the exit meeting. At this point, the audit reporting process is almost complete.

Management Comments

Upon completion, the auditor distributes the formal draft audit report to relevant management. This formal report requires a formal response, typically called *management comments* or the *management response*. Your auditor will indicate when your management comments must be formally received — one to two weeks is common.

The management response is your formal means for replying to each of the audit issues indicated in the audit report. The management response typically details the corrective action plan associated with the auditor recommendations, including a time estimate for completion and indication of who will be responsible for each action. In some situations, you may determine that the most appropriate action will require SAP changes that take time — in these situations, you'll likely indicate the desired state but also detail a short-term action plan that closes the gap between where you are today and where you need to be.

The auditor takes the formal draft and incorporates your final comments as part of the final report. As such, responding to each audit recommendation completely and clearly is critical. If a finding will not be resolved for a period of time, you should clearly state why, including cost estimates or work efforts required to make the change requested. Your response, or lack thereof, will be viewed by senior management and quite possibly by the board. If you've maintained a positive working relationship with your auditor throughout the process, and been engaged during the audit and various early reporting drafts, you may have already corrected each of the issues. Being able to demonstrate that issues have been resolved prior to the final report issuance demonstrates your diligence and desire to maintain a strong control environment by addressing issues quickly.

Final Report

Once your management comments have been received, the auditor prepares the *final report*. This report is typically similar to a formal draft; however, findings may be aggregated and summarized for senior management. The actual distribution of the final report depends on the type of audit and the category of auditor involved, as discussed in Chapter 1. Due to the importance of SAP in most organizations, the final report will commonly be received and discussed at the highest levels of the organization.

2.4.4 Follow-up

After the final audit report has been issued, your work is not over. It's now your responsibility to execute the action plan you detailed as part of your management comments. Most audit functions have a process for following up with management to ensure that issues have been resolved to audit's satisfaction. Given the risks associated with many common SAP audit findings, the auditor may also perform additional *follow-up* activities to ensure that issues have been resolved to satisfaction once management indicates that their resolution steps have been completed.

> **Being Proactive after the Audit**
>
> Auditors commonly interact with senior management, and as a result, are often asked about the status of issues reported in final audit reports. As a result, you may find it helpful to inform the auditor of any changes to the status of issues for which the resolution is your responsibility. This includes issues that have been resolved, as well as resolution dates that have been deferred or action steps that have changed. In this way, your auditor has the most current details and can follow up with you quickly if status changes raise any concerns.

The reporting process that the auditor follows for follow-up work often mirrors the pattern found in the reporting processes, and you have the opportunity to respond to the audit findings prior to issue of a follow-up report. Auditors, and internal auditors in particular, generally share the status of significant unresolved issues from prior audit reports at every audit committee meeting.

Audit issues identified in prior audit reports are almost always included in the scope of a new audit; thus, your diligence in ensuring not only that the cause of the problem has been addressed but also monitoring for future recurrence is important to keep out of audit trouble. Having the same issue appear on consecutive audit reports is generally a poor way to stay in management's good graces.

A summary of your expected involvement in each phase of the audit process is illustrated in Figure 2.3: Management Responsibilities in the Audit Process.

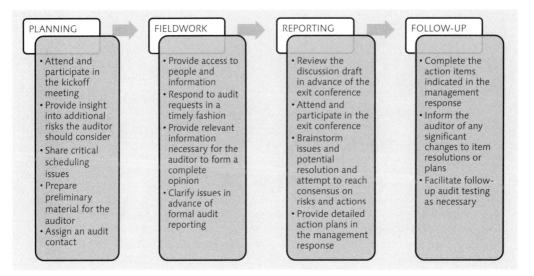

Figure 2.3 Management Responsibilities in the Audit Process

2.5 Summary

In this chapter, we've shared details specific to an SAP audit. We discussed the potential timing of an SAP audit, and then broke down the typical SAP audit into a series of interrelated components. We walked through specific problems common to many organizations when they first go through an SAP audit, and detailed specific recommendations for reducing the occurrence of these problems. We've also shared the process that a typical SAP audit follows, so you'll be prepared for what will be expected when the auditors come on-site.

In the next chapter, we'll talk specifically to those organizations going through an SAP implementation or significant upgrade, and share tips to ensure that risks are effectively considered and mitigated in SAP even before being identified through an audit. We'll also discuss the first foundation layer of the typical SAP audit — the SAP project management process.

The only thing we have to fear is fear itself.
— *Franklin Delano Roosevelt*

3   SAP Implementations and Upgrades

The most costly and time-consuming audit issues to resolve are those identified after go-live. Once SAP is live and running in production, making changes or enhancements becomes exponentially more difficult than if these same changes were considered during the initial development process. At best, problems identified in your production system expose your organization to significant risk. At worst, erroneous and inaccurate transactions flowing unchecked through your business systems can damage customer relations, lead to lost revenue or unrecoverable expenditures, or even result in regulatory fines and sanctions.

The more time that passes between your initial SAP design and configuration decisions and an audit finding associated with those decisions, the more challenging resolution becomes. Audit issues related to SAP configuration or business process design become more difficult, more time consuming, and more resource intensive to correct the greater the time frame between decision and audit finding. Even more problematic, certain configuration decisions are so integral to your ongoing usage of SAP (such as the structure of your general ledger chart of accounts or the setup of your organizational units), that any significant changes to these decisions are most easily made through an entirely new implementation.

Many organizations believe that putting great people on the implementation team will ensure that the right process decisions are being made. This is true to some extent; however, the reality of the typical implementation is that time is scarce, the list of items to do is long, and the entire area of governance, risk, and compliance (GRC) falls into a challenging category — those things that we know in the backs of our minds that we really should do but in the heat of the moment seem like things that we can deal with later. Similar to how many people treat preventative medicine, we know internal controls are important and yet often put them off until it's too late. Even when the implementation team wants to devote sufficient attention to GRC, many organizations still find themselves lacking — not by choice but rather by risk and control expertise on the implementation team. As a result, auditors commonly find a plethora of risk and control issues after system go-live.

The impact of such issues can be large. With an implementation team already burned out from the rigors of the implementation process, and the implementation budget exhausted, getting the momentum to mitigate audit concerns is often challenging at best. Additionally, the rework of going back and making changes to SAP or your related business process to address these issues detracts from daily operations and results in unnecessary distraction.

This chapter is about avoiding audit issues. By configuring SAP and designing your business processes to effectively manage the risks that can create audit concern, you can eliminate the majority of audit findings. This chapter is also about managing your implementation or upgrade such that the implementation team acts in unison, with a consistent understanding of these potential risks and their role as part of the implementation team for addressing them.

> ### The Importance of a Sound Methodology
>
> Given the complexity of SAP and the number of configuration and customization options available, it's not possible to discuss every possible configuration option that could lead to audit concern. Additionally, ongoing changes and improvements made by SAP to SAP applications make specific configuration advice an ever-changing target. Our goal for this chapter is not to tell you exactly how to configure SAP during the implementation but rather to provide you with a framework (independent of SAP component and version), that can help you make sound risk and control decisions. Our hope is that you understand the rationale for this approach, recognize how it can be applied to your organization, and adapt it as appropriate to fit your needs.

This chapter is designed for SAP project managers, administrators, and SAP team members looking to avoid audit headaches during or after the SAP implementation. We share techniques that, if performed well during an implementation or upgrade, can significantly decrease if not eliminate the number of audit concerns associated with SAP and the business processes it enables. We share tips on how to work with your auditors during the implementation or upgrade, including advice for using your auditor as an advisor to the SAP implementation team. We also outline a specific methodology for designing and documenting controls and control-related decisions in a way that should significantly reduce the time spent preparing for an audit.

If you have not yet started your SAP implementation or upgrade, you will likely find this entire chapter useful. If you are mid-way into the implementation, portions of this chapter are organized by implementation phase. Skip through the phases that you've already completed so that you have an idea of what you could have been doing, and take time to read about your current and upcoming phases. If you're nearing the end of your implementation or upgrade and cannot afford to implement the techniques that we've described, a section later in this chapter will highlight a few quick-hit areas that can at least prepare you more effectively than if you go live without considering these areas.

This chapter will close with a discussion of project management issues and tips. As mentioned in Chapter 2, the process for managing the SAP implementation or upgrade can be included in the audit scope if the audit occurs during or shortly after the implementation, so this section will outline the characteristics of a sound project management process (at least from an audit and control perspective).

By the end of this chapter, you should be well equipped to configure SAP and supported business processes to effectively manage your business risks. If you are currently going through an SAP implementation or upgrade, or anticipate doing so in the near future, this chapter is for you. If you have already completed your implementation and are looking for advice on how you can better approach your next implementation, you'll find insight in the discussion here. If you hope to never see an implementation again, but are still curious about how non-auditors can design processes that pass audit scrutiny, then read on.

For the rest of this chapter, when we use the word "implementation," we'll be referring to both implementations and upgrades. Because some upgrades are more complex and comprehensive than others, it's up to you to determine how the advice applies to your own process.

> **Before You Begin**
>
> This chapter assumes you are already familiar with the audit process, recognize the possible differences between different types of auditors and different types of audits, and understand the fundamentals of an SAP audit. If these topics are not familiar to you, revisit Chapters 1 and 2 before reading further.

3.1 Reasons for Considering Internal Controls During an Implementation

Organizations commonly talk about the desire to create a well-controlled business environment. Managers often understand the importance of monitoring operational activity and ensuring that employees are making appropriate decisions. Too often, however, by the time discussion of internal control reaches the ears of employees, people view controls only as an additional burden that it may cause them. Before embarking on your SAP implementation, everyone on your implementation team should understand why internal controls are important, whether any specific controls are required of your organization based on the business you are in, and how internal controls might enhance business operations.

3.1.1   Regulatory Requirements

Sometimes, maintaining and reporting on internal controls is mandated by law. Depending on the country or countries in which your organization operates, regulations may dictate the need for internal controls, either related to specific aspects of your business or across the business as a whole. Failure to comply with such regulations can lead to negative publicity, significant fines, and even potential jail time for executives.

The Foreign Corrupt Practices Act (FCPA) in the United States is one such regulation where fines in recent years have increased both in frequency and severity. FCPA makes it illegal for companies to make a corrupt payment to a foreign official to secure business, and requires companies with security listings in the United States to maintain adequate systems of internal controls over financial reporting. Companies facing non-compliance can be fined up to $2,000,000 per violation, and individuals can face fines of $250,000 and five years in prison for each violation. Some of the more well-publicized FCPA violations include:

► 2005: The Titan Corporation, $28.5M
► 2006: Schnitzer Steel Industries, $15.2M
► 2007: Vetco, $26M
► 2007: Baker Hughes, $44M
► 2008: Siemens AG, $450M+

These fines are anything but insignificant, and have increased significantly as enforcement becomes more common. Organizations sometimes question the cost of compliance — these figures make the cost of non-compliance abundantly clear. More than two dozen countries have implemented laws similar to FCPA, so this affects more than just organizations with operations in the United States.

> **We Have To...But Do We *Want* To?**
>
> Regulations are often cited as the most important reason to have internal controls. If you haven't come to the realization already, hopefully by the end of this chapter you will see how internal controls can directly and positively contribute to an organization's bottom line. Even in the absence of regulatory mandate, organizations with strong, well-designed internal controls should be more efficient, more competitive, and more profitable in the long run than organizations lacking a sound internal control environment.

The last decade brought about a slew of other regulations, and an entirely new category of regulation emerged, establishing standards over financial reporting and corporate governance. These regulations include the Sarbanes-Oxley Act of 2002 (SOX) in the United States, Bill 198 in Canada, the Combined Code in the United Kingdom, the Financial Instruments and Exchange Law (J-SOX) in Japan, CLERP9 in Australia, and Loi sur la Sécurité Financière (LSF) in France. These laws protect investors by linking business governance, and internal controls in particular, to the reliability of financial statements upon which investors base their opinions. The specifics of each regulation are different; many situations require that senior management state that they have implemented and specifically test and monitor internal controls over financial reporting.

The breadth of regulations requiring some form of internal controls is exhaustive. Some regulations establish standards for the security and privacy of data, such as the Health Insurance Portability and Accountability Act (HIPAA) and the Gramm-Leach Bliley Act (GLBA) in the United States, and the European Union Directive on Data Protection in Europe. Other regulations are industry-specific, governing issues such as quality control in chemical and pharmaceutical companies, gaming operations in (casino) gaming companies, and energy reliability in the utilities industry. Still other internal control standards are mandated by standard-setting bodies, such as Payment Card Industry (PCI) standards for organizations accepting credit cards as payment.

In addition to the specific penalties imposed by these regulations, failure to comply often results in a negative backlash from the major financial markets as well. In the early days of the Sarbanes-Oxley Act in the United States, companies reporting weaknesses in internal controls often saw double-digit percentage drops in their stock prices. While the market today is somewhat less volatile over such reporting, companies disclosing control weaknesses are likely to experience a market impact.

Regulatory References to System Implementations

Interestingly enough, certain regulations directly speak to the need for designing and delivering effective internal controls during an implementation. In the early days of SOX in the United States, a number of organizations argued that the nature, complexity, and resource-intensive nature of system implementations could make it difficult to have controls in place and fully tested — particularly if the scheduled implementation was near the regulatory reporting deadline. In a Securities and Exchange Commission (SEC) Frequently Asked Questions guide, the SEC stated that "companies are required to prepare reliable financial statements following the implementation of the new information systems." In essence, the SEC was reminding companies that financial reporting integrity is always expected, and that expectation does not change merely because a company undertook a challenging project during the year. The SEC went on to say that "the staff does not believe it is appropriate to provide an exclusion by management of new IT systems and upgrades from the scope of its assessment of internal control over financial reporting...With respect to system changes, management can plan, design, and perform preliminary assessments of internal controls in advance of system implementations or upgrades."

Given the large number of potential internal-control related regulations to which your organization may be subject, it's wise to seek advice from your legal counsel early in the SAP implementation planning phase. Provide each member of your implementation team with a summary of the regulations that should be considered during the implementation, briefly illustrated in Table 3.1: Sample Internal Summary of Regulatory Considerations.

Regulation	Brief	Legal Contact	SAP Implications
Sarbanes-Oxley	Controls over financial reporting process	B. Smith	Financial Accounting and Controlling Security
HIPAA	Storage and transmission of healthcare data	J. Williams	Security
Random Industry Regulation	Storage and disposal of regulated materials	K. Thomas	Materials Management in SAP ERP
Other Regulation	Description	Legal	Component

Table 3.1 Sample Internal Summary of Regulatory Considerations

3.1.2 Business Partner Relationships

Certain business partner relationships may also necessitate the need for strong internal controls. Usually, these result from contractual obligations and associated penalties (monetary or otherwise) for non-compliance. If your organization has any loans or lines of credit through your financial institution, for example, loan covenants may establish specific asset ratios or other metrics that you must maintain. Failure to comply with your loan covenants could result in those loans becoming due immediately.

Other business partner relationships may also be governed by contracts. Organizations providing services, for example, may be bound by documented service level agreements (SLAs) that guarantee a specified level of operational performance. Failure to meet the minimum standards set forth in the SLA could result in less favorable payment schedules, trigger special clauses, or even allow immediate contract termination. Government contracts often contain stringent clauses over billing schedules and terms, use of subcontractors, and information disclosure. Every time your organization has a formal or implied contract, and that contact contains undesired penalties for non-compliance, your need for internal controls increases.

One Big Mess

Contract compliance is particularly challenging because contract terms often differ widely. Additionally, many organizations struggle with even having visibility into the obligations under which they are governed by a contract. Centralizing contract administration under SAP can help, but you perpetually face the risk that an employee bypasses standard protocol and enters into a contract outside of standard methods, and thus invisible to SAP. Entire books can be written on contract compliance, so suffice it to say, this can be a particularly challenging issue and one where a base level of internal controls is an absolute necessity.

3.1.3 Cost to the Business

A typical audit may not occur until late in the implementation, or even after the implementation. As mentioned in the preface, this can make it difficult to incorporate audit-relevant suggestions into your SAP configuration and related process design decisions. These decisions can become difficult and costly to correct as time passes beyond the point of the initial decision. Most implementations have significant audit findings after go-live. Considering controls up front minimizes rework and eliminates audit concerns.

Not Merely About Audit Findings

While we all want the audit to go as quickly and painlessly as possible, and while this chapter is written in the context of reducing potential audit concerns, the benefit of these suggestions to your organization goes well beyond merely satisfying an auditor. If you're thinking only in terms of getting an auditor out of your hair, you are perhaps losing sight of the bigger picture. The process we describe has a direct impact on your organization's ability to manage your business effectively.

Most audit issues are merely an identification of situations where:

▶ A business condition potentially exposes the organization to more risk than management desires

▶ A process exists (or does not exist) that goes against management's stated or implied intentions

▶ An undesired error or anomaly has been specifically identified

Independent of any audit, all of these conditions affect your organization's ability to run efficiently and effectively, and should be both understood and addressed. By following the ideas discussed in this chapter, you can strengthen your SAP-enabled processes, reduce your organization's overall business risk, and enable your employees and management to focus on their designated roles (rather than retroactively fixing errors and problems).

While at first it may not seem like post-go-live audit issues could pose significant costs to your organization, consider the impact. During the audit, an audit finding increases the time that the auditor must spend by necessitating additional testing (where relevant to the issue), and adding to the list of items that will need to be formally reported to management. As discussed in Chapter 2, the audit reporting process consists of a series of phases designed to validate issues and communicate them fairly, so every finding also affects management time during the reporting cycle. Every reported audit issue must have an official management response, and this response will require work to effectively estimate the resources required to follow the audit recommendation. If the change affects SAP configuration, the IT change control process will kick in and likely result in the need for requirements documentation, design specifications, coding, testing, quality assurance (QA), documentation, and the slew of activities involved in making changes to a production SAP system. Thus, a single audit finding after go-live could require specific action by at least six people and take months to correct.

3.1.4 Process Verification

SAP implementation teams can be quite large, and functional teams often emerge with responsibility for specific process areas. For example, a procurement team may focus on SAP's MM component. An accounting team may take the lead on financial accounting. During the whirlwind that typically describes an implementation, control assumptions can be made that ultimately lead to control gaps. The procurement team may, for example, rely on the accounts payable department to double-check certain information before payment, whereas the accounts payable team may expect controls within procurement to eliminate the need for greater diligence.

As you'll learn later in this chapter, the technique for designing effective internal controls necessitates a method of process analysis sometimes lacking during traditional process design or reengineering. As a result, simply applying the approach for designing controls can often expose process design weaknesses much sooner than they would normally be detected. Control design techniques, which we discuss later in this chapter, force you to examine the things that can go wrong in a process and frequently identify process deficiencies — and, by focusing on the end-to-end process, can also expose gaps created by functional team silos. Even for processes new to your organization, a good control design framework will force you to think through potential issues and develop mitigation strategies up-front.

3.1.5 Control Redesign and Optimization

In addition to seeking robust operational and reporting capabilities, organizations often implement SAP as a means to re-engineer and improve business processes. In conjunction with improving specific business processes, the implementation is also the time to update or eliminate inefficient and ineffective controls. Controls should evolve and change as your business environment changes, and as new technology supports techniques that were not available when earlier controls were designed. For example, at one time, many companies set specific dollar limits above which invoices required secondary approval. Techniques such as stochastic invoice blocking, enabled by SAP, now allow organizations to get away from arbitrary limits and statistically hold invoices for additional verification. Additionally, controls typically consider management's risk appetite, which changes as management changes. The implementation is the best (and often the only practical) time to optimize your controls and fit them to your business without costly after-the-fact rework.

> ### "We've *Always* Done it That Way!"
>
> One of the best ways to stifle organizational efficiency is to apply the wrong level of control to a business process. Too often, an organization's internal control experts apply outdated, ineffective, time-consuming controls over processes because those are the controls that they've grown accustomed to. It's time for organizations to apply the same rigor to re-engineering controls as they do to the business processes those controls govern. If your controls in SAP feel surprisingly similar to your controls before SAP, it may be time to seek outside, independent advice.

Some of the more common opportunities for control re-design and optimization surround the following activities:

- Approvals and authorizations — commonly labor intensive or focused on static thresholds
- Report monitoring — too often require extensive review, rather than honing in on specific (potential) issues
- SOD monitoring — insufficient balance in the time spent on those rules actually being violated, and those that may but have not to this point
- Detective controls — over-reliance on detective vs. preventative controls, and/or controls to late in the process to allow meaningful recovery

3.1.6   Upgrade-Specific Benefits

In addition to the general benefits described in this section, SAP upgrades have their own unique issues. While upgrades are typically less challenging than full-blown implementations, considering internal controls during the upgrade process is no less important. Specific attention to three key areas is critical during the upgrade process:

- **Loss of internal control functionality**. Periodically, an SAP upgrade may result in the loss of certain functionality that your organization may have relied on for controlling certain activities. Companies using SAP's Reverse Business Engineering

(RBE) to monitor the risk of SOD violations and excessive SAP access, for example, needed to compensate when SAP removed this functionality from recent versions of the system. Whenever functionality loss affects existing internal controls, organizations must determine new ways of mitigating that risk.

▶ **Improved functionality.** Often, functionality introduced by SAP during a new release can allow organizations to eliminate or improve previously enacted controls and further streamline processes. Perhaps you created a custom report to monitor a specific exception condition, and the upgrade eliminates the potential that the exception can even exist. Alternatively, you may have built mitigation procedures in an area where the new functionality introduced can serve as a more effective internal control. Every functionality change introduced by the upgrade should be examined specifically with controls in mind, and how that change affects the way that risks can be managed in the upgraded component.

▶ **Custom ABAP programs.** Every upgrade has the potential to affect custom ABAP programs, and often this effect may not be intuitive, based on what is being changed. Where these custom ABAP programs serve as an internal control mechanism or in some way supports internal controls, these custom programs must be specifically tested to identify potential unexpected results from the upgrade. Additionally, custom ABAP programs can impact new functionality offered by the upgrade in unanticipated ways. Perhaps the upgrade introduces new control functionality as in the previous bullet, but the ABAP allows users to bypass that functionality (something that would not have been considered during the initial ABAP development because the functionality being bypassed did not exist prior to the upgrade). Every custom ABAP program must be examined during the upgrade to determine how it's affected by the upgrade, or how it affects the new functionality provided by the upgrade.

For all of these reasons, having a deep understanding of your business risks, control needs, and current control techniques and applying that knowledge to the upgrade process is essential to ensure an effective upgrade that can also withstand the rigors of an audit.

3.2 Creating a Control-Conscious Implementation

If money were no object, surviving an SAP audit could be assured merely by including SAP risk, audit, and control experts in every process design and configuration decision made during the SAP implementation. In the real world, however, blanketing the project with such personnel may not be practical and is certainly not cost effective. SAP implementations are a significant cost to any organization, and using full-time expert control advisors across every process affected by the implementation for the duration of the project is an expensive proposition. The obvious question then becomes, if internal controls are so key to SAP audit success, and establishing these controls before system go-live is easier than doing it after, how can organizations achieve an appropriate level of control without spending a fortune.

Fortunately, there is a solution. In this section, we introduce an approach that leverages a concept we term the *control-conscious implementation team*. Having a control conscious-implementation team allows you to leverage the direct involvement of typical SAP implementation team members into early-stage control design decisions, while supplementing their lack of SAP internal controls expertise with oversight from SAP risk and controls specialists. You effectively increase the effectiveness of your implementation process at audit-proofing SAP through a series of specific actions focused on the entire implementation team by:

- ▶ Educating them on basic control concepts
- ▶ Developing a common language and regular communication process
- ▶ Establishing a consistent approach for identifying and documenting risks to be addressed through the implementation
- ▶ Providing them with tools to help think through important control decisions during the traditional design phase
- ▶ Monitoring internal control progress through integrated project management activities

Such an approach requires commitment from your SAP project management team to take ownership of control design but pays dramatic dividends. Rather than needing a dedicated SWAT team to deal with specific control issues, the control-conscious implementation provides you with an entire army of staff on the lookout for audit-relevant risks and equipped with an appropriate process to address those risks once identified.

> **Using Experts in Governance, Risk, and Compliance for SAP**
>
> The control-conscious implementation team does not eliminate the need for SAP control expertise. Using advice from internal controls experts specializing in SAP is still key to ensuring you efficiently leverage SAP functionality to address all relevant risks. The control-conscious implementation team does, however, allow you to significantly reduce the number of true SAP controls experts involved with your implementation and allow a much smaller resource investment stretch a long way.

3.2.1 Implementation Team Skills and Knowledge

Designing effective internal controls requires a handful of skills and processes not historically required on implementation teams. These skills and processes can be added but require sufficient knowledge to effectively integrate them into the implementation process.

Risk Assessment and Management

The first new skill is that of risk assessment and management. Throughout the implementation, control-conscious team members should consider a variety of risk-related questions:

- What risks are associated with the process with which I'm currently dealing?
- Are previous decisions related to how we deal with these risks still necessary in light of SAP capabilities?
- If we've accepted a certain level of risk in the past as being too costly to effectively control, is this still appropriate in our new SAP environment?
- When we make process decisions, how do these impact our risk environment?
- What inherent and control risks must be addressed during process design?

> **Inherent Risk**
>
> Inherent risk describes the risk in a process that is always associated with that process, regardless of organization. Examples of inherent risk within any payment process include the risk of:
> - Over-/under-payment
> - Duplicate payment
> - Payment outside the timing specified in the contract
>
> These risks may be addressed by organizational procedures, process variations, and/or technology, but before mitigation procedures are applied, inherent risks affect the process regardless of organizational characteristics.

The answers from each of these questions directly affect the level of internal control emphasis that must be placed over the risk.

Let's consider an SAP implementation covering the payables process. The implementation team (or at least someone on the team with the ability to influence design decisions) should have knowledge of payables-related issues such as:

- ▶ Challenges that have resulted in past problems
- ▶ If the organization has been affected by fraud, the specific situations that allowed the fraud to perpetuate (information that may not be common knowledge across the organization)
- ▶ The current relevance of existing payables-related control tolerances (e.g., if controls focused on payments over $500, assessing how much risk remains in payments less than $500 and investigating possible SAP configurations that could add a level of control to these smaller payment types)

The team should consider the impact of these risk issues and determine how these can best be addressed through SAP or the processes built around SAP. The team should also be aware of not only those risks inherent to the process itself but also those specific to their business (e.g., a company doing business internationally may need to consider the FCPA risk of third-party payments), and those resulting from the process design choices being made, thereby creating control risks (e.g., as SAP workflow is introduced, new risks associated with workflow, such as the risk of the employee receiving the workflow being on vacation and holding up the payment process, need to be considered).

Control Risk

Control risk is the risk that an internal control (designed to mitigate an identified risk) is bypassed or otherwise not effective. To some extent, control risks are a type of inherent risk, associated not with the process but with the specific control technique being used. Examples of controls risks include:

- ▶ An SAP warning message is bypassed, allowing an erroneous transaction to be bypassed
- ▶ A forgetful employee posts his password under his keyboard, increasing the risk that security authentication procedures become ineffective for that employee
- ▶ An employee purchases goods on his corporate credit card, despite policy that that type of material must go through the corporate procurement process

Control risks must be considered whenever an internal control is applied to a process.

Control Design

Another new skill that needs to be included in the implantation team is that of *control design*. In addition to recognizing risk, and processes and situations that create those risks, the control-conscious implementation team must also understand effective control procedures for mitigating those risks. The team should consider the implication of answers to questions such as:

▸ When is the best point in the process for the control to occur?

▸ Does the control strike an effective balance between the risk it's intended to address, and the business impact it may introduce?

▸ What control risks do we introduce with this control, and should new controls be designed to address these risks as well?

▸ Are all variations of the process covered by this control, or must they be considered for other controls?

▸ After application of this control, is the level of remaining risk appropriate?

Remaining Risk

Remaining risk is the amount of risk to which an organization is exposed even after controls have been put into place. Also known as residual risk, remaining risks recognize that controls rarely perfectly mitigate a risk, and the organization may still be exposed to some level of risk (albeit smaller) after the application of the control. Examples of remaining risk include:

▸ SAP configuration prevents an employee from entering a single transaction over a single specified amount, but the employee could still have multiple transactions (split transactions) under that amount

▸ QA procedures select a sample of transactions for verification of accuracy, and it's possible that erroneous information exists in transactions not selected for QA procedures

▸ Employee verifications made before time of hire may miss legal convictions in-process at the time of hire and thus not on official records

Management should be aware of the level of remaining risks and involved in determining whether they are appropriate. Ideally, the remaining risk is communicated to and formally accepted by management, creating awareness of the potential exposure at a high level in the organization.

When discussing the need for risk assessment and management skills in the implementation team, we used an example in accounts payables. Continuing that same example, consider the situation where the implementation team identifies the risk of fraudulent payments to vendors as one that must be mitigated through internal control procedures. In thinking through possible ways to accomplish this, the team may decide that controls preventing fraudulent payments are preferable, because detective controls may not allow recovery of funds when dealing with fraud. As such, the team places controls over initial vendor setup, to ensure that only appropriate vendors get added to SAP. Perhaps the control is that only a handful of trusted employees are allowed to enter vendors, and an independent QA process ensures that all vendor details are entered accurately. Of course, when considering this process, the team assesses the impact of this process on the payment processing time for new vendors. Centralization and QA may result in higher quality and consistency but slow the overall setup time for new vendors and thus affect the speed at which payments to new vendors can be made.

When considering the effectiveness of this control, the team probably notices that this process would only affect fraudulent payments to fictitious vendors, and has no impact on the potential for fraudulent payments to approved vendors. Thus, the control-conscious team may need to consider additional controls over fraudulent payments to this category of vendors. Additionally, the team may recognize that centralized vendor management is contingent on SAP security controls being appropriately established to effectively segregate these duties. Finally, the team may recognize that this control works best for frequently used vendors but may not apply to one-time vendors and thus additional controls may need to be designed over this latter category of vendor. This entire thought process culminates in a series of controls that cover the risk of fraudulent vendor payments.

For those of you who have been through an implementation before, you may find this type of thinking to be new to your prior experience. Perhaps you applied similar concepts to one set of processes but not across the entire implementation. Later in this chapter, we share techniques for ensuring that such a process occurs effectively across the implementation.

3.2.2 Setting the Stage for Effective Control Design

To create the controls-conscious implementation team, you must consider effective ways for building skills in risk assessment and management, as well as *control design*. As a benchmark, before the implementation process gets too far along, every team member should possess a basic knowledge of risks and controls, and be provided tools for designing, communicating, and gaining consensus on appropriate controls to address the risks within. The specific ways for accomplishing this during your implementation may vary depending on your experience and that of your team. We suggest, at a minimum, holding a half-day information session with each functional team, during which an expert in SAP risk, audit, and control provides:

▸ An overview of internal controls and what they are intended to accomplish

▸ A review of techniques for ensuring effective control design

▸ Discussion on risks that the team should address through internal controls during the design phase of the SAP implementation

The idea is to empower each team member with the knowledge and tools to think through control issues in the processes for which they are responsible. In doing so, this enables the SAP risk, audit, and control experts who will work with the implementation team to mentor and provide QA and thus spread their time more effectively across the implementation.

Once the team has been provided with this new knowledge and an appropriate design methodology, the true risk and control experts can take on an advisory role to the implementation (rather than need to be in a lead role on the implementation). As team skills develop and each functional team proves capable at understanding risks and designing controls, your SAP risk, audit, and controls experts can moderate their time more effectively. Likely, these experts will spend a short amount of time with each functional team every week to ensure that the control design effort is on track and tools are used appropriately. If you design metrics appropriately and push your control-conscious team effectively, you can likely wean yourself almost entirely of these SAP risk, audit, and control experts as you progress into future phases of your implementation.

> **Organization Tip**
>
> Rather than restricting your SAP risk, audit, and control experts to specific functional lines, put them in a position to have visibility across all processes. This enables them to review and validate end-to-end process controls that may cross functional teams. Even in a project with strong cross-team communication channels, it's easy for control assumptions from teams operating in traditional component-specific silos to result in either duplication of controls or control gaps (which are even more detrimental to the overall control design process).

3.2.3 Reporting Issues and Progress

Early in your implementation planning cycle, determine how to incorporate the new risk and control activities into your implementation project plan and communication strategies. Organizations often have different approaches and philosophies to manage implementation tasks, so your specific technique for tracking these activities may vary. The key is to track and communicate the status of your control design (which depends on initial risk identification), and ultimately the configuration and testing of these controls.

> **A Word of Advice for Managing Control-Related Activities**
>
> We strongly suggest including control-related activities as specific line items in your SAP project plan, rather than considering these to be merely subcomponents of the related process design. Organizations often assume that once the importance of controls is communicated and the team is educated on control design, the controls will naturally be built as part of the process. Because the process of control design is new for most implementation teams, however, visibility into control-related activity status can be easily lost. As deadlines approach, diligence on designing controls may also diminish. If you are serious about designing effective controls during your implementation process, include control-related activities as specific tasks on your project plan.

The level of detail related you choose to track and communicate related to control considerations during the implementation is up to you. At a minimum, most organizations managing their SAP implementations in this way track the following milestones, for each process:

▶ Process risks identified and prioritized

▶ Risk assessment (prioritization) validated with internal and external audit

▶ Controls designed for each key risk

▶ Control design validated with SAP risk, audit, and controls specialist

▶ Configurable controls set up in SAP

▶ Configurable controls successfully pass testing

▶ Manual and process controls incorporated into user training and education

▶ Training attendance verified for all control performers

▶ Existing control-related documentation (such as Sarbanes-Oxley control lists) updated

Tracking at this level of detail is our suggested minimum. Tracking these activities for each individual internal control can also be of value, although sometimes organizations track this detail separately to not overburden the SAP implementation plan with too much detail.

By including your control design activities in your project plan, you reinforce the notion that control design is an integral component of the implementation, and not a separate initiative. This is important because it sets a strong tone for the project and will likely benefit you if and when auditors get involved. Additionally, including control-related activities on the project plan ensures a certain level of ongoing communication and status reporting through the normal project status reporting process. Merely including these tasks in the project plan will help to ensure controls are being considered, which puts you further ahead than many organizations.

Another area where SAP implementation reporting can be enhanced relates to key performance indicators (KPIs) related to the control design effort. With controls now specific line items on the implementation plan, you can begin to track, monitor, and report on statistics that will help drive success with an SAP audit. A few examples of KPIs include:

▶ Number of controls per process (more is not necessarily better)

▶ Ratio of preventive-to-detective controls

▶ Ratio of manual to automated controls

▶ Percentage of configurable controls that have been configured

▶ Percentage of configured controls that have been tested

▶ Percentage of manual controls that have been built into training programs

Several of these KPIs are possible only after specific phases of the implementation. As you refine your reporting process, however, these control-related KPIs can even be fed into management reporting dashboards.

3.2.4 Working with Auditors

At some point during the implementation, you will likely need to *work with your internal and/or external auditors*. While the thought may at first make you cringe, we encourage you to not only welcome audit participation but even suggest it if your auditors are not getting involved. In fact, get your auditors involved to limit surprises after the implementation.

Even if your auditors are not SAP experts, they can bring valuable experience and advice to the implementation team. Because auditors are generally involved in reviewing processes across your organization, they generally have a more in-depth knowledge of your business risks that few others possess. Your auditors are also a great source for identifying the inherent risk that should be addressed during your control design activities. In fact, most auditors have a list of risks that they often use as starting points for their audits, which they may give to you for your planning purposes. Even in the absence of such a list, your auditor can provide some valuable insight into your brainstorming process.

In addition to assisting the implementation team with risks identification, your auditors may assist in ways not immediately apparent. Many audit departments create process flowcharts of organizational processes that they audit, and these flowcharts provide valuable input when determining how processes will change under SAP. Audit also typically maintains relationships and communication lines within your organization that can prove extremely valuable if you are not getting the resources or cooperation that you need to be successful. To make the most of audit involvement, however, you must establish the right relationship early in the implementation and agree on specific rules of engagement. Each auditor involved in your implementation should understand these rules.

Integrated Planning

In the same way that we recommend including specific control-related activities in your SAP implementation project plan, we also recommend including your auditor's relevant activities in this plan as well. This approach reinforces the premise that all tasks necessary for a successful implementation be included in the project plan, and that for control design, auditor buy-in is as important as other QA procedures that you place over the SAP implementation. We are not suggesting that you need to include your auditor's own work program into your project plan (if they will be auditing your implementation, then it's unlikely you'll see the actual audit steps), but we are suggesting that you agree on some key audit milestones and add these to your implementation plan, assigning audit as the owner of those activities.

Key Meetings

During an implementation, time is a highly prized commodity. As such, the auditor should be participating in a manner that is highly respectful of the implementation team's time. This includes simple things like requiring the auditor to attend all relevant meetings for their full duration. Repeating meeting discussion to someone who was not present can be time consuming, and potentially having to revisit decisions made during the meeting because audit concerns were not available for the discussions can be severely detrimental to continued progress. If for some reason your auditor cannot attend a key meeting, he should provide any desired input in advance of the meeting so that it can be effectively considered, and then review meeting minutes and ask relevant questions within a defined period of time. Such interactions should be documented in a service level agreement that you make with your auditor.

> **Relocating the Auditor with the Implementation Team**
>
> Make space in your implementation team's area for any auditors who will be involved in the initiative, and encourage them to relocate to this area for the duration of the implementation. This creates a greater sense of teamwork and facilitates knowledge transfer.

Audit Reporting

Another important set of ground rules relates to audit concerns, and specifically how, when, and in what format these concerns are communicated. Ideally, audit concerns should be reported jointly and integrated into the standard implementation reporting process. This continues to reinforce the common goals that the organization is working on throughout the implementation. Additionally, the auditor and the implementation project manager should work together to identify proposed solutions to these issues to also be included in the reporting process. The goal of this process is not to make the project manager or implementation team look bad, nor is it to make the auditor look good. The goal is to quickly address implementation risk before delays increase the cost of correction. Audit may still choose to have separate audit reports for their work, but the better that audit information is communicated along with implementation-related communications, the greater the integrated nature of the project becomes clear to the organization.

Communication Speed

The timing for communication of audit concerns is also important, and you should come to agreement with your auditor early in the implementation about how and when potential issues will be shared. We have already discussed how on an implementation, the time between when a decision is made and when a change to that decision is deemed necessary, the more rework that may need to be performed, the greater the cost of the change, and the higher the likelihood of pushing the project behind schedule. Set the expectation with your auditor that any potential issue that affects project scope or configuration should be reported immediately, even if the auditor has not fully validated the issue. Such a process is likely a change for your auditor and may not come naturally, as most auditors issue findings after completion of the entire audit, rather than in near real time (we discussed audit reporting in more detail in Chapter 2). Depending on your auditor's experience, they may not even be aware of the impact that typical audit reporting cycles may have on an implementation. The importance of timely issue reporting makes this one of the highest-priority ground rules. The goal here is to ensure that there are no surprises.

The process for designing internal controls during an SAP implementation typically follows the illustration in Figure 3.1: The SAP Control Design Process. In general, an early scoping effort determines control design priorities. For the processes, locations, and risks determined to be in scope, a set of expected controls is developed and designed. These controls may be configured in SAP, fully manual outside of SAP, or system-dependent whereby an employee interacts with SAP to perform the control. The mechanism for assessing the controls depends on the type of control. The results of initial control assessment may cause the control to be redesigned, reconfigured, or retrained prior to SAP system go-live. Ultimately, ongoing controls monitoring will influence the evolution of these controls over time.

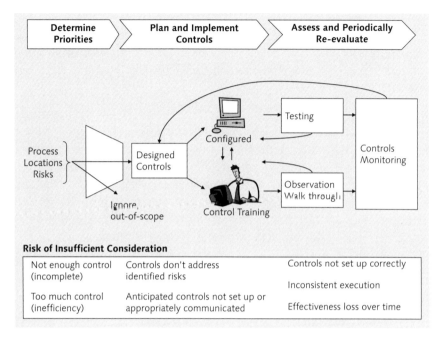

| Determine Priorities | Plan and Implement Controls | Assess and Periodically Re-evaluate |

Risk of Insufficient Consideration

Not enough control (incomplete)	Controls don't address identified risks	Controls not set up correctly
		Inconsistent execution
Too much control (inefficiency)	Anticipated controls not set up or appropriately communicated	Effectiveness loss over time

Figure 3.1 The SAP Control Design Process

3.3   Designing Effective Controls

Central to effective control design during your SAP implementation is a consistent process that each implementation team member with control design responsibility follows throughout the implementation. This process should facilitate easy documentation and communication of controls. Many documentation techniques capture risk and control-related information, and tools range from the simplistic to the fully automated. Over the last five years, SAP has even developed tools in this space, as part of what is now termed SAP BusinessObjects GRC solutions.

For purposes of this book, we use a simplistic template to illustrate core concepts and aid the thought process of your team members when they are thinking through control issues for their respective processes. A Microsoft® Excel®-based version of this template can be found online, and is a great starting point for helping your auditors understand how you have designed and configured controls as part of your implementation. Delivering a complete set of control documentation at the end of the implementation will be a tremendous benefit, and is a key step in surviving an SAP audit with as little pain as possible.

As we continue through this chapter, bear in mind that our examples are intended to be simple in order to illustrate the core concepts without burdening you with too much detail. During an actual implementation, the number of items identified and the level of detail for each item would be significantly greater.

3.3.1 Defining Relevant Processes and Sub-processes

Organizations typically collect a large amount of information during an implementation, and control design information is no exception. Information overload can occur quickly if you are not well organized from the start. Risk and control information is often commonly grouped under *processes and sub-processes*. You may find it helpful to align your control design processes and sub-processes with SAP terminology, and keep your information consistent with the organization of your business process procedures (BPPs) or other documentation created during your implementation.

You'd typically determine how you wish to organize your risk and control documentation during the planning phase of the implementation, well before design begins. This provides you with the opportunity to have a structure in place when you educate your team on how the control design process will work in your environment. For our simplistic example, we'll break the Purchase-to-Pay process into the following sub-processes: Procurement/Purchasing, Goods/Service Receipt, Payment, Vendor Master File, and Material Master File.

3.3.2 Creating the Risk Inventory

Once you have defined logical groupings (in this case, sub-processes), the next step is to determine the *risks* that will need to be addressed during the implementation. This determination is also best performed during the planning phase. An example of risks mapped to sub-processes can be seen at Figure 3.2: Illustrative Risk Mapping.

Identifying the key risks associated with each sub-process and documenting these before the design phase begins allows the control-conscious implementation team to focus on ensuring that each risk has been addressed either through configuration in SAP, or by a manual process governing the use of SAP. Each functional team would break their respective processes down into major sub-processes, and for each of these sub-processes list the risks related to that sub-process. In Figure 3.2, we illustrate three risks associated with the Procurement/Purchasing sub-process; however, in reality most sub-processes will have a dozen or more risks associated with them.

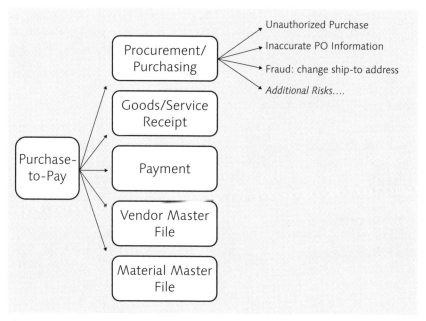

Unauthorized Purchase

Inaccurate PO Information

Fraud: change ship-to address

Additional Risks....

Figure 3.2 Illustrative Risk Mapping

Prioritize Your Risks

Although not included in this example, we also recommend adding a risk rating for each identified risk, and use this rating to allocate resources and determine priorities for control development. Ideally, this rating would be reviewed and discussed with your internal and external audit teams to ensure general agreement with these priorities. This rating would consider both the likelihood of the risk occurring and the potential impact if it did occur. You team would focus first on those risks with a higher risk rating, and address lower risk ratings as time permits.

Chapter 2 provided more detail on ways to think about risk, and may be a useful review if you are struggling at this point. Get assistance from your audit team when defining risk. Most audit departments, and all of the larger audit firms, have risk matrices associated with common business cycles. These matrices can serve as great starting points for the risks you need to consider.

Whether you have developed this risk inventory at the SAP project management level, or each functional team has worked to develop their own, once created, the risk inventory becomes the basis for your control design plan. You now have enough information to determine the control design effort and allocate appropriate resources. Changes to these risks (whether additions, deletions, or just changes to perceived priority) should follow a change management process similar to what you use for other parts of your implementation. This ensures that any changes to risks are vetted, approved, and communicated to the team so that everyone is working against a common set of risks.

3.3.3 Linking Controls to Risks

Moving into the design phase of the implementation, the control-conscious implementation team identifies and designs the controls that will address each of the risks in the risk inventory. Continuing with our earlier procurement example, Figure 3.3: Mapping Controls to Risks illustrates in a simplistic way how the control planning effort extends from the risk inventory. In this case, the risk of unauthorized purchase is mapped to four planned controls: SAP security, approval limits, SAP workflow, and the monitoring of a custom report. You will also note that each control has been given a reference number. This facilitates easier cross-referencing with other documents.

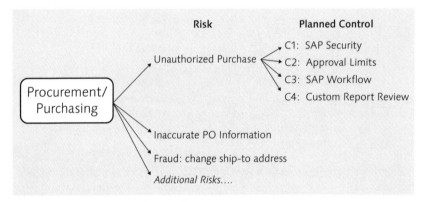

Figure 3.3 Mapping Controls to Risks

> **Relationship of Controls to Risks**
>
> In most situations, specific controls address multiple risks in varying degrees of reliance, and risks may be common across processes and sub-processes. Documenting these relationships and ensuring consistency when control descriptions change over time can become complicated as more risks and controls are added. As a result, using a purpose-built control documentation tool or creating a risk and controls database may help keep maintenance at an acceptable level.

As you study this example, you may wonder how we arrived at four controls. In Chapter 2, we discussed how controls mitigate risks, and the thought process that an auditor often uses when going through this analysis. Ultimately, each time a control is considered, the control-conscious implementation team makes an assessment as to whether that control is enough, or whether the risk warrants additional controls to create a stronger foundation.

Consider our fictitious example, with the team mitigating the risk of an unauthorized purchase. The team may have first looked at SAP security, and extended their analysis as follows, written as the team may be thinking through the process:

SAP Security

Limiting the number of individuals who can initiate and approve purchase is one way to reduce the risk of unauthorized purchases. Insufficient access control contributed to one of the purchasing frauds that we experienced in the past. By establishing appropriate roles within SAP security, we can ensure that only approved users make or approve purchases in SAP. This cuts the risk of unauthorized purchases dramatically but does not prevent unauthorized purchases from those employees who are allowed to initiate and approve purchases. While SAP security is important and a first step in mitigating this risk, we need to consider other controls as well.

Approval Limits

To supplement SAP security and provide greater internal control for those employees who have legitimate authority to initiate and approve purchases, the team next looks to establish approval limits. When combined with the SAP security, the addition of approval limits to the list of planned controls means that: (1) only a limited number of employees can initiate and approve purchases, and (2) each employee would have a specific cap on the purchases he can make. The team then assesses whether security plus authorization limits is sufficient control. For our example, the team recognizes that their organization has experienced fraud in the past, and thus enhanced controls over purchases may be necessary. The limits certainly put a cap on how much the organization is exposed, but there is still risk that expenditures under those limits are unauthorized. As a result, the team seeks an even greater level of control.

Workflow

The team decides that a good supplement to SAP approval limits might be using SAP workflow, in conjunction with these limits. Approval can be routed to specific levels of management depending on the dollar amount of the purchase. Thus, lower-dollar purchases can get one level of review, while higher-dollar purchases can be routed to the top levels of management for review.

Custom Report Review

With the three controls already planned (SAP security, approval limits, and SAP workflow), the team generally feels well covered. As they think through various scenarios, however, they realize that many of these controls are still heavily reliant on manual processes, and manual processes have a higher risk of failure. Security must be set up correctly to limit to the right employees, and changes must be made whenever employees transfer or leave the organization. Approval limits must be configured correctly, and adjusted as business conditions change. Managers responsible for approving workflow must be diligent in their reviews. Given the number of risk factors combined with problems that the organization had in this area in the past, the team decides to add one more control to be ultra-safe. In this case, they are developing a set of custom reports that the controller can review to hone in on potential problems. Because this control occurs after the transaction occurs, it will not prevent an unauthorized purchase, but it will help the controller detect potential abuse and limit the organization's overall impact.

> **Enough is Enough**
>
> As you can see, the number of controls necessary to mitigate an identified risk is somewhat subjective, and depends on the nature, timing, and assessed effectiveness of the controls being put into place. As you refine your list of proposed controls, getting advice from an SAP risk, audit, and controls specialist can help validate the integrity of the team's thought process. Consider running your thoughts by your internal and external auditors as well before configuration, to ensure everyone's specific concerns have been addressed by the proposed control design.

The control-conscious team follows this thought process for each risk identified within each sub-process, typically resulting in two to five controls for every identified risk. The brief control descriptions used in our example are good for illustrative purposes but are likely too brief to effectively communicate how the control works. Having an agreed-on standard for the detail to be included in a description will go a long way to ensuring a consistent understanding of the actual control mechanics, not only within the implementation team but also among auditors and employees who may need to perform the control. As a general rule of thumb, every control should include, at a minimum, the following information:

- ▶ When: At what point specifically is the control performed, or what triggers the control? Examples include: "upon login" or "before the transaction can be saved in SAP" or "prior to period close"
- ▶ Who: Who performs the control's action? Typically this would be a role or a system. Examples include: the CFO, accounting clerks, or SAP.

▶ What: The "who" is doing what specific action? The "what" should be specific enough to be repeatable. For example, "reviews Report ABC for reasonableness" is vague, whereas "reviews Report ABC for any item exceeding 150% of the month's average" is more precise.

▶ Because: What specifically gives assurance that the control is being performed? Examples include: "based on configured limits established in the IMG at <location in the IMG>," or "per corporate expense policies posted on the HR intranet site," or "as part of the closing checklist."

You may find that writing controls in this way, with each of the recommended components, forces you to think in a specific level of detail. Ultimately, having this level of detail is essential for communicating the control in a way that it can be configured and tested appropriately within SAP, or performed effectively by those interacting with SAP.

More than SAP Controls

When designing controls, it's vital that you consider not only controls in SAP but also SAP-independent controls that must be in place for the process to be effective. Even if the SAP implementation team is charged solely with SAP design and configuration, someone in the organization must look after controls outside of SAP to truly be ready for an audit. Using the technique we have discussed in this chapter will help ensure control completeness, regardless of whether these controls are manual or automated.

3.3.4 Tracking Control Design Progress

As the implementation progresses through the design phase into configuration and testing, you are in a position to begin *tracking* the status of each control. Between the point when the control is first envisioned and the point when the control is fully implemented, a number of key milestones exist:

▶ Control Documentation Complete

▶ Control Configuration Complete (N/A for manual controls)

▶ Control Testing Complete (N/A for manual controls)

▶ Control Training Complete (N/A for automated controls)

If your documentation process allows, track each of these details in a centralized location. If a process change occurs after the conceptual control design, you will likely need to reset the status of these milestones and rethink the controls to be applied over the process.

3.3.5   Additional Risks Resulting from Control Decisions

If you follow the process described in Sections 3.3.1, Defining Relevant Processes and Sub-processes, through 3.3.4, Tracking Control Design Progress, you are further ahead than most organizations implementing SAP when it comes to designing effective internal controls. Using this process, you are ready to survive your next SAP audit. If you are looking to do more than just survive, perhaps even to excel, then a few additional steps can help get you there. For every planned control, ask "What could cause this control to fail?" and document the response as an additional control risk. Then, for each control risk, identify additional controls that must be in place to mitigate these risks. These controls may be controls already existing in your organization, or controls that you need to further design during the implementation.

In Figure 3.4: Extending Control Design to Accommodate Control Risks, we illustrate this concept by continuing the example we have used in this section. In this case, the team considers additional risks for each control identified. In the case of SAP security, the team notes that invalid setup would affect the integrity of this control, as would an employee termination or transfer not being communicated to the security team so that access can be changed. Recognizing these risks, the control-conscious implementation team now must identify controls that mitigate these risks, and follow these controls through the control design process. Not every control risk needs to be identified by a new control — some may be addressed by other controls being designed, or by existing controls already in place throughout the organization.

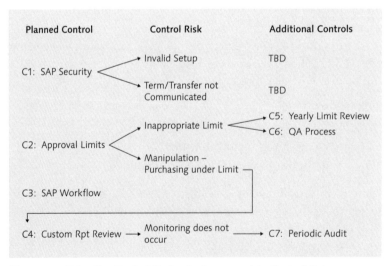

Figure 3.4   Extending Control Design to Accommodate Control Risks

3.3.6   Other Areas of Consideration

Thus far, we have presented control design related solely to the new business processes resulting from the SAP implementation. While this is certainly an important area for controls, it's not the only area where internal controls need to be considered. The processes and administrative procedures for supporting and maintaining SAP during the implementation should also be considered. This includes controls similar to the general computer controls (GCCs) that we discussed in Chapter 2, but rather than focusing on the production SAP environment, they are specific to the environment during the development process. Particular areas of focus should include:

▶ Change control — design decisions typically evolve during the implementation process, and effective change controls should ensure that controls relate to the final process design, not how the process may have been envisioned earlier in the implementation.

▶ Data cleansing — organizations often wisely choose not to migrate data with poor quality into SAP, instead editing and cleansing that data to enhance integrity; however, the mere process of data cleansing creates the potential that key data is intentionally or accidentally altered.

▶ Security — the increasing number of data privacy regulations means that even in the development environment, certain data must be restricted.

Obviously, other controls should exist over the implementation process; however, these three control categories will give you a great start.

Despite a variety of SAP implementation techniques, most implementations follow the general phases depicted at the top of Figure 3.5: Control Implementation Phases. Every phase of the standard implementation plan has a set of corresponding activities in the control implementation plan. As such, control design considerations occur throughout the SAP implementation.

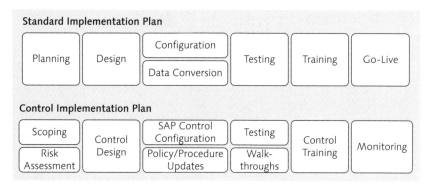

Figure 3.5   Control Implementation Phases

3.4 Control Considerations by Implementation Phase

In this section, we walk through each phase of the standard implementation lifecycle and recommend specific areas where control considerations should be included. We also share common issues related to each phase of the implementation lifecycle.

3.4.1 Planning

The *planning* process sets the foundation for effective control design throughout the implementation, and as such, considering the control design effort during the implementation planning phase is critical. This includes planning both for controls within the SAP-enabled processes resulting from the implementation, as well as control outside of SAP and also those controls supporting the implementation process itself.

During implementation planning, you are first and foremost setting the processes that will guide the rest of the implementation and ensure effective control design. This includes both developing controls over the implementation process itself, and establishing the procedures that will guide the control design effort. In the planning phase, you should be developing your risk inventory and from that inventory determining the level of control design effort required. You should be finalizing your control design process, and educating your team on their responsibilities in that process. You should also be working with your auditors to determine their level of involvement and ground rules for their participation on the project.

Intangible Benefit
Project management controls may at times seem difficult and time consuming; however, they serve an important function. In addition to keeping the project on track and ensure the achievement of desired outcomes, these controls also increase the likelihood that any inadvertent mistakes are either prevented or detected quickly before impacting the success of the project.

The planning phase is also where you will develop project controls that will dictate how the implementation effort proceeds, how decisions are made, how issues are tracked, and how status is communicated. While these activities have only limited impact on control design specifically, they are the project management controls that we discussed in Chapter 2, and they set the foundation for audit assurance during and shortly after the implementation. As such, being diligent in these processes is important, and getting your auditors involved in validating planned project-level controls can also be of benefit — ensuring the procedures that you enact over the implementation are sufficient for audit reliance later on.

The easiest way to gain audit assurance over the implementation process is to follow a robust, well-structured methodology. The Project Management Institute's guidelines set forth in the Project Management Body of Knowledge (PMBOK) are well recognized by auditors, and diligently managing your implementation according to these guidelines is sure to impress your auditor. Of course, the structure provided by SAP's ASAP implementation methodology also has many of these characteristics and can support a well-run implementation.

The ability to effectively consider the implications of many fundamental project management issues, and adapt your methodology appropriately, is central to having sound project management controls. Your auditor will typically be interested in the answers to these questions as well (this is an incomplete list):

▶ Who will be involved in key project-related decisions such as go-live readiness, and how will such decisions be made?

▶ As issues are identified during the implementation, how will we track these issues and ensure appropriate resolution? If any of these issues cannot be resolved before go-live, how will we make the determination as to whether go-live is still appropriate?

▶ How can we ensure control design consistency across the implementation team, and who will determine whether tools are being used appropriately?

▶ How will we track the status of control design and ensure that the effort is proceeding as intended?

▶ If different opinions exist, how will we ultimately determine whether controls effectively address key risks, and what the final controls to be implemented will look like?

▶ How do we ensure that late-stage process changes trigger an additional round of control design?

▶ Once controls have been conceptually designed, how do we ensure that they are implemented as intended and working as anticipated during control design?

By thoughtfully considering the answers to these questions, you have laid the foundation for a successful implementation. You have established the key processes that will guide your control efforts. You have also avoided some of the most common issues.

After the planning phase, auditors often find many organizations lacking. Common areas of concern include:

▶ Lack of project structure and standards

▶ Failure to include control design activities as line items in the project plan

▶ Inconsistent control design processes among team members

By following the guidelines and considerations in this section, you can avoid these issues becoming an audit concern during your implementation.

3.4.2 Design

Most of the work we discuss in this chapter occurs during the *design* phase of the SAP implementation. Because the primary activities in this phase were discussed in detail in Section 3.3, Designing Effective Controls, we'll avoid including great detail here, and highlight a few areas of importance.

During the planning phase, inventory your risks. Ensuring that all risks have been addressed by one or more controls is critical during the design phase. These controls may be in SAP, or may be the result of manual processes, but regardless, they should be sufficient to reduce the risk to an acceptable level.

Controls Documentation Using SAP's Business Process Procedures (BPP)

Many SAP implementations still follow the ASAP methodology, which includes a set of BPPs for documenting configuration details and process decisions. When using these documents, the tendency is to try to document controls within every BPP. While the idea seems conceptually sound, the reality is that many BPPs are written at a task level, and may not be suitable for an entire set of controls — in fact, designing controls at this granular level of detail could result in over-controlled processes and lead to process inefficiencies. While it can be useful to reference controls within the BPPs, the original control documentation is best kept outside the BPPs and linked only by reference number — so that multiple controls addressing the same risk can be changed in a single place without the need to edit every relevant BPP. Keeping a separate controls summary document also allows you to find controls quickly, without reviewing every BPP document.

Re-engineering is a useful mindset to have when designing controls. SAP provides many sophisticated options when it comes to controls, and thinking about how your internal controls can be enhanced using SAP functionality will help you create efficient controls. It can be easy to fall into the trap of designing the same controls that you have had in the past, and hard to break auditors (and other employees) of controls to which they have become accustomed. Spending the right amount of effort redesigning controls actually helps to ensure that controls continue to work properly over time — reducing the likelihood that employees bypass an inefficient control because of the time or effort involved in performing it.

As you are designing controls, considering the future can play a part in effective control design. Many organizations, driven independently or through their audit departments, are considering techniques such as continuous auditing and/or continuous monitoring. If your organization is moving in this direction, considering these processes in advance as part of your control design will save a lot of effort in the long run, even if continuous auditing and/or monitoring is several years into the future. At the point you are in the midst of the implementation, you have the best visibility into details and data easily lost or forgotten after the implementation — capturing it as part of your control documentation can make future improvements significantly easier.

As you finalize control design activities, you may also find it useful to track and communicate remaining risks with management and your audit team to ensure agreement and buy-in before go-live. SAP implementations can be time consuming, and management's risk tolerance level can change during the implementation process. Communicating these remaining risks in a formal setting ensures that everyone understands each risk and has a chance to influence how it's addressed before the system goes live.

Because the design phase is where much of the internal control work takes place, problems here can cascade throughout the implementation. Some of the most common audit concerns related to the design phase include:

▸ Failure to consider process-level controls outside of SAP
▸ Ineffective tracking of remaining risks
▸ Re-engineered processes hindered by outdated controls
▸ Poor visibility into control design status

3.4.3 Configuration

Once your proposed set of controls has been developed, you can begin *configuring* these controls in SAP. Typically, this involves going into the IMG and modifying settings to either enable a specific control-related function, or change specific parameters for a function turned on by default. Control configuration can also include developing any custom ABAP programs necessary for the proposed control design. Have a process for verifying that every proposed control in your design specifications is configured during configuration — a common audit step compares design specifications to configuration.

As you are configuring each control, you may also find it helpful to capture setup details (such as the specific location in the IMG where the control is configured) and include this in your control documentation as well. When your auditors begin reviewing SAP, being able to direct them precisely to where each control is configured will save a lot of time during the audit process.

> **Why Did We Do That Again?**
>
> Another best practice related to your control documentation is to retain information, where relevant, for the rationale for specific control decisions. If questions arise during the audit where the auditor is looking to understand why a specific decision was made, this information will come in handy. Additionally, it can be a useful internal reference after go-live as personnel change and memories fade.

Another configuration opportunity during this phase is the setup and configuration of audit-specific functionality. This specific configuration is focused not on your proposed internal controls but rather on SAP tools or other functionality you may need to maintain those controls (e.g., SAP BusinessObjects Process Control, if included with your SAP purchase) or that your auditors may use to review the controls (the Audit Information System, AIS, which comes with every SAP instance). While these can often be set up after the implementation, addressing them while knowledge is fresh eases implementation effort.

Some of the common challenges that organizations face during the configuration phase include:

▶ Insufficient documentation of configuration decisions and related settings

▶ Controls identified in design documents but not configured to specifications

▶ Failure to configure AIS and other audit-centric functionality (where relevant)

3.4.4 Data Conversion

Over the last several years, data privacy has become a much more visible issue, and as a result a typical implementation team no longer has access to the entire set of organizational data for testing and development purposes. This can make the *data conversion* effort more challenging than in the past, because security and change control procedures, even in the development environment, need to be strong.

If you will be doing any data cleansing (modifying data to add information required by SAP but not previously recorded in your legacy system, or changing data to eliminate duplicate or invalid information), you should also establish strong control procedures over the data cleansing process. These procedures should be designed to ensure that:

▶ Data is modified accurately, and no errors are introduced during the data cleansing process

▶ Only data that should be changed has been changed

▶ An audit trail allows the new set of data to be mapped back to the original set of data for audit purposes

Taking Advantage of the Tools That Audit Uses

Many audit departments use specialized audit tools (like *ACL* with *Direct Link for SAP ERP*) to identify errors and indicators of data integrity problems within data. These audit tools contain specialized functions to quickly find potential errors, omissions, and inconsistencies. If your organization uses such a tool, leverage your auditors to assist in the data cleansing process. There is no better way to avoid surprises than to validate your system using the tools that your auditor will use in his testing.

The most common audit issues related to data conversion are:

▶ Rushed, incomplete process (often due to significantly underestimating the effort during the planning stage)

▶ Failure to cleanse data before moving it to SAP, resulting in invalid master data affecting SAP transactions

▶ Loss of audit trail during data cleansing

▶ Ineffective monitoring of changes to master data during conversion process

3.4.5 Testing

If you have integrated your control documentation into your system design documentation, control *testing* likely flows through your standard testing process. Ideally, your test scripts include tests of your configured controls, and any issues identified during testing are recorded in your standard issue-tracking system. The controls you have established are designed to address your organization's risks, so any testing concerns related to controls should be thoroughly investigated and resolved prior to implementation.

Some regulatory compliance audits, like those in the Sarbanes-Oxley Act in the United States, may allow an auditor to place reliance on the testing performed during the implementation if certain criteria are met. Check with your auditors to see if this is the case in your situation, and if so, work with them to ensure your testing processes are sufficient for their purposes. While testing in a manner that allows greater reliance by your auditors likely adds time to your own testing process, in the long run, it can pay dividends by reducing the time necessary for the audit. Given the importance of your internal controls, have your audit team perform independent testing of your key controls before go-live, enhancing assurance that your new SAP system is ready.

Common audit issues resulting from an incomplete testing phase include:

▶ Inconsistent testing procedures across teams or rollouts

▶ Failure to test using the security roles as they will be implemented in production

▶ Poor follow-up on issues identified during testing (under the assumption that the test failure is an "isolated incident")

3.4.6 Training

We cannot emphasize enough the importance of effective *training* during the implementation. Many SAP audit findings result from insufficient user understanding or knowledge of the system. Other audit issues may be easier to pinpoint, but poor training can have a pervasive effect on the integrity of your processes. Even if the majority of your controls are configured directly in SAP, some of these controls still require a level of manual interaction and thus necessitate proper employee training.

The goal of training is to ensure a successful outcome — employees who understand how they should be using SAP have the skills and knowledge to perform their functions proficiently. As such, training is about more than just attendance at a training event — it's about ensuring that employees walk away with the ability to do what is intended of them. Training evaluations, attendance records, and other metrics are important, but consider also procedures for monitoring employee activity after training to ensure effective retention.

> **Integrated Training**
>
> Control training is best when integrated as part of the training that employees receive on SAP. Treating control training as a separate event de-emphasizes the value of internal controls and their importance to the implementation.

Your training should include enough information for employees to perform their activities as intended. This means training on more than just navigation within SAP. For example, it's common for an organization to train employees on how to get to a specific control-related SAP report. As we discussed in Chapter 1, however, the control is not accessing the report, but rather the action that is taken from the report. Thus, for the employee responsible for reviewing an SAP report as part of his assigned control activities, the employee needs to not only understand how to access the report in SAP, he also needs to know how often to review the report, what specifically to look for on the report, and how to leverage SAP to investigate and resolve anything that catches his attention during the review.

Common audit concerns related to training include:

▶ Focused solely on SAP rather than also including manual controls surrounding the use of SAP

▶ Designed primarily around SAP system navigation vs. usage

▶ Failure to monitor the effectiveness of training and ensure user retention

3.4.7 Go-Live

If you have followed the process that we have described in this chapter, by the time you are ready for *go-live*, you should be comfortable with your ability to pass any audit. Prior to go-live, however, there are a few activities you should consider to validate your readiness. If you have any open issues, particularly if they affect control effectiveness or are the result of control testing, these issues should be assessed in light of the risks they pose. Because these issues affect controls, and controls are intended to mitigate risks, communicate these open issues to management and allow sufficient discussion and determination as to whether the implementation should be delayed until these issues are resolved.

Most audit issues are the result of insufficient effort in earlier phases of the implementation, but two concerns commonly occur:

▶ Readiness based on date/budget

▶ Inadequate risk assessment for open issues

3.4.8 Summary of Control Considerations by Phase

Each phase of the implementation lifecycle is important to the overall integrity of the control design process. Insufficient effort during any single phase is likely to have a cascading effect across all phases, resulting in increased effort late in the implementation or insufficient controls at go-live. Not appropriately considering risk and control issues during each phase is likely to have the following impact:

▶ Planning — hinders your ability to have the right balance of controls, potentially focusing too much attention on areas of low risk resulting in effort spent designing unnecessary or overly complex controls, or neglecting to account for certain risks resulting in complete lack of control.

▶ Design — can result in uncontrolled processes, or controls not appropriately configured to your specific business needs. This increases your organization's exposure to risk, and directly impacts management's perception of implementation success.

▶ Configuration — may result in the false belief that planned controls were set up in SAP as intended.

▶ Data conversion — may fail to identify data problems that could impact every transaction processed in SAP.

▶ Testing — increases the risk that controls configured in SAP are not working as intended, and decreases your ability to identify transactions and situations where controls may inadvertently be bypassed.

▶ Training — presumes, potentially falsely, that employees will inherently know their control responsibility for manual controls or system-related controls requiring manual interaction, or that the process will be intuitive enough that employees naturally perform the intended actions to the degree of precision desired.

▶ Go-live — increases ongoing audit effort by not fully capturing and documenting implemented controls while details are still fresh in the mind of the implementation team.

Is it too Late to Start?

If you are already in the middle of an implementation and are nearing go-live, you may not have the luxury of going back through each implementation phase and completing each of the steps we have described. If you simply do not have the ability to complete what we have described in this chapter, consider focusing on the following areas:

▶ Consistency of controls across entities and rollouts (one audit "red flag" is two similar areas with different setup/configuration), unless supported by clear logic

▶ Customization of default SAP parameters and tolerances to your organization's risk

▶ Master data maintenance procedures

▶ Security, including overall SAP security administration, controls over powerful roles and IDs (SAP*, SAP_ALL, etc.), and restrictions over developer access to production

▶ Monitoring of exception processes (e.g., inventory adjustments or sundry invoice processing, to name a few)

▶ User education and understanding of key control processes

▶ Integrity of data conversion and cleansing

▶ Change control and transport process (governing the new production SAP system)

Focusing on these areas is no substitute for following the process that we have described in this chapter. If time and resources permit, follow the guidance that we have described even if it means postponing the go-live. Focusing on the areas in this list will not ensure a clean audit report but will likely reduce your number of post-implementation audit issues.

3.5   Summary

Failure to consider controls during an SAP implementation or upgrade leaves your organization exposed to a potentially serious level of risk. It can also result in excessive costs and rework, and make audits of SAP time consuming and burdensome to your organization. Creating a control-conscious implementation team and providing a consistent set of tools and processes ensures proper control design. Include your auditor in the process, but set ground rules early and manage and report on audit issues through traditional project status reporting. By following a simple set of guidelines and focusing on designing internal controls commiserate with the level of risk to your organization, you can significantly enhance the quality of your implementation and complete your implementation effort with minimal impact to overall project activities.

"It is not the beauty of a building you should look at; it's the construction of the foundation that will stand the test of time." — *David Allan Coe*

4 The Foundation for an SAP Audit: General Computer Controls, SAP Basis Settings and Security

By now you should have a good understanding of the audit process, a general outline for a typical SAP audit, and a methodology for dealing with internal controls during the implementation itself. In this chapter, we dig into specific details of an SAP audit, starting with two areas that we identified in Chapter 2 as being foundational components of a typical SAP audit: general computer controls (GCCs) and SAP Basis settings and security. As mentioned in Chapter 2, having strong controls and processes within each of these areas is critical to surviving an SAP audit — an auditor is unlikely to place any merit on SAP functionality or processes if either of these two areas appear weak.

By the end of this chapter, you should understand the basic principles of GCCs, list several key control areas important for an SAP audit, and have sufficient knowledge to speak effectively with your auditor about potential issues in this area. You should also know where to find GCC-related information in advance of the audit, and understand the standards related to IT controls that your auditor is looking to validate. From an SAP Basis and SAP security perspective, you should recognize several key areas and have sufficient information to validate your own SAP settings. Following the advice in this chapter should ensure that your auditor gains sufficient comfort to place trust in the reliability of your SAP environment.

4.1 General Computer Controls

Depending on your auditor, you may also hear GCCs referred to as *IT general controls* (ITGC). You'll likely encounter some form of GCC assessment on every SAP audit. Like the name suggests, GCCs are general — they address risks common to every system, regardless of vendor, application, or platform. The specific way that these risks are addressed may vary by system, but the fundamental concept is universal. Unlike auditing SAP, where audit guidance is limited and general audit knowledge is often restricted to specialists, GCCs are well understood in the auditing profession. This is a huge benefit when dealing with the GCCs portion of an SAP audit, because specific standards and guidelines are prevalent.

A Double-Edged Sword?

The fact that GCCs are widely understood in the auditing profession also poses a downside related to the SAP audit. Auditors new to IT auditing are typically assigned GCCs reviews as their training ground, and some auditors may spend years doing this type of review before progressing into more advanced application or hardware reviews. Many auditors become comfortable working with GCCs, and as a result some fall into the trap of spending a lot of time focused on this area even when drawing a direct link to SAP risks may be challenging. Understanding GCCs can help you better discuss issues with your auditor if they arise.

Due to the prevalence of available information on GCCs, we'll not attempt to re-write texts in this section that have already been written. Instead, we'll highlight some of the more common GCC areas for an SAP audit, and point you to additional reference material if you wish to learn more.

4.1.1 Overview

GCCs are a type of internal control broadly associated with the management, processes, and general operations of the IT function as a whole. In most organizations, IT operates as a shared service function to the business, supporting the organization by providing IT infrastructure and support to applications like SAP. Some of the common services that the IT function often provides to support the SAP application include:

▶ Maintenance and administration of the hardware, databases, and networks upon which SAP runs

▶ Management and operations of the data center in which the servers running the SAP application components and databases reside, including physical and environmental controls over that data center

▶ Management of the organization's help desk, through which SAP-related support calls may first be placed before any necessary escalation to the SAP support team

▶ Maintenance and administration of user authentication processes, such as network IDs and passwords, which may ultimately feed directly into SAP through single-sign on processes or similar procedures

▶ Management and control of backup and archival processes, including storage and handling of tapes and other archival media

- Monitoring and maintenance of system interfaces and connections, including security over interim temporary files staged for import into SAP
- Strategic planning processes and decisions affecting organizational IT strategies, such as IT budget allocation
- Monitoring of system and network performance

Because of this relationship, the integrity of these support processes is critical to the reliable and effective operation of SAP processes. If database management and maintenance procedures, for example, are insufficient to ensure that the corrupt data is not created or introduced at the database level, then all the controls in the SAP application itself become irrelevant. If network access procedures are weak, then SAP security and segregation of duties controls (which are typically strong) can be compromised. If the data files being pulled into SAP from other systems are incomplete, than SAP processing becomes inherently incomplete. GCCs address these issues and more.

An analogy is to think of SAP as a race car, and the IT support processes as all the behind-the-scenes operations that go into supporting the car and driver during the race. The best car and driver in the world require a lot of support to perform at their fullest. The gas going into the car must be pure and high quality. The wheels and other parts must be optimized for the vehicle. The pit crew must be trained and ready to support the car on a moment's notice. The track must be designed for the type of racing that the car is geared to, and be clear of any obstacles before the race starts. The race officials must all agree on the rules. The car must be protected before the race, for fear that ill-intended individuals may do it harm unbeknownst to the driver. In our SAP example, it's the GCCs that support SAP in the background, making sure it's able to perform at its finest.

GCCs are rarely managed by a single area of the organization, and often have independent but related layers depending on how the organization that manages IT hardware, databases, and applications. Consider Figure 4.1: GCC Relevant Process & Procedure Stack. At the highest level, certain IT processes and procedures affect all applications. These may include IT hiring and training policies, IT budgeting and prioritization processes, or company-wide security standards. In larger organizations, various IT management functions exist, each with their own discrete set of procedures, typically aligned with corporate processes and procedures but often with subtle differences between one another. For example, IT management functions may be managed by geographic location, with North America having slightly different processes than EMEA. Functions may differ by business unit, with one division's IT managed by a separate group than another's. Eventually, the SAP system management function may also have subtleties that differentiate the performance of certain GCCs from other similar applications (perhaps security within SAP allows for more tightly managed security processes than a legacy system also within the organization, and thus procedures recognize these differing capabilities). In the case of a GCCs review related to an SAP audit, the auditor would be interested in the controls in each component of the stack that eventually support SAP, and ignore any stack that is not relevant to the SAP environment. Different stacks may exist for hardware, networks, databases, and other similar IT-specific management functions, and the auditor would consider each of these as part of the review.

If an organization's IT processes and procedures looked roughly like Figure 4.1, the auditor would focus on GCC characteristics in the organization-wide, IT management area A, and SAP-specific functions. Differences in procedures within IT management area B or within System ABC or System XYZ would be irrelevant to the SAP audit process. The auditor would be interested not only in the relevant procedures at each layer of this stack but also any differences when moving from layer to layer. As a general rule of thumb, it would be acceptable for SAP-specific processes and procedures to be more stringent (from an internal control standpoint) than procedures at IT management area A as well as organization-wide processes and procedures, but it would not be acceptable for the reverse to be true.

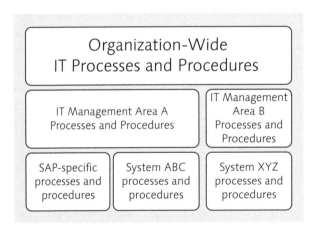

Figure 4.1 GCC Relevant Process & Procedure Stack

4.1.2 Standards

Numerous frameworks exist for auditing GCCs. Some of these relate specifically to GCCs, while others have been adapted for this usage by auditors. In this later case, these frameworks may not specifically reference GCCs but rather include similar characteristics as part of their *standards*. Sometimes, an auditor may rely on certain standards for a portion of a GCCs audit, to help put structure and guidance around a particular area like software change control. For the remainder of this chapter, we'll refer to GCCs in the broad sense, whether or not specifically named by the relevant assessment framework.

CobiT®

The most common IT control framework addressing general computer controls from an audit perspective is called CobiT, which stands for Control Objectives for Information and related Technology. CobiT is published by the IT Governance Institute (a spinoff of ISACA, the leading organization for IT auditors) and has been in place for well over a decade. With the onset of the Sarbanes-Oxley Act in the United States, CobiT (or at least the portions of CobiT related to financial reporting systems) took on greater importance in practice. Whereas auditors in the past had referenced portions of CobiT in their work, much more emphasis is placed today on the guidance contained in the framework.

The CobiT framework groups control objectives into four primary categories:

- ▶ Plan and organize
- ▶ Acquire and implement
- ▶ Deliver and support
- ▶ Monitor and evaluate

Each of these categories consists of 4 to 13 processes, and these processes ultimately lead to a series of more than 200 control objectives. Each of these control objectives would ultimately be addressed by one or more GCCs within your organization.

Because of the increasing visibility and usage of the CobiT framework, we suggest investing some time reading, at a minimum, the CobiT summary documents maintained by the IT Governance Institute at *www.itgi.org*. CobiT consists of multiple manuals and hundreds of pages of text, all readily available for public consumption (some for a nominal fee). Rather than attempt to map CobiT control objectives to the GCC portion of the typical SAP audit, we'll instead later in this chapter highlight some of the most relevant areas that can ultimately be mapped to CobiT.

GAIT

The GAIT framework, first published in 2007 by the Institute of Internal Auditors (IIA), is one of the newest frameworks that address IT auditing. Rather than delineating specific IT-related control objectives, GAIT defines a risk-based methodology for prioritizing the importance of those controls. The first version of this framework was intended to facilitate scoping of IT controls for Sarbanes-Oxley testing. The most recent addition to this framework, GAIT-R, broadens this approach to cover the interaction between IT and business risks in general, including those related to efficiency and effectiveness. GAIT recognizes that not all risks need to be addressed in an automated way, or by IT processes — and specifically that some IT-related risks may be mitigated by monitoring procedures or other processes in the business area rather than within IT itself.

Different Approaches to Auditing Standards

For the longest time, the IIA and ISACA (the leading standard-setting body for IT auditors) have co-existed without much overlap. The IIA set standards and practices for internal auditors, and left those standards and practices related to IT auditing primarily up to ISACA. In recent years, the IIA has taken a stronger stance on IT audit-related issues. Whereas ISACA focuses on controls within the IT function, the IIA raises more awareness around how IT risks may be addressed by complementary controls in the business areas (not just in IT). The standards from both organizations are still fairly aligned at the present time, yet there is growing debate as to how, and if, these two organizations will ultimately merge their thinking. As mentioned in Chapter 1, knowing the standards and frameworks that your auditor is using for your audit will go a long way to understanding the focus of his approach during your review.

ITIL

In the last few years, IT has embraced guidance by the IT Infrastructure Library (ITIL) for effectively managing IT service functions. Many IT auditors have also embraced ITIL as a benchmark against which they can audit. Audit-specific frameworks like CobiT typically do not prescribe specific procedures to be followed but rather broadly discuss the general risks that IT procedures should address. As a result, industry-standards like ITIL provide objective guidance that an auditor can measure against to determine if the IT processes under review are in line with industry best practices. Auditors referencing ITIL are typically interested in the efficiency and effectiveness of IT processes and in many cases have a broad IT background.

CMM®

The Software Engineering Institute (SEI) Capability Maturity Model (CMM) has been the de-facto standard for systems design and development processes. When reviewing GCCs related to application changes, many auditors look to CMM as the benchmark similar to the discussion of ITIL above. In fact, the last few major versions of CobiT have incorporated an IT controls maturity model into the framework, recognizing that control-related processes may mature over time, and depending on the relationship of the process to the overall business, not all processes need to be at an optimized state. Auditors referencing CMM are typically seasoned IT auditors with a solid understanding of the systems development process.

ISO 27000

From a security perspective, the de-facto standard is often the ISO 27000 series of guidance, also known as ISO27k. This set of security standards evolved from what was originally British Standard 7799 (BS-7799), a standard covering Information Security Management. The ISO27k series is often used by auditors to benchmark security practices, many of which fall into the broader category of GCCs. Auditors referencing this standard are typically security savvy and are likely to do a more in-depth security review than a typical auditor assessing GCCs.

4.1.3   GCC Highlights for an SAP Audit

To be best prepared for any SAP audit, have controls that effectively address each of the control objectives identified in the standards mentioned above, and particularly in CobiT. For many organizations, this can take years to progress to a sufficient point of maturity to be covered across all relevant CobiT areas. Because, as we described in Chapters 1 and 2, the specific nature and depth of audit testing will depend in large part on the type of audit being performed, applying the GAIT methodology in the context of that audit can reduce the initial set of high-priority controls to a more manageable level. For some organizations, this may still seem like a monumental task. This section highlights some of the most critical areas for focusing GCCs effort during an SAP audit.

As you read through this section, keep in mind that these are just a few of the highlights, and not the comprehensive set of controls on audit tests that you'll likely encounter during an SAP audit. Once you have addressed these areas, you can then turn your attention to some of the other control objectives addressed in the CobiT framework. GCCs generally refer to the broader set of IT controls, not only those specific to SAP.

As you review this section, remember also from the overview of the audit process in Chapter 1, and the methodology for designing controls during an implementation described in Chapter 3, that these areas fundamentally help to address certain risks (the "what could go wrong" answers) that could cause controls or processes within SAP to not be working effectively. Thus, as you think about your own organization, ask yourself questions like "What could cause this control to not work as intended in SAP?" or "What other processes must we have in place for this to work correctly?"

Doing so may lead to other GCCs or procedures that you may wish to consider in the high-priority category within your organization.

Some of the more common problem areas for most companies in general computer controls related to SAP include:

▸ Policies and procedures

▸ Security

▸ SAP change control

▸ Interface management and monitoring

We'll next look at each of these in more detail, and provide tips for getting around some of the more common audit issues related to these areas.

Policies and Procedures

Typically early in the audit cycle, your auditor will ask to see policies and procedures related to specific areas of interest. From an SAP standpoint, later in the audit cycle (such as in the SAP Basis settings and security portion of the review) your auditor will look at specific SAP configuration settings and processes to ensure compliance with these policies and procedures. This is the easiest type of audit finding — if settings or procedures don't comply with the standards that your own organization set, the audit finding is an easy one.

Before digging into SAP specifics, however, your auditor will look for a few specific things:

▸ Existence of documented policies and procedures

▸ Completeness within these policies and procedures

▸ Obvious discrepancies between standards and industry benchmarks

Any issues with any of these three items could result in a "red flag," that if not resolved by other settings or practices that the auditor observes during the SAP audit could ultimately lead to an audit finding. Independent of specific settings or processes in SAP, the following tips can help you avoid common audit issues related to policies and procedures:

▸ Ensure policies and procedures are up-to-date — Audit findings often result from procedures that were appropriate when first drafted but that are no longer reasonable given current technological capabilities or other business issues. As a result, the business adapts, but the policies and procedures remain outdated. A good example of this is a company that I once worked with in the early 2000s that still had a policy in their procedures manual that defined how short an employee's pencil should be before requesting a new one from the supplies manager. Clearly, that policy is a bit outdated now and probably has been for the past 30 years, yet a review process never took place for this organization's policies that would have allowed it to be purged. Ensure that a periodic review process occurs over all policies and procedures to help confirm the appropriateness as business needs change. An organization is also at risk of falling into a negative policy cycle when they do not periodically review their policies. A negative policy cycle is a phenomenon occurring when employees don't read the policy manual because it's out of date, yet the policies aren't updated because the employees aren't reading the policy manual.

▶ Have a process for approving exceptions to policies and procedures — For a variety of reasons, following documented policies and procedures may not always be possible. Create a formal process for approving exceptions to policies, and document in detail each of these exceptions (particularly if they affect SAP). Such documentation shows the auditor that you are aware of and have made a conscious decision to address the related business risks resulting from non-compliance with stated policies.

If the Documented Policy is Wrong, Change It

An organization can sometimes find themselves in audit trouble even when they think they are operating with management's intent in mind. Business areas may choose not to comply precisely with a policy or procedure, feeling that if they are close enough to address management's intent, it's fine. The deviation is a clear audit exception without a formal validation from management that the proposed process really is sufficient (in the form of a policy exception). Employees should not be arbitrarily choosing whether to follow policy, or how to interpret policy — which is why the exception process is so critical. If the policy is inappropriate, then that policy should be changed rather than setting a precedent that rules can be violated.

As an example, assume that your security standards say that all passwords must have a minimum length of 10 characters and be changed every 28 days. It may be tempting to argue that the 9 character and 30-day setting that you have within SAP is good enough, but that's not for audit to decide. While these SAP settings may still provide strong security, the mere fact that SAP does not match your corporate policy (and no exception has been documented) is an issue. If an approve policy exception has been made and signed off by appropriate management, however, the potential issue disappears from the auditor's radar. As such, having a policy exception process is critical to ensuring SAP audit success.

▶ Periodically communicate and re-approve exceptions — If any policy exceptions affect SAP, periodically re-evaluate these exceptions and ensure they are still appropriate. Your organization's risk tolerance may change as people and the business changes over time. Additionally, advances in technology may allow you to more effectively address risks. Lastly, over time, the costs of compliance may change, again resulting in the need to re-evaluate exceptions to management's defined process. Typically, re-evaluating policy exceptions on a 12-month cycle is appropriate for most organizations.

▶ Self-audit against your policies — One of the easiest findings for an auditor is where settings and processes don't match corporate policy. Because policies change over time, and the people supporting those policies also change over time, self-auditing is the best way to ensure that your policies and procedures don't get out-of-sync. Self-auditing may be through manual audit process, or as the result of automated monitoring (using features within SAP BusinessObjects Process Control, for example).

Security

Security is an important control enabler. Strong security ensures that only approved individuals can affect business-relevant data, allows duties to be segregated, and enables transactions to be tied back to individual users. Some security settings will be within the SAP application, and we'll address these in the SAP Basis Settings and Security section later in this chapter. Other security settings and standards apply at a broader level than just SAP. These include:

▶ Privileged system access

▶ User access assignment, maintenance, and removal

▶ Segregation of duties

We'll address specific SAP security settings later in this chapter as part of the SAP Basis Settings and Security section. At a general level, the following recommendations can help you avoid trouble with the security portion of a GCCs review:

▶ Limit and monitor privileged access to SAP infrastructure components — IT users with administrator privileges or other super-user type privileges to IT infrastructure that supports SAP should be tightly controlled. Additionally, their activities should be monitored and audited. This includes users with privileged access to the servers upon which SAP components reside, users with the ability to directly update the databases on which SAP stores data, users with the ability to change critical network settings, and other such activities across all of the SAP infrastructure set.

▶ Change user access upon change in responsibilities — One of the most common IT audit findings is actually one of the easiest to detect and resolve: users with active system access even after they have left the organization. Auditors will typically match recent employee terminations and transfers to system access, and the frequency at which findings occur is astounding. Make sure that your processes ensure that user access is updated whenever a change in responsibility occurs, whether through termination, transfer, or shift in responsibilities. This includes not only SAP access but also access to other applications and components that affect SAP.

Physical and Network Access Controls May Not Be Enough

Organizations with terminated or transferred employees still with access to critical applications often argue that this application access cannot be abused. Perhaps those employees no longer have physical access to the facilities, and even if they did no longer have network access to access the network and sign into the application to begin with. Even if this is the case, this argument makes several assumptions, which often make it invalid. First, it assumes that the only way an individual can access an application is if he is physically in the building. With the persistence of remote access applications today, this is often not the case. Second, it assumes that only the only individual that might be abusing the application access is the one with the expired network ID. Because the ID is still active on the application, however, colleagues who may have shared the ID and password (against company policy) or individuals who found the ID and password can still gain unauthorized access. While additional controls could mitigate these risks, the best approach is to modify application access as user access needs change.

▶ Validate user access against a segregation of duties (SOD) matrix — Every organization should have an SOD matrix, defining abilities that should not be granted in combination to a user (see Figure 4.2: Simple Segregation of Duties Matrix for a basic example). This matrix should be independent of the system, because, often, access within two independent systems can create segregation of duties concerns. This matrix should be also periodically be validated by management, and each ability should be mapped to its respective transactions, authorizations, and authorization objects so that security personnel can effectively identify which users have these abilities. SAP BusinessObjects Access Control can greatly enhance an organization's ability to identify and monitor possible SOD issues by automating much of this process.

Simple SOD Matrix (Y = Violation)

	A	B	C	D
A	N/A	Y	Y	N
B	Y	N/A	Y	N
C	Y	Y	N/A	N
D	N	N	N	N/A

A = Create/Modify Pricing Master Data
B = Create/Modify Sales Orders
C = Apply Cash Receipts to Customer Accounts
D = Create/Modify Purchase Orders

Figure 4.2 Simple Segregation of Duties Matrix

Change Control

No matter what type of SAP audit you experience, some level of change control assessment is usually part of the audit procedures. Change control refers to the processes for initiating, creating, reviewing, and approving changes to the SAP application and related infrastructure components. Within SAP, change control is critical because it provides the auditor with comfort that the SAP settings he is validating today will be the same tomorrow. We'll discuss specific SAP Basis and security settings in SAP later in this chapter. At a broader level, a few things can help ensure a strong change control process that will survive audit scrutiny:

▶ Remove unnecessary programmer access from production — Allowing programmers to process anything more than innocuous transactions in production is generally a segregation of duties issues. In fact, practically every IT audit text will suggest that programmers should never have access to production. At times, however, you may need to give certain individuals access to transactions and other SAP abilities that they may not typically need (or they should not have, given typical SOD requirements). For example, a programmer may need emergency access to SAP production to fix a time-sensitive problem. Rather than grant privileged access as part of the user profile definition (and risk that these privileges could be used when not intended by management), provide a means to grant access only when needed, and audit the access actually used. We recognize that in many SAP environments, particularly shortly after go-live, such a strong stance can be challenging, and thus recommend that if programmer access to the production SAP client is necessary, it be severely limited to a small number of employees, their actions be monitored, and this access be time-bound and removed as soon as possible.

> **Control Programmer Access to Production Using SAP**
>
> Super User Privilege Management (SPM) functionality within SAP BusinessObjects Access Control allows organizations to better control programmer access to production and can generally eliminate any audit concerns. The ability for certain employees to check out enhanced privileges when necessary ensures continuity of your business processes in time of need, while the tracking, logging, and automatic expiration of these privileges provides the control that auditors generally expect.

▶ Use standard change request forms — Good business practices (and many audit checklists) require that every change to SAP be validated in light of security and control implications. Using standard request forms, ideally with specific questions related to potential security and control issues, ensures at a minimum that these have been considered. When creating a customer transaction in SAP, for example, consider how it may affect SAP workflow, for example, whether the transaction could create any segregation of duties concerns and the types of edit checks and tolerances which should be applied to the transaction to validate user input. By placing such items on a standardized form, the auditor can be assured that they are consistently considered.

▶ Maintain a pre-transport checklist — We discussed the importance of having sufficient audit evidence in Chapter 1. The change control process includes many evidence-related items important to an auditor — from the initial change request and requirements through approvals, testing and QA results, and ultimately the go-ahead for transport into production. Because any of these could be required for audit support, ensuring each of these have been gathered with appropriate signatures and supporting documentation prior to moving any change into SAP production is essential. Of course, retaining this information so that it can be associated with the transport is also important.

▶ For emergency changes, complete skipped steps post-implementation — Every organization experiences emergency changes, where code must be moved into production more expeditiously than through the standard change process. Emergency changes often involve less up-front diligence to streamline the process, and some emergency changes may completely bypass controls. Following up after the change to ensure that the emergency change meets production standards is critical to satisfy audit requirements. Additionally, inform affected business management of the emergency change so that they can monitor operations for potential impact.

▶ Develop test plan details commensurate with the complexity of the change and experience of those involved in testing — Some changes are less complex than others. For example, adding a field to a report has potentially less inherent risk than changing the essence of a calculation. Even simple changes, however, should be tested. But the complexity of the change isn't the only factor that should affect the level of detail in the test plan. Some testers may be more familiar with SAP testing procedures than others. By ensuring that test plan detail considers both the complexity of the change and the experience of the testers, you have better assurance that testing will be performed effectively to catch the issues it's meant to catch.

▶ Resolve unsuccessful tests prior to go-live — Although this may seem obvious, we've seen situations all too frequently where organizations did not fix every problem identified during testing prior to approval and transport of the change. If management has been appropriately informed and accepts the risk associated with the test failure, make sure this information is thoroughly documented — not just for audits but also for troubleshooting and problem resolution if issues are identified down the road.

Interface Management and Monitoring

Rarely does an organization use SAP as its sole application system, and as a result, interfaces to and from SAP are common. Interface procedures should ensure that:

▶ Information is received and processed completely

▶ Data is only processed once, and any re-processing procedures (when necessary) ensure data is not duplicated

▶ If stored in a holding area between systems, data is protected from modification

▶ Monitoring procedures both detect and resolve potential file completeness and integrity issues

The responsibility for monitoring SAP interfaces often differs by organization, typically with SAP personnel monitoring batch jobs within SAP through Computer Center Management System (CCMS), and other IT personnel reviewing interface status and monitoring procedures through other tools. Because multiple people can be involved in interface processing, consider the following:

▶ Ensure resolution, not just notification, of interface problems — If an interface issue occurs, business management is often consulted to determine appropriate resolution. We have seen situations where IT communicates the potential problem, and then considers their job done until (or unless) receiving additional instruction from the business area. From an audit perspective, the most important thing is that something was done rather than the information was communicated. If the business manager did not see the notification, if he responded and the right information did not make it back to IT, or other similar issues, the former process would cause problems.

▶ Control and monitor changes to job scheduling — Interface and other job scheduling can pose a risk to the integrity of SAP processing, particularly if jobs are processed in the wrong order. As such, auditors often pay close attention to the scheduling process and the monitoring of changes to the schedule. Remove any unnecessary access and ensure you have a process in place to monitor and approve changes to the schedule.

4.1.4   GCCs Summary

As discussed in this section, GCCs provide a foundation for audit assurance. These controls often consist of processes for overseeing and managing an organization's systems in general, and may not be specific to just SAP. Having effective GCCs is important, because it allows the auditor to gain comfort that specific configuration settings and processes in SAP are reliable, and cannot be circumvented through processes outside of SAP.

In the next section, we discuss how SAP Basis settings and security often support these GCCs with specific configuration in SAP.

4.2   SAP Basis Settings and Security

As discussed in Chapter 2, part of the SAP audit process includes examination and validation of certain SAP Basis settings and security parameters within SAP. To some extent, these settings and parameters are an extension of the GCCs that we just discussed — supporting these controls within the SAP environment. This section will dive into specific SAP Basis settings and security parameters that often fall under audit scrutiny, and share tips and techniques for configuring SAP appropriately.

Like the section on GCCs, a lot of documentation has been written on SAP Basis settings and security. One of the better SAP audit guides is a publication written by SAP in 1997 called *SAP – Audit Guidelines R/3*. This publication for years has only been available on the SAP Germany website. A search on the keywords "SAP" and "Audit" in any Internet search engine find it in the initial set of hits, and most recently it was found at: *www.sap.com/germany/about/company/revis/pdf/plf-fi-e-30d.pdf*. While this text is older, from an SAP Basis standpoint it's still highly relevant — the risks posed within the SAP Basis system as described in this book are still largely relevant. We are unsure why SAP never updated and maintained this guide; however, it still is an excellent reference when preparing for an audit of the SAP Basis system.

Guidance on the security front is prevalent. Entire books have been written on SAP security alone, including SAP Security and Authorizations, published by SAP Press. This book goes beyond the administrative side of security to discuss risk and compliance issues, and techniques for supporting regulatory requirements with SAP security.

Given the prevalence of information on SAP Basis settings and security, in this section we'll simply highlight a few of the key areas that may come up during an SAP audit. We encourage you to spend additional time with some of the reference material mentioned above to get a more comprehensive understanding of the issues and better prepare your SAP system for an eventual audit.

4.2.1 SAP Basis System Audit Highlights

Certain technical SAP Basis system settings are important to provide the auditor with assurance that SAP will continue to work as intended, and/or ensure that effective monitoring within SAP can occur. Depending on the technical depth of your SAP audit, an SAP Basis review could range from a few preliminary audit checkpoints to a thorough multi-week review. We'll leave the discussion of a comprehensive review to the texts mentioned previously, and instead provide a few highlights here.

Securing the Production Client

Changes should not be allowed directly in the production client, and SAP settings should be configured to prevent any such changes. Allowing changes directly in the production client could lead to changes that are not fully tested, or even unauthorized changes. During an audit, the auditor will likely want to view the production client settings, which you can obtain through transaction SCC4. You can see an example of these settings in Figure 4.3: Production Client Settings.

An auditor reviewing these settings will look for five specific characteristics of the production client:

1. The Changes and Transports for Client-Specific Objects setting should be set to No Changes Allowed
2. The Cross-Client Object Changes setting should be set to No Changes to Repository Objects
3. The Protection: Client Copier and Comparison Tool setting should be set to Protection Level 1: No Overwriting
4. The CATT and eCATT Restrictions setting should be set to eCATT and CATT Not Allowed
5. The Last Changed by Date should be reasonable given the implementation date.

In Figure 4.3, notice that each of these settings is as desired, with one possible exception. The production client settings were changed on September 16, 2009, which is fairly recent. The auditor would likely look for further explanation of what was changed and why.

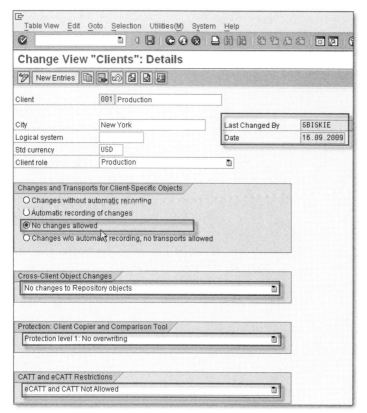

Figure 4.3 Production Client Settings

As a final point related to securing the production client, once the auditor has obtained comfort that the settings are appropriate, he will likely also look to ensure the ability to change these settings is limited. Security access to transaction SCC4 should be highly restricted, and ideally logged and monitored.

Enabling Table Logging

In the example above, we noted that the auditor would likely investigate the recent changes to the production client settings. If table logging has been turned on, the auditor would want to examine table T000 to see specifically which production settings were changed and what the prior values had been. Without table logging, the auditor (or anyone investigating the nature of the change) is left to guess what happened. As such, enabling table logging is a good practice and will help facilitate an SAP audit. Due to performance reasons, care should be taken as to which tables should be logged. Most organizations select a handful of key tables on which to enable logging, and also put processes in place for periodic review of those logs (rather than waiting for an auditor to be the first to detect a potential problem).

Defining the Enterprise Structure

The Enterprise Structure, sometimes also referred to as the Corporate Structure, the SAP Hierarchy, or the Organization Management Model (OMM), defines key enterprise settings that affect companies, profit centers, and locations. Because the Enterprise Structure directly affects the organizational categories available for reporting, failure to effectively map the business and define an appropriate structure can pose a significant risk — limiting reporting views available to the organization. As such, the auditor will seek assurance that the Enterprise Structure defined in SAP is appropriate to meet the reporting needs of management, and supports sufficient regulatory reporting. Typically he will compare the Enterprise Structure to the organizational structure at the current time, and discuss any differences in structure with management, including any challenges that may result from the currently configured SAP Enterprise Structure.

Changing the Enterprise Structure after the initial SAP implementation can be complex, and thus addressing any potential audit concerns before go-live is important. Refer to the advice in Chapter 3 for more information on obtaining auditor buy-in before SAP go-live.

Follow SAP Naming Conventions

As a company, SAP reserves certain name ranges for SAP-developed objects, and recommends that any custom-developed objects an organization creates starts with a Z or a Y. Custom-developed objects include ABAP code, roles and profiles, reports, and others. Failure to comply with this naming convention raises the risk that customizations are lost during an upgrade. Auditors will typically look to see that internally developed SAP objects are named appropriately, and raise a red flag if not.

4.2.2 SAP Security Highlights

As we have discussed, SAP security is a very important control enabler in the SAP system. Depending on the technical depth of your SAP audit, a security audit could range from a few preliminary audit checkpoints to a thorough multi-week review. We'll leave the discussion of a comprehensive review to the texts mentioned earlier in this section, and instead provide a few highlights here.

Default Parameters

Several of the security parameters provided by SAP as default settings are typically not appropriate for many organizations, and should be changed. These security parameters relate to password requirements, actions that SAP takes on invalid logins, and other such criteria. The right setting for your organization will depend on your industry, your regulatory environment, and your own security policies, but you may need to change certain settings to establish a minimum level of security.

Typically, an auditor will request report RSPARAM to review these settings. In Figure 4.4: Report RSPARAM, a number of parameters begin with "Login/." Each of these parameters controls specify security settings, many of which are of interest to an auditor. A few key settings to consider modifying include:

Display Profile Parameter

Parameter Name	User-Defined Value	System Default Value	N	Comment
login/fails_to_session_end		3	3	Number of invalid login attempts until session end
login/fails_to_user_lock		5	5	Number of invalid login attempts until user lock
login/isolate_rfc_system_calls		0	0	
login/min_password_diff		1	1	min. number of chars which differ between old and new password
login/min_password_digits		0	0	min. number of digits in passwords
login/min_password_letters		0	0	min. number of letters in passwords
login/min_password_lng		6	6	Minimum Password Length
login/min_password_lowercase		0	0	minimum number of lower-case characters in passwords
login/min_password_specials		0	0	min. number of special characters in passwords
login/min_password_uppercase		0	0	minimum number of upper-case characters in passwords
login/multi_login_users				list of exceptional users: multiple logon allowed
login/no_automatic_user_sapstar	0	1	1	Control of the automatic login user SAP*
login/password_change_for_SSO		1	1	Handling of password change enforcements in Single Sign-On situ
login/password_change_waittime		1	1	Password change possible after # days (since last change)
login/password_charset		1	1	Zeichenmenge für Kennwörter
login/password_compliance_to_cu		0	0	Kennwort muß aktuellen Kennwortregeln genügen
login/password_downwards_comp		1	1	password downwards compatibility (8 / 40 characters, case-sensiti
login/password_expiration_time		0	0	Dates until password must be changed
login/password_history_size		5	5	Number of records to be stored in the password history
login/password_logon_usergroup				users of this group can still logon with passwords
login/password_max_idle_initial		0	0	maximum #days a password (set by the admin) can be unused (idl
login/password_max_idle_product		0	0	maximum #days a password (set by the user) can be unused (idle)

Figure 4.4 Report RSPARAM

▶ Login/password_expiration_time — by default, passwords are set to not expire

▶ Login/min_password_diff — by default, new passwords only need to have a single character difference between the passwords that they are replacing

▶ Login/min_passwrod_lng — by default, the minimum required password length is six characters (less restrictive than the security requirements of many organizations)

You can also force strong passwords by requiring a specified minimum number of digits, letters (upper or lower case), and special characters in passwords. These are controlled by parameters Login/min_password_digits, Login/min_password_letters (including Login/min_password_lowercase, and Login/min_password_uppercase), and Login/min_password_specials, respectively. By default, these settings are set to 0, meaning that there is no requirement.

Defining Restricted Password Lists

Security-conscious organizations recognize that users may try to circumvent the intent of password controls by creating weak passwords. While this can be mitigated to some extent using default parameter settings as discussed above, a good security practice is to also maintain a list of restricted passwords. For example, a company in Green Bay, Wisconsin, may want to restrict easily guessed passwords based on the football team "Packers" or any of its players. Such restrictions might include: Packers1, Pack3rs, Packer5, or similar variations that are relatively easy to guess. Table USR40 is where SAP maintains the organization's restricted password list, and an auditor will likely review this table and recommend that entries be added if it's not already being used.

Limit Access

Not surprisingly, access to sensitive tables, transactions, and reports will also be on the auditor's radar. As such, security should restrict access to SAP customizing tables, prevent unauthorized changes to SAP's data dictionary, and be set to provide other similar functions. The security guides referenced earlier in this section are a good source of information related to this topic.

Change Default Passwords

Like every system, SAP comes with a series of powerful user accounts and default passwords for initial login. It should go without saying, but these default passwords should be changed to prevent the risk of unauthorized access (audit findings in this area are still surprisingly common). At a minimum, the passwords for the following IDs should be changed:

- SAP*
- DDIC

▸ SAPCPIC

▸ EARLYWATCH

▸ TMSADM (where relevant)

Restrict Access to Powerful Roles

Certain profiles in SAP allow for super-user type access and/or contain powerful privileges. If you cannot eliminate the usage of these roles, severely restrict them, as an auditor will be reviewing to see if and how they are being used. A few of these include:

▸ SAP_ALL

▸ SAP_NEW

▸ SAP_A.USER

▸ SAP_A.ADMIN

Ensure Role Names are Accurately Descriptive

When defining new security roles and profiles, the names should appropriately describe the role or profile and are not misleading. An auditor will raise a large red flag if he finds names that are not reflective of the accrual role, capabilities, or profiles, because it raises the concern that someone may be intentionally attempting to mislead a security review. We have seen instances, for example, where a role name indicating "inquiry only" was anything but that.

Locking Sensitive Transactions

Certain SAP transactions are extremely powerful, and generally should be locked from use in production except when needed. One example of such a transaction is SCC5, which allows for the deletion of an SAP client. You should determine which transactions are appropriate for locking in your organization, design procedures for locking and unlocking these transactions, and restrict and monitor this functionality.

During an audit, the auditor is likely to request a listing of locked transactions to see if sensitive transactions such as SCC5 have been blocked from usage. Report RSAUDITC, shown in Figure 4.5: Report RSAUDITC, is typically where the auditor will look for this information.

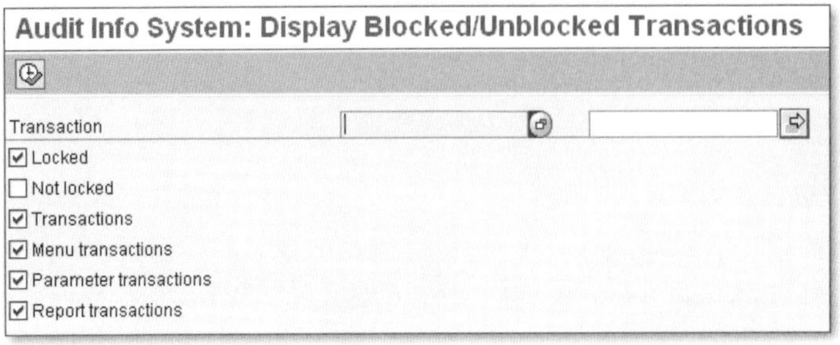

Figure 4.5 Report RSAUDITC

4.3 Summary

In this chapter, we reviewed the importance of GCCs that govern IT processes and hardware, networks, databases, and other applications affecting SAP. We shared information about various audit frameworks against which auditors may perform their assessments related to GCC. We also highlighted specific areas within a GCC assessment for an SAP audit that prove problematic for many organizations, and shared tips for avoiding potential audit concern.

For SAP Basis settings and security, we provided several useful references for obtaining more information about this topic. We walked through specific configuration settings that often crop up during an audit, and discussed potential red flags that could raise audit concern.

With the information that we have shared thus far in this book, you have the tools necessary to lay an appropriate foundation for a comprehensive SAP audit. In the next few chapters, we'll look at specific settings and controls within select SAP components that support strong business processes and help eliminate errors and abuse.

"Balanced budget requirements seem more likely to produce accounting ingenuity than genuinely balanced budgets." — Thomas Sowell

5   Financial Reporting Cycle

The financial reporting cycle is different from most other key business cycles supported by SAP. Whereas the purchase-to-pay cycle results in material acquisition for ultimate customer fulfillment, and the order-to-cash process results in receipt of payment for satisfying a customer need, the financial reporting process plays the role of a necessary evil — designed to merely communicate the transactions that have happened within the period. Despite being primarily an after-the-fact documentation event, however, the financial reporting process is a core part of many SAP audits. Management often relies on financial and operational reports produced by SAP for decision-making purposes, and the auditor acquires valuable process-related information through financial analysis. In the case of publicly traded companies, specific financial reporting audits are frequently a regulatory requirement.

In this chapter, we explore the SAP financial reporting cycle in detail, with particular emphasis on the SAP ERP Financials Financial Accounting component (part of the SAP ERP Financials Suite). Within SAP ERP Financials Financial Accounting, we address the SAP General Ledger, FI-AR receivables, FI-AP payables, and FI-AM asset management. We discuss the risks inherent in the process, and review a sampling of SAP configurable controls and commonly expected during an SAP financial reporting audit. We also highlight a series of processes and procedures, which, if applied consistently, can mitigate a number of financial reporting risks and put you in a better position for an audit.

5.1   Risks

The business impact of *risks* within the financial reporting process can be significant. Reporting is often tied to regulatory or contractual obligations from which fines and prohibitions can result from non-compliance. As such, controlling the integrity of the financial reporting process is absolutely critical.

In Chapter 1, we discussed the concept of risk and how internal controls are designed to mitigate specific business risks. When preparing for an SAP audit covering financial reporting, think through some of the things that could go wrong in the SAP financial reporting process that could affect reporting integrity. A few of these risks include:

- Insufficient reporting structures — The organizational model, chart of accounts, and other relevant SAP structures must be appropriately configured to support the capture and reporting of transactions required by financial reporting rules. Regardless of the effectiveness of other processes, if the configured financial-related structures do not allow transactions to be categorized and reported appropriately, financial reporting compliance can be difficult to achieve.

- Inaccurate postings — While SAP automatically completes the accounting entries associated with many transactions, other postings rely wholly or partially upon user input. Certain accounting estimates, such as reserve calculations, may be based on information within SAP but are ultimately posted to SAP manually. Other accounting postings may be fully calculated and posted by SAP but based on appropriate user transaction input or classification (such as assignment of asset class). User errors during these processes can result in incorrect postings to the SAP General Ledger.

- Incomplete SAP General Ledger processing — A variety of circumstances can result in transactions not being fully processed in SAP. SAP General Ledger transactions that have been put on hold or parked will not be posted. Incomplete documents, where SAP detects missing information required for complete posting, will also remain off the books. These issues must be investigated and resolved for financial reporting to be complete.

- Postings to the wrong accounting period — Near the end of a reporting period, specific rules govern the period to which a transaction must be posted. Obligations incurred before period end, for example, may need to be recognized even if not yet invoiced or otherwise visible to SAP. Even if postings are quantitatively accurate, if they are made to the wrong posting period, then the transaction is technically inaccurate.

- Inaccurate or incomplete management reports — The integrity of cost center or profitability information with the SAP ERP Financials Controlling component or within an SAP NetWeaver Business Warehouse (SAP NetWeaver BW) can affect the integrity of SAP ERP Financials Financial Accounting transactions, even if not initially apparent. Reporting from SAP ERP Financials Controlling or SAP NetWeaver BW can be used by management to make determinations that ultimately lead to manual journal entries or adjustments. As a result, while these components do not directly feed SAP General Ledger, they can indirectly affect the integrity of certain SAP General Ledger postings.

▶ Unauthorized document changes — Initial SAP document entry can often be thorough. If document changes (made after initial approval) do not go through the same level of scrutiny, unauthorized or inaccurate transactions can be posted to the SAP General Ledger.

▶ Fraudulent transactions — The Association of Certified Fraud Examiners (ACFE) estimates that corporations, on average, lose 7% of revenue to fraud. Whether the result of earnings manipulation to reach incentive thresholds or through outright theft, the existence of fraudulent transactions can cause financial reporting to fall out of compliance with regulatory guidelines.

Of course, each of these risk categories is broad. As mentioned in Chapter 3 on the discussion of designing appropriate controls during an implementation, effectively managing risks requires understanding specific situations for which controls can then be applied. For example, we mention above how incomplete SAP General Ledger postings can result from legitimate transactions being parked or on hold when the financial statements are generated, and thus be missing from the resulting reports. Other situations could also result in incomplete processing. An interface into SAP may fail during a nightly processing run and not be detected and resolved. A contract with financial reporting ramifications may be entered into by the business areas but not yet communicated to the accounting function. A batch of invoices may be sitting on a clerk's desk waiting processing. During an SAP audit where the financial reporting process is in scope, an auditor will be interested in how each of these risks have been addressed by SAP or by business processes surrounding the use of SAP.

Later in this chapter we provide suggestions for SAP configurable controls that can help mitigate some of the risks inherent in the financial reporting process, and highlight important processes that can also strengthen control. Before that, however, we'll discuss SAP master data and security issues critical to the integrity of the financial reporting process.

5.2 Security and Master Data

SAP security can provide a powerful level of control by limiting abilities to only a small group of authorized users. Master data controls are also critical due to the effect that master data has on business transactions. When preparing for an audit, ensuring strong *security and master data* processes are in place is a good first step toward audit success.

5.2.1 Preventing Segregation of Duties Conflicts

A segregation of duties review is a core component of most types of SAP audits. In Chapter 4, we discussed *segregation of duties* in the context of general computer controls (GCCs) and the IT function. Appropriate segregation of duties is also important within the financial reporting process. Insufficient segregation of duties could lead to unapproved journal entries (requiring time to correct and resolve), undetected errors (potentially leading to poor management decisions based on inaccurate information), or even outright fraud.

Table 5.1: SAP ERP Financials Financial Accounting Segregation of Duties Highlights illustrates some of the abilities that should be segregated within the SAP ERP Financials Financial Accounting component. This is by no means a complete list, because complete rule sets within security management tools like SAP BusinessObjects Access Control can have hundreds of rules for SAP ERP Financials Financial Accounting alone. To survive an SAP audit where financial reporting is part of the review, however, at least ensure these common violations have been addressed.

The Ability To:	Should Not Be Combined with the Ability To:
Post SAP General Ledger transactions	Create/maintain SAP ERP Financials Financial Accounting master data
Post SAP General Ledger transactions	Open/close posting periods
Post SAP General Ledger transactions	Enter/modify currency rates
Post SAP General Ledger transactions	Modify data validation rules
Post SAP General Ledger transactions	Receive/reconcile cash
Post SAP General Ledger transactions	Receive/manage fixed assets
Post abnormal or high-value general ledger transactions	Approve abnormal or high-value general ledger transaction
Create/maintain SAP ERP Financials Financial Accounting master data	Create/maintain financial statement structures
Create/maintain FI-AR master data	Post customer invoices
Create/maintain FI-AR master data	Process customer receipts
Create/maintain depreciation areas	Post fixed asset transactions
Post fixed asset transactions	Receive/manage fixed assets

Table 5.1 SAP ERP Financials Financial Accounting Segregation of Duties Highlights

> **Dealing with Small Teams**
>
> The best way to deal with segregation of duties is to prevent potential conflicts using SAP security. In some situations, however, traditional security-enabled segregation may not be possible. Perhaps a single employee manages a group of functions in a remote location, and as a result his duties cannot be effectively segregated. Many auditors understand such business realities. However, if this describes your situation, have monitoring and review procedures in place (and working) to mitigate the risk of insufficient security.

5.2.2 Restricting Postings to Functional Areas

The large majority of SAP General Ledger postings occur through normal daily transaction processing in SAP — often without the user recognizing the accounting entries created in the background. Goods receipts post items to inventory or expense and recognize an obligation to pay for those items. Shipments subtract from inventory and trigger an expectation of customer payment. Common transactions like these occur every day without any need for a user to go into SAP ERP Financials Financial Accounting and post directly to the SAP General Ledger. Inevitably, however, some transactions require manual posting and thus some accounting users need to create journal entries. This ability should be limited, because manual postings create the exposure for manual error.

Within the accounting and finance functions, the ability to post SAP General Ledger transactions may require an even further level of control. Small organizations with only a few employees in the accounting function can probably get by with allowing accounting employees to post most types of SAP ERP Financials Financial Accounting transactions. In larger organizations, however, additional segregation should be considered. By *restricting* the type of transaction that a user can post to his specific area of responsibility, you can further reduce the risk of errors or unauthorized transactions.

> **Guilty Until Proven Innocent?**
>
> In additional to reviewing how you have leveraged SAP security to control SAP ERP Financials Financial Accounting master data and postings to SAP General Ledger, your auditor will also likely question those techniques you did NOT use. For example, if you restrict SAP General Ledger postings by company code, business area, and document type, your auditor will likely ask why you have not further restricted postings by account. Be prepared to discuss this issue in terms of how you have managed business risks and what factors in your environment lead you to believe that current security settings are appropriate.

Most organizations find it appropriate to, at a minimum, restrict SAP General Ledger postings by document type using authorization object F_BKPF_BLA. Further restrictions can be placed on company code and business area using authorization objects F_BKPF_BUK and F_BKPF_GES, respectively. Restricting access to account types or specific SAP General Ledger accounts using authorization objects F_BKPF_KOA and F_BKPF_BES, respectively, is also a common practice.

5.2.3 Limiting Access to Powerful Transactions

When assigning security privileges, ensure that powerful SAP transactions and abilities within the SAP ERP Financials Financial Accounting component have been *limited* to a small number of personnel. Even if these functions are never used, the ability of a user to perform them poses risk to the organization and thus creates audit concern. A few of these transactions include:

- The ability to open and close accounting periods (S_ALR_87003642)
- The ability to perform mass transaction reversals (F.80)
- The ability to post to periods that most users find blocked for posting (authorization object F_BKPF_BUP)

In addition to limiting access to these abilities through security, you can further strengthen controls by monitoring their usage. This monitoring should be independent of the group able to perform these transactions. Being able to show an auditor that the use of powerful transactions is both limited and effectively monitored is ideal.

> **Raising the Bar: Better Control over Powerful Transactions**
>
> Organizations looking to overachieve and virtually eliminate the risks of powerful transactions should consider removing these abilities from all users, and only assigning them at time of need. Once the relevant transaction has been completed and verified, access can once again be removed.

5.2.4 Establishing Controls and Security over Master Data

Master data tables drive SAP transaction processing. Strong controls over master data, whether it be creation, modification, or deletion, are necessary for audit success. As it relates to master data in the financial reporting process, the auditor will generally be looking to ensure that:

- The ability to change master data is limited to a core group of employees (for each type of master data)
- Employees who make changes to master data have sufficient knowledge of financial reporting and training on organizational policies and SAP usage to understand the issues and implications

▸ Procedures exist for authorizing changes to master data that can affect financial reporting (typically in advance of the change)

▸ Independent quality assurance processes validate master data changes

▸ Master data is periodically reviewed for relevance (i.e., outdated accounts are blocked for posting or marked for deletion)

Organizations may choose to manage SAP General Ledger master data centrally or locally. Auditors often view centralized maintenance as providing stronger control with more consistency; however, business circumstances will dictate which is right for you.

Restricting Changes to SAP General Ledger Master Records

SAP provides a variety of mechanisms to restrict changes to SAP General Ledger master records. Security permissions can be set to restrict changes based on a specific chart of accounts, on company code, and/or on a number range within a given chart of accounts. SAP General Ledger master data contains both information specific to a given chart of accounts, as well as information that can be company-code specific (such as posting currency, tax category, and field status groups). Due to the impact that account assignments and other details can have on the financial reporting process and the roll-up of management information, tighter restrictions are generally preferable to more open security models. In general, restrict the ability to create, change, delete, block, and unblock SAP General Ledger master records to only a small handful of trained employees, and only within their defined areas of responsibility (e.g., a controller in one company code should not be able to change accounting data for all company codes). Some of the key authorization objects for doing this are shown in Table 5.2: SAP General Ledger Account Authorization Objects.

Auth. Object	Name	Purpose
F_SKA1_KTP	GL Account: Authorization for Charts of Accounts	Restrict modifications to SAP General Ledger master data by chart of accounts
F_SKA1_BUK	GL Account: Authorization for Company Codes	Restrict modifications to SAP General Ledger master data by company code
F_SKA1_BES	GL Account: Account Authorization	Restrict modifications to SAP General Ledger master data by account number
F_SKA1_AEN	GL Account: Change Authorization for Certain Fields	Restrict modifications to SAP General Ledger master data to defined fields

Table 5.2 SAP General Ledger Account Authorization Objects

Restricting Changes to Customer Accounting-Related Master Records

While often thought of in the context of sales, the customer master record also contains important SAP ERP Financials Financial Accounting–related data, including both accounting information and credit management details. Specific information such as customer reconciliation accounts, bill-to addresses, and bank data can be important for both general internal control as well as fraud prevention. As such, maintenance over certain customer master data fields is important to financial reporting.

If you are using the Sales and Distribution (SD) component, customer master data is generally managed centrally through SD, with specific permissions related to accounting details. Customer data can also be managed directly within SAP ERP Financials Financial Accounting. From a segregation of duties perspective, the entry and maintenance of accounting-related customer details should be segregated from the sales function. SAP provides a variety of mechanisms to restrict changes to Customer master records, including account, application, company code, account group, or specific fields within the customer master. Some of the key authorization objects for doing this are shown in Table 5.3: Customer Master Authorization Objects.

Auth. Object	Name	Purpose
F_KNA1_BED	Customer: Accounts Authorization	Restrict modifications to customer master data by customer account range
F_KNA1_APP	Customer: Application Authorization	Restrict the ability to modify customer data to SD or financial accounting data (SAP ERP Financials Financial Accounting)
F_KNA1_BUK	Customer: Authorization for Company Codes	Restrict the ability to change the customer by company code
F_KNA1_KGD	Customer: Change Authorization for Accounts Groups	Restrict the ability to change the customer account group
F_KNA1_AEN	Customer: Change Authorization for Certain Fields	Restrict modifications to customer master data by defined fields

Table 5.3 Customer Master Authorization Objects

Restricting Changes to Customer Credit Master Records

Although it may not seem like it at first blush, credit management is as important to the accounting and financial reporting function as sales forecasting is to the planning function. Special accounting rules apply to valuing accounts receivable. If, for example, a customer is only able to pay half of what he owes your organization, then the value of the customer receivable is what you can reasonably expect to receive from him, not the value of what he owes you. Because of this, customer credit management is closely managed, in many organizations by the finance department.

SAP provides a variety of mechanisms to restrict changes to Credit Management master records. Security permissions can be set to restrict changes to a base account, credit control area, and specific fields within credit management. Some of the key authorization objects for doing this are shown in Table 5.4: Credit Management Authorization Objects.

Auth. Object	Name	Purpose
F_KNKK_BED	Credit Management: Accounts Authorization	Restrict modifications to credit management data by customer account range
F_KNKA_KKB	Credit Management: Authorization for Credit Control Area	Restrict the ability to change the credit management based on credit control area
F_KNKA_AEN	Credit Management: Change Authorization for Certain Fields	Restrict the ability to modify specific credit management fields on the customer record

Table 5.4 Credit Management Authorization Objects

Restricting Changes to Vendor Accounting-Related Master Records

Similar to customer records, vendor master records also contain important SAP ERP Financials Financial Accounting–related data. Specific information such as vendor reconciliation accounts and bank data can be important for both general internal control as well as fraud prevention. As such, maintenance over certain vendor master data fields is important to financial reporting.

If you are using SAP purchasing, vendor master data is generally managed centrally through the purchasing component, with specific permissions related to accounting details. Vendor data can also be managed directly within SAP ERP Financials Financial Accounting. From a segregation of duties perspective, the entry and maintenance of accounting-related vendor details should be segregated from the purchasing function. SAP provides a variety of mechanisms to restrict changes to vendor master records, including account, application, company code, account group, or specific fields within the vendor master. Some of the key authorization objects for doing this are shown in Table 5.5: Vendor Master Authorization Objects.

Auth. Object	Name	Purpose
F_LFA1_BEK	Vendor: Accounts Authorization	Restrict modifications to vendor master data by vendor account range
F_LFA1_APP	Vendor: Application Authorization	Restrict the ability to modify vendor data to purchasing data (PUR) or financial accounting data (SAP ERP Financials Financial Accounting)
F_LFA1_BUK	Vendor: Authorization for Company Codes	Restrict the ability to change the vendor by company code
F_LFA1_GRP	Vendor: Accounts Group Authorization	Restrict the ability to change the vendor based upon account group
F_LFA1_AEN	Vendor: Change Authorization for Certain Fields	Restrict modifications to vendor master data by defined fields

Table 5.5 Vendor Master Authorization Objects

Restricting Changes to Banking Master Records

The ability to change banking data should also be tightly restricted, because bank account information can be highly susceptible to fraud. SAP provides a variety of mechanisms to restrict changes to Banking master records. Security permissions can be set to restrict changes to a bank account, credit control area, and specific fields within credit management. Some of the key authorization objects for doing this are shown in Table 5.6: Banking Authorization Objects.

Auth. Object	Name	Purpose
F_BNKA_BUK	Banks: Authorization for Company Codes	Restrict modifications house banks and bank accounts company code
F_BNKA_MAN	Banks: General Maintenance Authorization	Restrict the general ability to maintain bank master data

Table 5.6 Banking Authorization Objects

5.3　SAP Configurable Control Considerations

In Chapter 2, we reviewed the typical process for auditing SAP and introduced a series of audit assurance "layers" upon which an auditor will typically build his confidence in SAP processing. In this section, we explore the Component-Specific Technical Settings layer related to SAP ERP Financials Financial Accounting and Controlling. Specifically, we introduce a number of *SAP configuration suggestions and considerations* that can enhance processes over the SAP financial reporting cycle.

This list is by no means exhaustive, and we fully expect that you will utilize many more configurable SAP controls than are mentioned herein. This section highlights some of the control features within SAP that, in our experience, could be more comprehensively used by organizations running SAP applications. Regardless of whether you agree with the control technique, consider the risks being addressed by these recommendations and ensure, where appropriate, that you have addressed these risks within your organization.

> **Assess Your Own Risks**
>
> The recommendations provided here are suggestions only, and should be reviewed in the context of your own business risks and anticipated value. You may find some of these suggestions unreasonable for your business environment, and you may choose to address the underlying risks in different ways. Effective SAP control is not a one-size-fits-all situation.

5.3.1 Configure SAP Data Quality Checks

Data quality problems affect many organizations. While SAP supports strong data integrity checks, many of these need to be turned on and configured for your business. Failure to take advantage of these capabilities places reliance on user diligence during document entry, and after-the-fact reviews to detect any errors or abuse. Many auditors now use specific tools to detect potential data problems in both master and transactional data, so utilizing these techniques on your most important data elements can help prevent audit embarrassment.

Define Important Fields as "Required Entry"

By default, the fields that SAP requires for transaction processing or master data entry may not be all the fields you need to fully process business transactions in your environment. Configuring SAP to flag situations where additional information may be required can help ensure a high level of data integrity.

For example, in FI-AR, you may choose to require the reconciliation account, ensuring that whenever a posting is made to the FI-AR sub-ledger, an automatic posting is made on a real-time basis to the related SAP General Ledger reconciliation account. You may also choose to require the currency and exchange rate fields so this information is available when it comes time for processing.

Figure 5.1: Maintain Field Status Groups shows an example where a company using Controlling may require the entry of cost centers to ensure sufficient information is available to flow to the SAP ERP Financials Controlling component. This particular setting is available in the IMG under ENTERPRISE CONTROLLING • CONSOLIDATION • INTEGRATION: PREPARATION FOR CONSOLIDATION • PREPARATION IN THE SENDER SYSTEM • FURTHER SETTINGS FOR BUSINESS AREA CONSOLIDATIONS • FINANCIAL ACCOUNTING • MAINTAIN FIELD STATUS GROUPS FOR G/L ACCOUNTS.

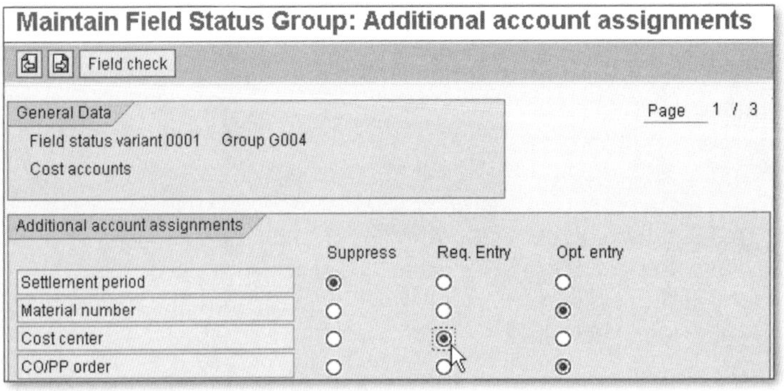

Figure 5.1 Maintain Field Status Groups

Field status groups within SAP enable additional data handling procedures over individual fields and field groups based on the type of transaction (e.g., create, change, display). For controlling key data, the field status groups you'll most likely use are "Required Entry" and "Display." Use "Required Entry" to specify those fields that must contain data, and "Display" for those fields that you wish the user to see but not have the ability to change. Change any fields that are not used to "Suppress" to prevent user confusion.

Create SAP General Ledger Validation Checks

Beyond just ensuring that data is entered in specific fields, SAP also validates data entry based on simple or complex criteria. While SAP already contains many standard edit and validation checks, additional validation or substitution rules can strengthen financial reporting controls. Data validation for SAP General Ledger entries helps limit the potential for errors, and can also minimize opportunity for fraud and abuse.

At a minimum, implement SAP validation procedures over account combinations during journal entry processing. Specific rules may vary by organization, but certain account combinations are not possible from an accounting perspective. For example, debiting depreciation expense and crediting cash does not make logical sense (and could be an attempt to mask fraud). Impossible combinations such as these should be set with a validation message of either "Error" (allowing the user to correct the transaction), or "Cancel," resulting in the transaction being cancelled. For account combinations that are unusual but not impossible, set the message level to "Warn" to allow the user to verify appropriateness before proceeding.

Warn vs. Error

When setting data validation rules, avoid the temptation to use "Warn" messages over "Error" messages for clearly illegitimate entries. From an internal control perspective, user warnings are only useful for catching unintentional mistakes. Because warning messages can be bypassed, they are meaningless for preventing fraud and abuse.

Validation rules are set using transaction GGB0, or by navigating the IMG through FINANCIAL ACCOUNTING • SPECIAL PURPOSE LEDGER • TOOLS • MAINTAIN VALIDA-TION/SUBSTITUTION/RULES • MAINTAIN VALIDATION (Refer to Figure 5.2: Creating Document Validations). For SAP ERP Financials Financial Accounting documents, validations can occur at the document header, for individual line items, or upon document completion. The validation generally consists of three parts: an optional prerequisite, the validation check procedure (which results in a true or false answer), and the message resulting if the check is true.

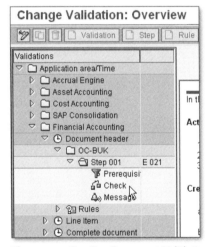

Figure 5.2 Creating Document Validations

In addition to validating account combinations, other helpful validation procedures for SAP General Ledger entries include:

▸ Verifying that a specific company code is posting to only authorized business areas during document posting

▸ Ensuring that the SAP General Ledger description field contains reasonable text (e.g., text length exceeds a specified number of characters)

- Checking that entries in excess of expectations for a specific account are legitimate (e.g., a multi-million dollar entry to reserves for an insurance company may be appropriate, but a multi-million dollar entry to prepaid expense may not).
- Warning on transaction postings to accounts marked for deletion

If you have configured any substitutions in SAP, the substitution is performed before validation procedures. As such, any data changed during the substitution process is checked against validation rules.

Set Reasonable Posting Tolerance Levels

SAP data validation rules can be extremely powerful; however, defining a robust set of rules can be time consuming and may not be practical for small SAP configuration teams. A good early step is to use SAP posting tolerance functionality. Defining posting tolerances, shown in Figure 5.3: Posting Tolerances by Company Code, allows you to limit postings by:

- Maximum amount (dollar or percentage) for a single document
- Maximum amount (dollar or percentage) for a single line item within a document

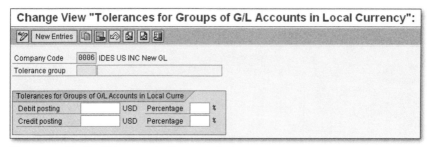

Figure 5.3 Posting Tolerances by Company Code

Posting tolerances can differ by tolerance groups, with individual users assigned to these tolerance groups. By defining a posting tolerance but leaving the tolerance group blank, you are able to create a rule that applies to all users. You can then establish a tolerance group for a limited set of users with the ability to exceed standard limits, while at the same time restricting these users from posting clearly erroneous transactions. The tolerance levels defined in a default SAP installation are substantially higher than typical postings by most organizations (in the hundreds of millions of dollars), and thus auditors will often look to ensure that settings have been changed from the default.

Define Maximum Exchange Rate Differences

Foreign currency exchange rates can have a dramatic effect on the financials for companies that operate internationally. Fluctuations in exchange rates can be dramatic, and in larger organizations can affect the bottom-line by millions if not billions of dollars — clearly affecting operations projections and business decisions. For both financial and operational reporting, SAP allows foreign currency transactions to be revalued to a defined local currency based on exchange rates entered in the system. To protect from erroneous reporting or decision making based on inaccurate information, configure a maximum exchange rate difference in SAP. This tolerance establishes the largest percentage that a manually entered exchange rate can differ from one stored in SAP, at either the company code level or the individual foreign currency level. If a foreign exchange rate entered during manual document entry differs from the rate stored in SAP, the system generates a warning message. You configure this tolerance in the IMG through FINANCIAL ACCOUNTING • FINANCIAL ACCOUNTING GLOBAL SETTINGS • DOCUMENT • DOCUMENT HEADER • MAXIMUM EXCHANGE RATE DIFFERENCE • DEFINE MAXIMUM EXCHANGE RATE DIFFERENCE [PER COMPANY CODE/ PER FOREIGN CURRENCY].

5.3.2   Enhance Controls over SAP General Ledger Postings

In addition to configuration, which directly affects data quality, additional configuration techniques can also reduce risk and increase confidence in SAP General Ledger postings.

Implementing Park and Post

To ensure that all manual postings to the SAP General Ledger receive a secondary review, many companies implement a technique called *park and post*. To implement park and post, configure SAP so that users who have the ability to create SAP General Ledger entries do not have the ability to post those entries. A second group of experienced and knowledgeable users who do not have the ability to create SAP General Ledger entries would then review each parked document and post those that have been deemed appropriate. For the park and post technique to be effective (and pass audit scrutiny), the review process has to be consistent and reliable, not merely a formality.

Configuring Accounts for Automatic Posting, Where Appropriate

For certain types of transaction amounts, such as exchange rate differences, cash discounts paid, output/input tax, and cash discounts received, SAP automatically posts amounts to relevant SAP General Ledger accounts. Because the posting is automatic, this reduces the potential for user error. To take advantage of this functionality, configure relevant accounts to allow automatic postings.

Preventing Field Changes after Initial Posting

Subsequently changing a document that has been posted to the SAP General Ledger can affect the ease of an audit trail. The general rule of thumb from a control perspective is that the original document should be reversed, and the correcting document posted. This process allows full transparency into all transactions affecting the SAP General Ledger. If document fields are changed after the fact, determining what information as initially entered and approved by management can be difficult. To ensure proper control, define rules that prohibit changes to sensitive fields after initial posting.

Document change rules in SAP are defined in Transaction OB32, and an example can be seen in Figure 5.4: Document Change Rule Settings. If the "Field Can Be Changed" setting is unchecked, the field cannot be changed. If it's set, the field may be changed after initial entry, subject to any stipulations checked as part of the rule (in essence, making the field changeable only in certain circumstances). The available stipulations vary by account type and transaction type.

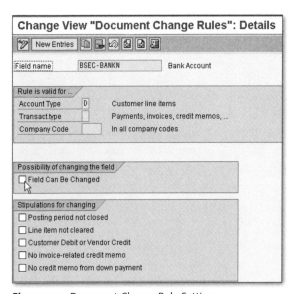

Figure 5.4 Document Change Rule Settings

5.3.3   Reduce Asset Management Errors

From an accounting perspective, recording assets in an appropriate manner can be challenging. Depending on the countries in which you operate, asset valuation rules can vary greatly. Even in low-complexity organizations, the treatment of issues like depreciation (where the value of an asset is reduced to recognize the decreasing real value over time) can be highly error prone. Whether dealing with large fixed assets like property, plants, and equipment, or small assets that are eventually used in production the Asset Management component of SAP ERP Financials Financial Accounting component has a number of configurable characteristics that can help improve overall control. For organizations where asset management has a significant effect on financial reporting, the following configuration options may be helpful.

Requiring All Fields Necessary to Complete the Asset Record

In the same way that field status configuration can be set to require certain fields for SAP General Ledger accounts, field status can also be used to require fields within the asset master record. By default, SAP requires a Company Code, Asset Class, and Description for every asset. Depending on business need and applicability, you may also choose to require entry of fields such as Cost Center, Business Area, Plant, and Location.

Setting Default Values for Asset Classes

Typically, items within a given asset class follow a common set of accounting rules, especially when it comes to depreciation activities. Configuring SAP to default to the appropriate depreciation key for any new assets added to the asset class, for example, helps to ensure consistency as well as minimize the potential for error. Default accounts can also be established to automatically select the appropriate SAP General Ledger accounts for asset transaction postings.

Configuring Asset Transfer and Retirement Transaction Types

When configuring transaction types for asset transfers (available for types 300 to 399) and asset retirements (available for types 200 to 299), define transaction types to control parameters such as depreciation treatment, account assignment, and timing for the relevant transfer/retirement. For retirements in particular, configuration should ensure that the system automatically logs an asset retirement date (or requires a past retirement date from the user), and changes the asset status to "retired" to prevent further postings.

Defining Low-Value Asset Maximum Amounts

Assets defined as low-value assets (LVAs) (sometimes referred to as "pooled" assets) can often be treated differently from traditional, individual assets. Specific rules apply to these LVAs, and they can be accounted for in bulk rather than by individual asset. Because the use of LVA treatment is often limited to defined characteristics, you can configure SAP to validate that assets included in LVA categorization do not exceed specified rules. Configuring SAP's LVA check (using Transaction OVY2 as shown in Figure 5.5: Testing LVAs upon Acquisition), tells SAP to check, for each asset acquisition posting, whether the asset value exceeds the LVA maximum for the company code or depreciation area. SAP will reject posting to asset acquisition postings to an LVA asset class if the defined criteria is not met (requiring that the user would then record the asset to a non-LVA asset class).

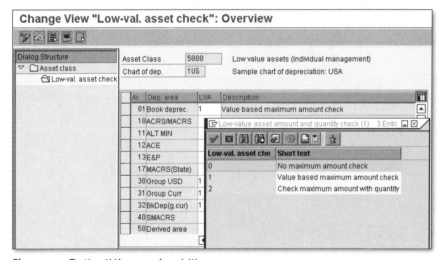

Figure 5.5   Testing LVAs upon Acquisition

5.3.4   Other Configuration Tips

The previous suggestions are the most critical from an audit and control perspective. Depending on your organization and business processes, the following ideas may also help enhance your internal control environment and allow better risk management. As with all other suggestions, the relevance of each of these to audit success is tied to your business risks:

▶ Alternate payment currencies — When alternate payment currencies may be used, configure SAP to maintain automatic account assignments, including clearing accounts, for payment differences that may arise as a result of payment currency.

▶ Duplicate business partners — Enable SAP functionality for detecting potential duplicates when customers or vendors are entered. Duplicate business partners within SAP ERP Financials Financial Accounting can lead to duplicate payments, extending too much credit, and other undesired issues. SAP will create a warning message if the address entered is the same as the one in the system, and present the user with a list of potential duplicates that he can review before completing processing.

5.4   Additional Procedures and Considerations

As we have discussed earlier in this book, configuring SAP the "right" way is often not enough. User interaction with the SAP system plays a large part in the effectiveness of business processes managed by SAP. This section highlights additional procedures and considerations that can help you further strengthen your financial reporting processes and withstand audit scrutiny.

5.4.1   Maintain and Follow a Closing Checklist

Even in smaller organizations, the closing process can be complex, with a lot of dependencies and potential for error. As a result, many organizations create closing checklists of all steps, and their relative order, required to close the books at required intervals (daily, monthly, quarterly, and/or yearly depending on business circumstances). These procedures typically include items such as:

▶ Ensuring parked/held journal entries have been assessed and posted, where appropriate

▶ Reviewing and reconciling key reports (a number of which we discuss later in this chapter)

▶ Revaluing open accounts paid in foreign currency

▶ Posting accrual entries and depreciation

SAP includes some basic functionality for managing the closing process, such as the Schedule Manager accessed through Transaction SCMA. Certain functionality in SAP BusinessObjects Process Control can also be used to validate the completeness of closing procedures. Third-party add-ons to SAP have also become popular, although in our experience built-in SAP functionality combined with manual checklists are still the most common method for managing closing.

5.4.2 Implement Procedures to Resolve All Parked and Held Documents Prior to Closing

SAP journal entries that have been put on hold or parked will not update any SAP General Ledger account balances until they have been posted. This can lead to incomplete financial statements and reports if these issues are not resolved before period close. Your closing procedures should include processes to ensure that all relevant parked or held documents have been processed (as appropriate) before period close.

Designated employees should run reports showing parked documents and ensure that any documents relevant to the current period have been resolved and posted. This may include running reports like the Compact Document Journal (ACCOUNTING • FINANCIAL ACCOUNTING • GENERAL LEDGER • INFO SYSTEM • GENERAL LEDGER REPORTS • DOCUMENT • GENERAL • COMPACT JOURNAL REPORT), report RFBELJ00, with the "Parked Documents" option checked. For held documents, a communication to all employees with the ability to post to the SAP General Ledger should request that any holds be cleared before period close so that the amounts can be posted in the correct accounting period.

> **In-Process Documents: Parking vs. Holding**
>
> While parked documents can be viewed by other authorized users, held documents can only be processed by the user who initiated the transaction. As such, documents on hold pose a risk to financial reporting completeness. Employees should be trained to never hold documents — to always park them instead. Because sudden illnesses or emergencies cannot be predicted, by parking documents, you can ensure that others can always complete processing if transaction originators are unavailable.

5.4.3 Confirm Receivables and Payables Account Balances

For financial statement auditing, most auditors send out what are known as *confirmation letters* to independently verify the balances of customer receivables accounts (and sometimes vendor payable accounts as well). Confirmation letters help the auditor independently validate the value of the account balance, ensuring that there are no disputed or missing items included in the total.

Because auditors are likely to confirm balances anyway, a good practice is to use standard SAP functionality to confirm your own customer and vendor balances in advance of the audit. Depending on the process used, the information you receive back may even allow the auditor to reduce his testing. Transaction F.17 generates customer confirmation, and Transaction F.18 generates vendor confirmation. These can also be accessed through menu path ACCOUNTING • FINANCIAL ACCOUNTING • [ACCOUNTS RECEIVABLE / ACCOUNTS PAYABLE] • PERIODIC PROCESSING • PRINT CORRE-SPONDENCE • BALANCE CONFIRMATION • PRINT LETTERS. Both forms of confirmations are similar, allowing you to select customers or vendors meeting certain criteria (e.g., one-time vendors, those with balances between specified amounts, those with recent postings, etc.) or even take a random sample.

When using confirmations, one of the most important settings is the Confirmation Procedure, under the Output Control section of the form, as shown in Figure 5.6: Generating Confirmations. SAP allows three different types of confirmations to be generated:

▶ Balance Notifications

▶ Balance Requests

▶ Balance Confirmations

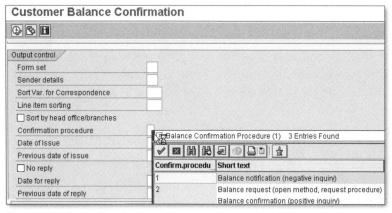

Figure 5.6 Generating Confirmations

The strongest confirmation procedure is the Balance Request, because it requests that the customer or vendor respond with the balance shown in his system without influencing him with what you show within SAP. A more common and still strong confirmation procedure is the Balance Confirmation, commonly known as the positive confirmation or positive inquiry. The Balance Confirmation requests that the customer respond to the confirmation letter, indicating that he either agrees with a balance or shows a different balance (included in the response). This type of confirmation is not as strong as the Balance Request, because some customers may simply check the box and respond that the balance is correct if it seems reasonable, without necessarily confirming in their own systems. Balance Notifications are not usually effective confirmation procedures. The Balance Notification requests a response only if the balance differs from their records, thus making the potentially incorrect assumption that non-receipt of a response indicates agreement with the balance (in reality, it could also indicate that the letter was never received, or the recipient has not had time to respond).

5.4.4 Establish Procedures for Verifying Asset Management Activities

Asset management can be performed inconsistently or incorrectly if procedures for acquisition, maintenance, transfer, and retirement of assets not performed appropriately. Policies, procedures, and user training should show relevant users how assets should be allocated to various asset classes, including LVAs, Procedures should cover reconciliation processes for verifying the accuracy of SAP General Ledger postings (such as reconciling the fixed asset sub-ledger to the general ledger fixed assets control accounts) and the physical existence and condition of assets (through physical verification).

For assets created or modified during the period, procedures (typically a quality assurance process by an independent party) should ensure that the correct asset class is applied to the asset. Among other things, applying the wrong asset class can result in incorrect deprecation treatment. Additionally, incomplete assets (viewed through Transaction AUVA) should be reviewed and completed prior to period close.

5.5 Management Monitoring: SAP Report Highlights

Monitoring procedures are a core part of an effective internal control structure. SAP contains numerous reports that you can use to identify and monitor potential risks within the financial reporting cycle. Diligent review of these reports and investigation of suspicious items complements the configured controls within SAP, and rounds out your ability to survive a financial reporting audit. This section highlights a few examples.

5.5.1 Reports Identifying Changed Data

SAP reports that highlight changes to sensitive data are valuable for ensuring that all changes (including initial creation) have been authorized and entered accurately. These reports provide valuable information, because they show both the old values and the new values that replaced them. The frequency that these reports should be reviewed will depend on the risk that inappropriate changes to the relevant data elements could pose to your operations. Data change reports should be reviewed by someone other than employees who can make changes to data.

Each review should at a minimum cover the period since the last review, which you can select using the "Changed On" general selection criteria in the reports below. Limiting "Changed By" selections to individual employees or small groups of employees can highlight suspicious activity, but when filtering selections using additional criteria, ensure that by the end of the review process that you have covered every change made during the review period.

Each of the reports in this section can be found under menu path ACCOUNTING • FINANCIAL ACCOUNTING.

SAP General Ledger Account Changes

Review the *Display Changes to G/L Accounts* report RFSABL00 to display changes both to SAP General Ledger accounts as well as sample accounts used for creating new master data records. This report can be found under submenu GENERAL LEDGER • PERIODIC PROCESSING • CLOSING • REPORT • GENERAL LEDGER REPORTS • MASTER DATA, or accessed directly through Transaction S_ALR_87012308.

Accounting Document Changes

Review the *Display of Changed Documents* report RFBABL00 to display changes to accounting documents. Pay particular attention to changes made to recurring entry documents (one of the Document Type selection options). Given that recurring entries post automatically over time, inappropriate changes can have a lasting impact on financial reporting. This report can be found under submenu GENERAL LEDGER • PERIODIC PROCESSING • CLOSING • REPORT • GENERAL LEDGER REPORTS • GENERAL, or accessed directly through Transaction S_ALR_87012293.

Bank Master Data Changes

Review the *Display of Bank Changes* report RFBKABL0 to display changes to banking master data. Reviews can be performed by country; however, because the number of banking changes should be minimal (except in the case of specific known business events), you will unlikely use this filter. This report can be found under menu BANKS • MASTER DATA • BANK MASTER RECORD, or accessed directly through Transaction S_P00_07000008.

Customer Changes

Review the *Display Changes to Customers* report RFDABL00 to display changes to customer records. Reviews can be filtered by company code and sales area data, if desired. Although this report can be large, once data has been returned you can filter on fields most relevant from an accounting and reporting perspective (such as tax jurisdiction). This report can be found under menu ACCOUNTS RECEIVABLE • INFORMATION SYSTEM • REPORTS FOR ACCOUNTS RECEIVABLE ACCOUNTING • MASTER DATA, or accessed directly through Transaction S_ALR_87012182.

Customer Credit Changes

Review the *Display Changes to Credit Management* report RFDKLIAB to display changes to credit management data, including changes to credit limits and removal of customer credit blocks. Reviews can be filtered by credit control area, if desired. This report can be found under menu ACCOUNTS RECEIVABLE • CREDIT MANAGEMENT • CREDIT MANAGEMENT INFO SYSTEM, or accessed directly through Transaction S_ALR_87012215.

Vendor Changes

Review the *Display Changes to Vendors* report RFKABL00 to display changes to vendor records. Reviews can be filtered by company code and purchasing organization, if desired. Although this report can be large, once data has been returned you can filter on fields that are most relevant from an accounting and reporting perspective. This report can be found under menu ACCOUNTS PAYABLE • INFORMATION SYSTEM • REPORTS FOR ACCOUNTS PAYABLE ACCOUNTING • MASTER DATA, or accessed directly through Transaction S_ALR_87012089.

5.5.2 Incomplete Information

Some SAP reports highlight situations where data is missing. In some cases, missing data may indicate processing problems, and in other cases, missing data could result in transactions that have not been fully captured in the SAP General Ledger system. The frequency that these reports should be reviewed will depend on the risk that having *incomplete* data could pose to your operations.

Incomplete SAP General Ledger Postings

Review the SAP ERP Financials Financial Accounting Document: List of Update Terminations report RFVBER00 to display terminated postings that have not been completed. Update terminations can occur for a variety of reasons, and this report should be run prior to any period closing to ensure all documents have been posted.

Missing Customer Data

Initiate the Customer Master Data Comparison transaction (F.2D) to identify customer records that have been created in SD but not in SAP ERP Financials Financial

Accounting (or vice versa). Identification of customers who have not been maintained in SAP ERP Financials Financial Accounting could indicate processing problems, and SAP ERP Financials Financial Accounting customers not in SD could be indicative of fraud.

Missing Credit Data

Initiate the Customers with Missing Credit Data transaction (F.32) to identify customer records with incomplete credit management information.

Assets Not Yet Capitalized

Review the Directory of Unposted Assets report RAZUGA01, to identify assets that have not yet been capitalized. Results will display the opening date of the asset, the user who created the asset, and the asset description. Follow up on items noted to ensure that appropriate postings have been made to the SAP General Ledger before period close.

5.5.3 Potential Issues

Certain SAP reports highlight potential issues that should be investigated. These issues could result from processing problems, fraud, or errors. Two common examples include:

- ▶ Gaps in Document Numbers (Transaction S_ALR_87012342)
- ▶ Invoice Numbers Allocated Twice (Transaction S_ALR_87012341)

Review these reports periodically (at least once per period), to investigate issues and determine and resolve root causes.

5.6 Summary

In this chapter, we reviewed risks within the SAP financial reporting cycle. To mitigate those risks, we highlighted a series of controls across four main categories. Related to security and master data, we explored segregation of duties, critical transactions, and important authorization objects. We then highlighted a series of configurable SAP controls that may be reviewed during an SAP audit. We reviewed a series of process-based controls and procedures that can strengthen risk management of financial reporting, and closed with an overview of key SAP reports.

In the next chapter, we will look at the order-to-cash process and examine similar control categories related to the SAP SD component.

"It's not the employer who pays the wages. Employers only handle the money. It's the customer who pays the wages." — Henry Ford

6 Order-to-Cash Cycle

In the order-to-cash cycle, customers receive goods and services while your organization receives compensation for meeting customer needs. The process itself sounds simple. Customers indicate a desire to purchase, and you fulfill their requests in exchange for payment. In reality, however, the order-to-cash process can be highly complex. Customers can be finicky. Orders and requests may be non-standard. Pricing models can be complicated. Payments may be late or for the incorrect amount. And despite the hassle, the order-to-cash process is a core business necessity — allowing organizations to make enough to continue ongoing operations.

In this chapter, we explore the SAP order-to-cash process, supported by the SAP SD component (part of the SAP ERP Operations Suite). Within SD, we address order processing, shipping, invoicing, returns, and collections. Similar to the approach used for the financial reporting cycle in Chapter 5, we review the risks inherent in the process, and a sampling of SAP configurable controls commonly reviewed during an SAP order-to-cash audit. We also highlight a series of processes and procedures that, if applied consistently, can mitigate a number of order-to-cash risks and put you in a better position for an audit.

> **Note**
>
> If you have read Chapter 5, you will see some overlap between the controls recommended for the financial reporting cycle and those recommended for the order-to-cash cycle, particularly related to customer master data and credit management. Because not all SAP SD customers use the SAP ERP Financials Financial Accounting component, the information is also included here to ensure complete coverage of the order-to-cash process.

6.1 Risks

Unlike the financial reporting cycle, where the business *risks* are heavily compliance oriented, the business risks in the order-to-cash cycle are primarily operational in nature. That is, they directly impact the efficiency and effectiveness of the *way* your organization operates and how likely management goals and objectives are to be realized. Because the order-to-cash cycle is highly customer facing, the quality of day-to-day operations can have a significant impact on customer perceptions and buying behavior.

In Chapter 1, we discussed the concept of risk and how internal controls are designed to mitigate specific business risks. When preparing for an SAP audit covering the order-to-cash process, think through some of the things that could go wrong in the SAP order-to-cash process that could affect reporting integrity. A few of these risks include:

▶ Missed sales opportunities — SAP can greatly enhance the sales process by consolidating customer information collected from a variety of sources and making it available to the sales function. Failure to fully capture customer information, late entry of data, and inaccurate interpretation of information can all lead to missed sales opportunities.

▶ Inaccurate quotations — Customers often rely on quotations for making buying decisions. Whether the result of misunderstanding the customer need, selecting the wrong product or service SKU, or failing to limit the duration of quotations, providing inaccurate pricing information to the customer can have negative consequences. Inaccurate quotations can lead to either missed sales opportunities, or result in being obligated to fulfill orders at unwanted price points.

▶ Pricing errors — SAP contains powerful pricing options and capabilities. With this power comes complexity, and maintenance of various pricing conditions combined with manual entry errors or incomplete updates can result in pricing problems. Additionally, management of customer-specific discounts and rebates can be complex and prone to error.

▶ Unauthorized discounts — Use of discounts not intended by management can result in lost revenue and set pricing precedents that are difficult to change. SAP controls restrict the ability to apply discounts, but certain transactions and processes within SAP allow discount-like functionality to be applied if not effectively restricted.

▶ Processing duplicate orders — SAP can ensure that a customer order is not duplicated or has not already started as part of a quotation; however, certain conditions apply. Failure to apply controls over order entry could result in duplicate processing of customer orders even when the SAP system is doing what it can to prevent this problem.

▶ Missed delivery dates — SAP can ensure that customer delivery dates can be met; however, this relies on the diligence of sales professionals. Failure to account for product backorders, inaccurate due date entry, and other such mistakes can lead to missed delivery dates and order cancellations. Lack of diligence when resolving sales document blocks can also lead to the inability to meet customer expectations for delivery, and possibly result in order cancellations.

▶ Late or missed billing — Failure to completely enter key information in SAP can result in late or missed billings. Depending on contract terms and customer circumstances, this can result in late payments and missed opportunities for interest income, or even reduce collectability.

▶ Inability to reconcile customer payments to orders — SAP contains strong matching functionality; however, ineffective cash application processes and reconciliation procedures can make it difficult to tie incomplete customer payments to the orders for which they apply. As a result, customer balance inquiries may be difficult to answer, interest due may not be fully collected, and the collectability of receivables balances can become questionable.

▶ Insufficient customer credit but goods shipped anyway — SAP checks credit at multiple points during the sales order process. If not configured appropriately, however, customer credit may change during processing and yet goods are still shipped. For example, a payment applied to the customer account may come back as NSF (non-sufficient funds) after the order has been entered into the system, and based on available credit before the NSF event.

▶ Revenue not recognized when allowed — While this risk primarily affects the financial reporting cycle discussed in Chapter 5, revenue recognition starts with the order-to-cash cycle. SAP records accounting entries on shipment of goods; however, these entries do not affect revenue until the bill is created, and blocked billing documents among other conditions can prevent creation of the appropriate accounting entries. Not only can failure to recognize revenue impact financial reporting, it can also influence management decision making.

▶ Inaccurate customer activity reporting — In the age of business intelligence, management decisions around marketing strategies, customer care, pricing, and support is dependent on the accuracy of information. Data quality issues such as duplicate customers can skew reporting and decision making. SAP contains numerous controls to help maintain data quality; however, many of these need to be configured appropriately to be relevant to your organization.

▶ Fraudulent transactions — The Association of Certified Fraud Examiners estimates that corporations, on average, lose 7% of revenue to fraud. Whether associated with the diversion of goods to illegitimate sources, unauthorized preferential treatment for a group of customers, or manipulation to reach sales bonus targets, the existence of fraud in the order-to-cash process can have a noticeable impact on profitability.

Of course, each of these risk categories is broad. As mentioned in Chapter 3 on the discussion of designing appropriate controls during an implementation, effectively managing risks requires understanding specific situations for which controls can then be applied.

For example, we mentioned above how unauthorized discounts could occur from transactions that may not be intuitively associated with SAP pricing. Sales personnel issuing free of charge deliveries (SAP functionality for shipping free goods to customers intended to replace damaged shipments) can, in essence, use this functionality to allow preferred customers to get additional goods for a lower price. Other transactions could also allow sales to manipulate pricing beyond that intended by management. For example, the ability to issue customer credits, if inappropriately used, could also allow pricing manipulation. For each of the risks that you identify in your environment, understand how they could come about and how you have addressed them in your SAP implementation or surrounding processes.

Later in this chapter, we provide suggestions for SAP configurable controls that can mitigate some of the risks inherent in the order-to-cash process, and highlight important business processes that can also strengthen control. Before that, however, we'll discuss SAP master data and security issues critical to the integrity of the order-to-cash process.

6.2 Security and Master Data

SAP security can provide a powerful level of control by limiting abilities to only a small group of authorized users. Master data controls are also critical due to the effect that master data has on business transactions. When preparing for an audit, ensuring strong *security and master data* processes are in place is a good first step toward audit success.

6.2.1 Preventing Segregation of Duties Conflicts

A segregation of duties review is a core component of most types of SAP audits. In Chapter 4, we discussed *segregation of duties* in the context of general computer controls (GCCs) and the IT function. Appropriate segregation of duties is also important within the order-to-cash process. Insufficient segregation of duties could lead to unauthorized pricing (creating revenue loss or resulting in lost sales opportunities), undetected errors (potentially leading to poor management decisions based on inaccurate information), or even outright fraud.

Table 6.1: SD Segregation of Duties Highlights illustrates some of the abilities that should be segregated within the SAP SD component. This is by no means a complete list, because complete rule sets within security management tools like SAP BusinessObjects Access Control can have hundreds of rules for SD alone. To survive an SAP audit where order-to-cash is part of the review, however, at least prevent violations such as these.

The Ability To:	Should Not Be Combined with the Ability To:
Process sales orders	Maintain pricing conditions
Process sales orders	Issue free of charge deliveries
Process sales orders	Process customer credit memos
Process sales orders	Post customer payments
Process sales orders	Release blocked documents
Create billing documents	Maintain customer master data
Create billing documents	Post customer payments
Create customer credit memos	Release blocked documents (for customer credit)
Create customer credit memos	Maintain pricing conditions
Create customer credit memos	Post customer payments
Maintain pricing conditions	Post customer payments

Table 6.1 SD Segregation of Duties Highlights

Dealing with Small Teams

The best way to deal with segregation of duties is to prevent potential conflicts using SAP security. In some situations, however, traditional security-enabled segregation may not be possible. Perhaps a single employee manages a group of functions in a remote location, and as a result his duties cannot be effectively segregated. Many auditors understand such business realities. However, if this describes your situation, have monitoring and review procedures in place (and working) to mitigate the risk of insufficient security.

6.2.2 Restricting Transactions to Functional Sales Areas

Within many organizations, the sales function can be highly complex. Selling may take place through a direct labor force or through a variety of distribution channels. Sales teams may be organized by product, by product category, by target industry, or by geographic region. Depending on industry, customer organizations can be in the tens of thousands, and the number of contacts managed within that customer base can reach hundreds of thousands if not millions. Managing this volume of information can be complex.

Whether managing customers or managing customer orders, segregating the ability to create and maintain data can help reduce the potential for errors and abuse. Most organizations find it appropriate to restrict customers by sales areas and sales organizations using authorization objects V_KNA1_VKO and V_KNA1_BRG. Sales activities can be further restricted through authorization object V_VBAK_VKO, which allows segregation by Sales Organization, Distribution Channel, and Division, and V_VBAK_AAT, which allows segregation by sales document type.

> **Guilty Until Proven Innocent?**
>
> In addition to reviewing how you have leveraged SAP security to control SD master data and sales transactions, your auditor will also likely question those techniques you did NOT use. For example, if you restrict sales transactions postings by sales organization and distribution channel, your auditor will likely ask why you have not further restricted postings by division. Be prepared to discuss this issue in terms of how you have managed business risks and what factors in your environment lead you to believe that current security settings are appropriate.

6.2.3 Limiting Access to Powerful Transactions

When assigning security privileges, ensure that powerful SAP transactions and abilities within the SD component have been *limited* to a small number of personnel. Even if these functions are rarely used, the ability of a user to perform them poses risks to the organization and thus creates audit concern. A few of these transactions include:

▸ The ability to perform mass maintenance (XD99)

▸ The ability to delete customer master data (VD06)

▸ The ability to perform mass changes on customer credit limits (program RFDKLI50)

▸ The ability to unblock business partners (VD05)

▸ The ability to unblock sales orders with a credit block (VKM1)

▸ The ability to enter customer credit memos (FB75)

In addition to limiting access to these abilities through security, you can further strengthen controls by monitoring their usage. This monitoring should be independent of the group able to perform these transactions. Being able to show an auditor that the use of powerful transactions is both limited and effectively monitored is ideal.

> **Raising the Bar: Better Control over Powerful Transactions**
>
> Organizations looking to overachieve and virtually eliminate the risks of powerful transactions should consider removing these abilities from all users, and only assigning them at time of need (particularly in the case of mass-maintenance transactions). Once the relevant process has been completed and verified, access can once again be removed.

6.2.4 Establishing Controls and Security over Master Data

Master data tables drive SAP transaction processing. Strong *controls* over master data, whether it be creation, modification, or deletion, are necessary for audit success. As it relates to master data in the order-to-cash process, the auditor will generally look to ensure that:

▶ The ability to change master data is limited to a core group of employees (for each type of master data)

▶ Employees who make changes to master data have sufficient knowledge and training on organizational policies and SAP usage to understand the issues and implications

▶ Procedures exist for authorizing changes to master data that can affect the order-to-cash cycle (typically in advance of the change)

▶ Independent quality assurance processes validate master data changes

▶ Master data is periodically reviewed for relevance (i.e., credit limits are current, pricing conditions are relevant, etc.)

Organizations may choose to manage certain order-to-cash master data, such as customer data, centrally or locally. Auditors often view centralized maintenance as providing stronger control with more consistency; however, business circumstances will dictate which is right for you.

Restricting Changes to Business Partners

SAP provides a variety of mechanisms to restrict changes to business partner master records. Security permissions can be set to restrict changes by specific field values (e.g., names beginning with A to D), to specific fields within the business partner record, on authorization groups, by business partner role, on relationship category, or by relationship field groups. Due to the impact that the quality of business partner data can have across the organization, tighter restrictions are generally preferable to more open security models. In general, restrict the ability to create, change, delete, and in some cases even view specific business partner data to only a small handful of trained employees, and only within their defined areas of responsibility. Some of the key authorization objects for doing this are shown in Table 6.2: Business Partner Authorization Objects.

Auth. Object	Name	Purpose
B_BUPA_ATT	Business Partner: Authorization Types	Restrict modifications to specific business partners based on the value of any business partner field
B_BUPA_FDG	Business Partner: Field Groups:	Restrict modifications to fields within business partner maintenance, or viewing of those fields
B_BUPA_GRP	Business Partner: Authorization Groups	Restrict modifications to business partners by authorization group
B_BUPA_RLT	Business Partner: Roles	Restrict modifications to business partner roles
B_BUPA_BZT	Business Partner Relationships: Relationship Categories	Restrict modifications to business partner relationship categories
B_BUPA_FDG	Business Partner Relationships: Relationship Field Groups	Restrict modifications to specific fields within business partner relationships

Table 6.2 Business Partner Authorization Objects

Restricting Changes to Customer Master Records

Customer master data is generally managed centrally, with specific permissions related to sales and accounting details. Customer data can also be managed directly within SD and SAP ERP Financials Financial Accounting, although when doing so, there should be procedures to ensure that SD and SAP ERP Financials Financial Accounting data remains in sync. From a segregation of duties perspective, the entry and maintenance of accounting-related customer details should be segregated from the sales function. SAP provides a variety of mechanisms to restrict changes to customer master records, including account, application, company code, account group, or specific fields within the customer master. Some of the key authorization objects for doing this are shown in Table 6.3: Customer Master Authorization Objects.

Auth. Object	Name	Purpose
F_KNA1_BED	Customer: Accounts Authorization	Restrict modifications to customer master data by customer account range
F_KNA1_APP	Customer: Application Authorization	Restrict the ability to modify customer data to sales data (SD) or financial accounting data (SAP ERP Financials Financial Accounting)
F_KNA1_BUK	Customer: Authorization for Company Codes	Restrict the ability to change the customer by company code
F_KNA1_KGD	Customer: Change Authorization for Accounts Groups	Restrict the ability to change by customer account group
F_KNA1_AEN	Customer: Change Authorization for Certain Fields	Restrict modifications to customer master data by defined fields

Table 6.3 Customer Master Authorization Objects

Restricting Changes to Customer Credit Master Records

SAP provides a variety of mechanisms to restrict changes to Credit Management master records. Security permissions can be set to restrict changes based on account, credit control area, and specific fields within credit management. Some of the key authorization objects for doing this are shown in Table 6.4: Credit Management Authorization Objects.

Auth. Object	Name	Purpose
F_KNKK_BED	Credit Management: Accounts Authorization	Restrict modifications to credit management data by customer account range
F_KNKA_KKB	Credit Management: Authorization for Credit Control Area	Restrict the ability to change the credit management based on credit control area
F_KNKA_AEN	Credit Management: Change Authorization for Certain Fields	Restrict the ability to modify specific credit management fields on the customer record

Table 6.4 Credit Management Authorization Objects

Restricting Ability to View / Maintain Payment Card Data

Data privacy issues have taken the headlines in the last few years. When dealing with payment card information such as credit cards, risks extend beyond the ability to maintain the information and migrate into the ability to view the data as well. SAP provides a variety of mechanisms to restrict access to payment card master records. Security permissions can be set to restrict display or maintenance not only on the card data but also the encryption used to protect that data. Some of the key authorization objects for doing this are shown in Table 6.5: Payment Card Authorization Objects.

Auth. Object	Name	Purpose
B_CARD_SEC	Payment Cards: Authorization Encryption Card Master	Restrict the ability to encrypt or decrypt payment card data
B_CCARD	Payment Cards: Payment Cards	Restrict the ability to maintain (or even view) payment card data

Table 6.5 Payment Card Authorization Objects

Restricting Ability to Maintain Pricing Conditions

The integrity of pricing conditions is critical to sales processing. SAP provides a variety of mechanisms to restrict access to pricing condition master records. Security permissions can restrict pricing condition maintenance by sales organization or by condition type. SAP security can also restrict the ability to generate condition tables. Some of the key authorization objects for doing this are shown in Table 6.6: Authorization Objects for Conditions.

Auth. Object	Name	Purpose
V_KONH_VKO	Condition: Authorization for Sales Organizations	Restrict the ability to maintain conditions by sales organization distribution channel, and division.
V_KONH_VKS	Condition: Authorization for Condition Types	Restrict the ability to maintain conditions by condition type
V_KONG_VWE	Generation of Conditions: Authorization for Usage/Application	Restrict the ability to generate condition tables

Table 6.6 Authorization Objects for Conditions

6.3   SAP Configurable Control Considerations

In Chapter 2, we reviewed the typical process for auditing SAP and introduced a series of audit assurance "layers" upon which an auditor will typically build his confidence in SAP processing. In this section, we explore the Component-Specific Technical Settings layer related to SD. Specifically, we introduce a number of *SAP configuration suggestions and considerations* that can enhance processes over the SAP order-to-cash cycle.

This list is by no means exhaustive, and we fully expect that you will utilize many more configurable SAP controls than are mentioned herein. This section highlights some of the control features within SAP that, in our experience, could be more comprehensively used by organizations running SAP applications. Regardless of whether you agree with the control technique, consider the risks addressed by these recommendations and ensure that, where appropriate, you have addressed these risks within your organization.

> **Assess Your Own Risks**
>
> The recommendations provided here are suggestions only, and should be reviewed in the context of your own business risks and anticipated value. You may find some of these suggestions unreasonable for your business environment, and you may choose to address the underlying risks in different ways, perhaps even outside of SAP. Effective SAP control is not a one-size-fits-all situation.

6.3.1   Configure SAP Data Quality Checks

Data quality problems affect many organizations. While SAP supports strong data integrity checks, many of these need to be turned on and configured for your business. Failure to take advantage of these capabilities places reliance on user diligence during document entry, and after-the-fact reviews to detect any errors or abuse. Many auditors now use specific tools to detect potential data problems in both master and transactional data, so utilizing these techniques on your most important data elements can help prevent audit embarrassment.

Define Important Fields as "Required Entry"

By default, the fields that SAP requires for transaction processing or master data entry may not be all the fields you need to fully process business transactions in your environment. Configuring SAP to flag situations where additional information may be required can help ensure a high level of data integrity.

For example, you may choose to require a full ship-to and bill-to address, ensuring that whenever an order is placed that sufficient information exists to ship the order and send the invoice for payment. You may also choose to require a reconciliation account for all customers, making it easier to reconcile customer payments to orders.

Figure 6.1: Maintain Status Groups shows an example where a company requires entry of the bill-to address, including street and postal code. This particular setting is available in the IMG under FINANCIAL ACCOUNTING • ACCOUNTS RECEIVABLE AND ACCOUNTS PAYABLE • CUSTOMER ACCOUNTS • MASTER DATA • PREPARATIONS FOR CREATING MASTER DATA • DEFINE ACCOUNT GROUPS WITH SCREEN LAYOUT (CUSTOMERS).

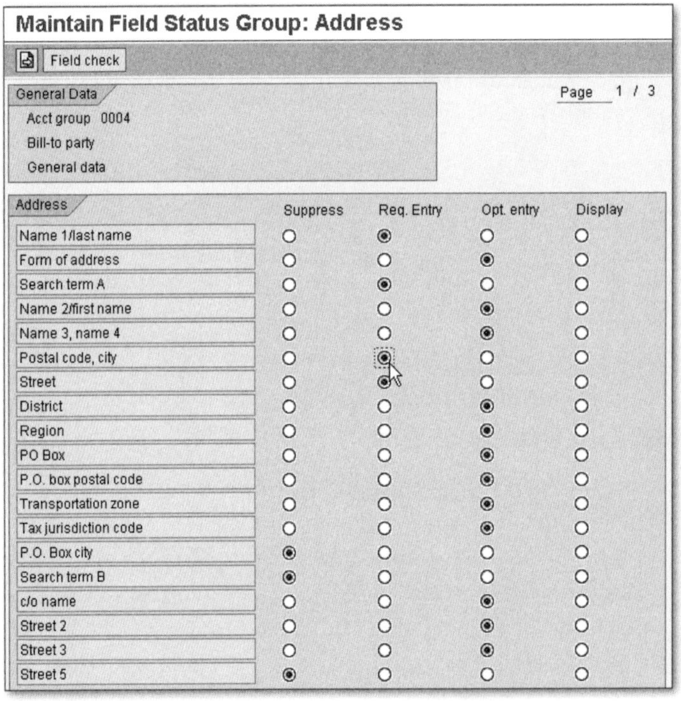

Figure 6.1 Maintain Status Groups

Similar functionality exists for Business Partners. Figure 6.2: Business Partner Required Fields shows how a Commission Recipient partner type should Bank Details as a required entry, so that direct deposit transactions can occur. Business Partner field attributes are available through the IMG under: CROSS-APPLICATION COMPONENTS • SAP BUSINESS PARTNER • BUSINESS PARTNER • BASIC SETTINGS • FIELD GROUPINGS • CONFIGURE FIELD ATTRIBUTES.

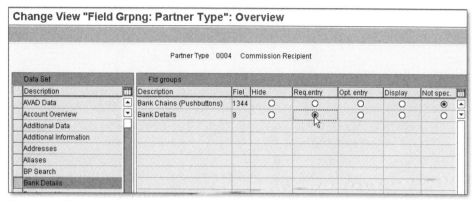

Figure 6.2 Business Partner Required Fields

Field status groups within SAP enable additional data handling procedures over individual fields and field groups based on the type of transaction (e.g., create, change, display). For controlling key data, the field status groups that you'll most likely use are "Required Entry" and "Display." Use "Required Entry" to specify those fields that must contain data, and "Display" for those fields that you wish the user to see but not have the ability to change. Change any fields that are not used to "Suppress" or "Hide" (depending on the screen) to prevent user confusion.

Define and Assign Incompletion Procedures

Sometimes, it may not be possible to require important fields as described above, because, depending on your business procedures, certain information may not be available at initial customer entry. In these cases, configure Incompletion Procedures to ensure that the data has been captured early enough in the process to prevent delays. As you process sales documents, incomplete fields are logged per configuration, and depending on configuration, you can force SAP to capture the missing data before further processing can occur. This configuration also allows easy reporting on missing data. Incompletion procedures are defined in the IMG at: SALES AND DISTRIBUTION • BASIC FUNCTIONS • LOG OF INCOMPLETE ITEMS. From here, you define the procedures, assign these procedures to incompletion objects, and then define status groups to describe functions that are carried out based on the incompletion status.

Configure Customer Payment Tolerances

At times, customers may pay amounts that are slightly different than what is owed. Depending on your business preferences, you may choose to write off small differences rather than invest time and energy in resolving small-dollar discrepancies.

Using tolerances also ensures that employees do not write off more than acceptable per company policy, and is thus a control over both entry errors and intentional policy circumvention.

Within SAP, you can define these tolerances at the customer level and for individual employees (perhaps giving receivables managers greater discretion than staff). Preferences are defined in tolerance groups, which are then assigned to each customer or employee. Payment differences are automatically posted to appropriate expense accounts, if open item clearing is used. Customer tolerances are defined through the IMG using: FINANCIAL ACCOUNTING • ACCOUNTS RECEIVABLE AND ACCOUNTS PAYABLE • BUSINESS TRANSACTIONS • INCOMING PAYMENTS • MANUAL INCOMING PAYMENTS • CLEARING DIFFERENCES.

6.3.2 Configure Minimum Pricing Rules

Define *minimum prices* for all goods intended for sale. The minimum price tells SAP that no matter what combination of pricing conditions and discounts are applied to an order, the price should never fall below the defined minimum. This helps ensure that you don't inadvertently sell products for a loss.

The SAP condition type PMIN establishes minimum pricing levels. To configure a minimum price, use menu path LOGISTICS • SALES AND DISTRIBUTION • MASTER DATA • CONDITIONS • SELECT USING CONDITION TYPE • CREATE, or enter Transaction VK11. Select condition type PMIN, and click on "Key Combination," as shown in Figure 6.3: Creating a Minimum Price Condition. From this screen, select materials and assign minimum pricing to those materials, with optional validity dates. Referring to Figure 6.4: Adding Minimum Pricing to a Material, material T-F499 has an established minimum price of $250.00 USD, valid between March 10, 2009, to December 31, 2009. Regardless of other discounts, SAP will not allow material T-F499 to be sold for under $250. If, during order entry, discounting would have normally caused the price to drop below this threshold, condition PMIN will add a surcharge on the sales order to gross up the material price to $250.

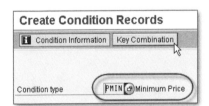

Figure 6.3 Creating a Minimum Price Condition

Figure 6.4 Adding Minimum Pricing to a Material

As with all pricing conditions, periodically review established minimum prices to ensure that they are reasonable in light of current market conditions.

6.3.3 Establish Dual Control over Sensitive Fields

Certain data fields can be particularly sensitive — either because entry errors can cause significant harm, or because they are particularly susceptible to fraud. Customer bank accounts (if applicable to your organization's processes), for example, could be manipulated for fraudulent purposes. To protect against inappropriate changes to sensitive fields, SAP provides a "dual control" setting that places a block on certain types of transactions (such as payment transactions) whenever a field defined as being sensitive is changed. The block can only be removed by someone with a user ID other than the ID that changed the data. While such a control will not mitigate collusion, it does ensure that at least two individuals agree with the change.

You establish dual control by defining sensitive fields in the IMG using FINAN-CIAL ACCOUNTING • ACCOUNTS RECEIVABLE AND ACCOUNTS PAYABLE • CUSTOMER ACCOUNTS • MASTER DATA • PREPARATIONS FOR CREATING CUSTOMER MASTER DATA • DEFINE SENSITIVE FIELDS FOR DUAL CONTROL (CUSTOMERS). Figure 6.5: Dual Control over Customer Fields illustrates the simple process used to set the fields that will have this additional checking in place. Over 200 fields within the customer record are available for dual control; however, many would not usually be considered sensitive. While dual control is a great way to validate changes over truly sensitive data, it can slow the process for maintaining customer information. Configure the most critical and sensitive fields for dual control, but do not go overboard.

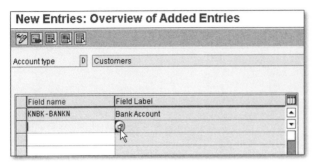

Figure 6.5 Dual Control over Customer Fields

6.3.4 Configure Credit Checking to Minimize Business Risk

Customer credit management is a standard process within most organizations aimed at minimizing exposure to customer payment default. Failure to effectively manage customer credit can lead to questions regarding receivables valuations on financial statement audits, and raise profitability concerns for operational audits. Inappropriate controls over credit management can also help facilitate fraud — whereby someone maliciously sets up a fictitious customer, establishes credit for that customer, and then receives goods. During a typical order-to-cash review, the auditor will be looking to ensure that:

▶ Credit management is used to manage credit risk (and depending on industry, all customers have been assigned credit limits)

▶ Procedures and analyses for assigning credit limits are reasonable, including authenticating customers before granting credit

▶ Credit limits have been accurately entered into SAP

▶ Credit checking procedures (procedure type and point within the sales process) are effective at minimizing exposure

To help ensure audit success, you can configure a number of credit management-related controls within SAP.

Defining Credit Checking by Sales Document

For all sales documents that result in a customer order (and resulting payment), configure SAP to verify customer credit. You define this check through Transaction OVAK. Figure 6.6: Credit Limit Check by Sales Document illustrates an example where credit checking has been enabled for document type AGIS. When enabling credit checking, you can select between one of two broad options: simple checking (based on credit at the time of sales order entry), or dynamic checking (based on credit as it exists at order entry, at delivery, or with other additional options). From a control perspective, dynamic checking is the ideal, and condition "A" (Run Simple Credit Limit Check and Warning Message) is the least effective.

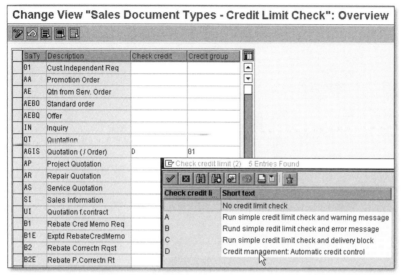

Figure 6.6 Credit Limit Check by Sales Document

Defining Credit Checking by Delivery Order

For all sales documents that result in a customer order (and resulting payment), consider configuring SAP to verify customer credit at the point of delivery creation and/or goods issue. You define this check through Transaction OVAD. Configuring credit checking both at delivery creation and goods issue extends the greatest level of control.

Defining Automatic Credit Control

Automatic credit control, also known as dynamic credit control, is the most powerful and versatile option within SAP, and thus the one most likely to stand up best to audit scrutiny. Automatic credit control settings are defined through Transaction OVA8. Figure 6.7: Dynamic Credit Control shows an example of automatic credit control options.

Some of the more powerful capabilities within automatic credit control include:

- Ability to assess the existing sales order along with other open orders and open delivery items when checking credit
- Ability to automatically block the sales document for further review based on certain conditions

▶ Automatic blocking of sales and delivery (or inability to save sales document) for customers with outstanding invoices beyond a specified number of days

▶ Automatic blocking of sales and delivery (or inability to save sales document) for customers exceeding a defined dunning level

▶ Ability to re-check credit upon change to critical fields such as payment terms

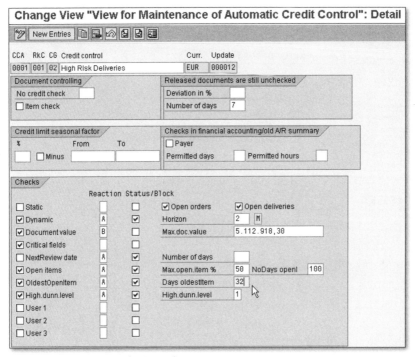

Figure 6.7 Dynamic Credit Control

How and where you apply dynamic credit control will depend greatly on your organization, your customer base, and a variety of factors. Be prepared to justify to your auditor why features have not been used if you choose not to exert the highest level of control.

6.3.5 Establish Document Flow Control

During the typical order-to-cash process, SAP sales documents are often related to each other. For example, a customer quotation may turn into an order. That order is eventually associated with a delivery document. And that delivery could, for various reasons, result in a return. Document flow displays information about how much of the source document quantities and values have been copied into the target document.

Figure 6.8: Establishing Document Flow Control for Delivery shows where this is configured for each delivery type and sales document type relationship. You can access this screen through transaction VTLA (delivery types to sales documents). Figure 6.9: Establishing Document Flow Control for Billing shows where similar controls can be established for billing documents, established through transaction VTFA (billing types to sales documents).

Using delivery as an example, select a target delivery type or billing type and source sales document type and expand the Item folder in the dialog structure. Next select one or more item categories and click on the Details icon. Check the UPDATE DOCUMENT FLOW box within the form's Control Data section. The effect on the target document quantity (positive, negative, or no effect) is set using the POS./NEG. QUANTITY field. Typically, the following relationships should be established:

- ▶ Quotation to Sales Order = Positive
- ▶ Contract to Return = Negative
- ▶ Sales Order to Sales Order = No Effect
- ▶ Delivery to Invoice = Positive
- ▶ Delivery to Cancellation = Negative
- ▶ Deliver to Pro-Forma Invoice = No Effect

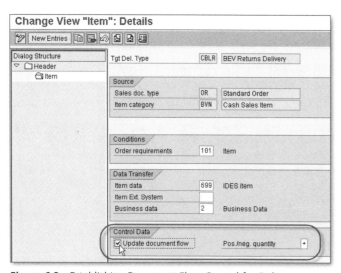

Figure 6.8 Establishing Document Flow Control for Delivery

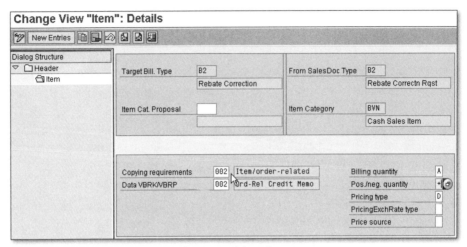

Figure 6.9 Establishing Document Flow Control for Billing

If for some reason you choose not to establish document control for a particular relationship, be prepared to explain this decision to your auditor and how you have mitigated any resulting business risk.

6.3.6 Enhance Controls over Returns and Credits

Configure all credit memos, returns, and similar sales order types to require reference to the original billing document. This ensures that invalid or inaccurate returns cannot be processed, such as giving credit for items not ordered or in excess of what was ordered. Establish this requirement through Transaction VOV8. On the *Change View "Maintain Sales Order Types": Overview* screen, select all sales order types corresponding to returns and credits and click on the Details icon. You'll be presented with a screen similar to Figure 6.10: Requiring Mandatory Reference Documents. By default SAP configuration, the "Reference Mandatory" field is blank. Set this field to the value "M" to require reference to an SAP billing document.

New Implementations and Mandatory Reference Documents

Upon initial SD implementation and for a period of time thereafter, the reference document field likely cannot be set to mandatory, because the source documents (i.e., the order the return references), may be in your legacy system instead of SAP. After sufficient time has passed for SAP to be the book of record, change this flag to mandatory. This reduces the risk of unauthorized or inappropriate credits to customer accounts.

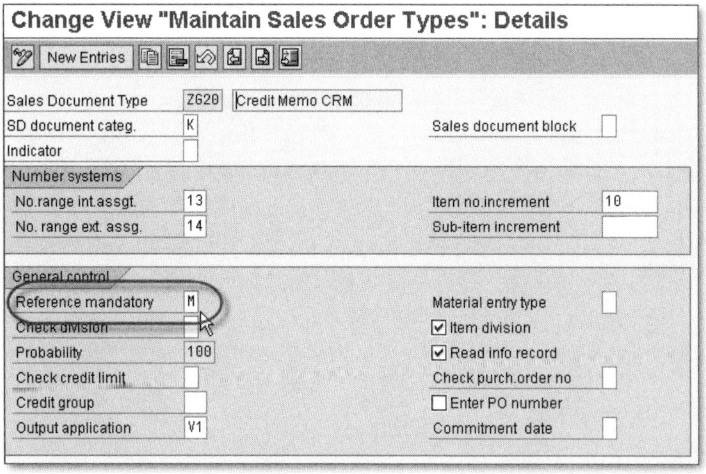

Change View "Maintain Sales Order Types": Details

New Entries

Sales Document Type	Z620 Credit Memo CRM
SD document categ.	K
Indicator	

Sales document block

Number systems

No.range int.assgt.	13	Item no.increment	10
No. range ext. assg.	14	Sub-item increment	

General control

Reference mandatory	M	Material entry type	
Check division		☑ Item division	
Probability	100	☑ Read info record	
Check credit limit		Check purch.order no	
Credit group		☐ Enter PO number	
Output application	V1	Commitment date	

Figure 6.10 Requiring Mandatory Reference Documents

To further enhance control over customer credits, ensure that SAP is configured to automatically block customer credit memos so that these can be reviewed and released by an independent reviewer. By default, standard SAP automatically provides a billing block for customer credit and debit memo requests. To verify that your system settings have not been changed, navigate the IMG to SALES AND DISTRIBUTION • BILLING • BILLING DOCUMENTS • DEFINE BLOCKING REASON FOR BILLING. Figure 6.11: Automatic Credit Memo Blocking illustrates how this should look in your system.

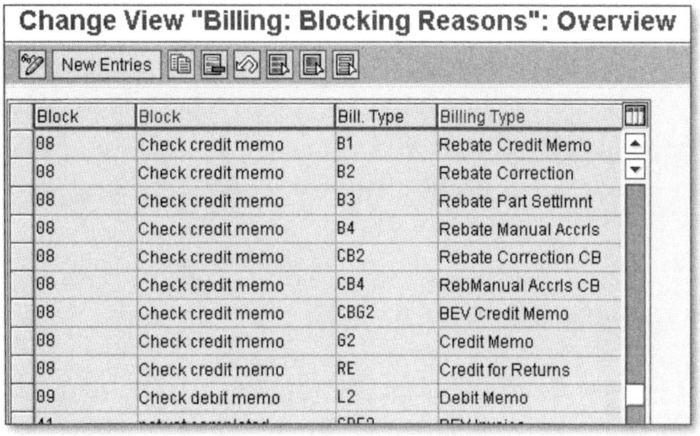

Change View "Billing: Blocking Reasons": Overview

New Entries

Block	Block	Bill. Type	Billing Type
08	Check credit memo	B1	Rebate Credit Memo
08	Check credit memo	B2	Rebate Correction
08	Check credit memo	B3	Rebate Part Settlmnt
08	Check credit memo	B4	Rebate Manual Accrls
08	Check credit memo	CB2	Rebate Correction CB
08	Check credit memo	CB4	RebManual Accrls CB
08	Check credit memo	CBG2	BEV Credit Memo
08	Check credit memo	G2	Credit Memo
08	Check credit memo	RE	Credit for Returns
09	Check debit memo	L2	Debit Memo

Figure 6.11 Automatic Credit Memo Blocking

6.3.7 Define Appropriate Dunning Procedures

At times, customers may for various reasons not pay for goods or services received. SAP contains dunning procedures that allow you to continuously communicate with customers to attempt receivables collections. Depending on configuration, these communications can get more forceful over time. When configuring dunning processes, local laws can regulate dunning procedures. Dunning is configured in SAP through the IMG at: FINANCIAL ACCOUNTING • ACCOUNTS RECEIVABLE AND ACCOUNTS PAYABLE • BUSINESS TRANSACTIONS • DUNNING • DUNNING PROCEDURE. Dunning may not be part of every SAP audit, but operational audits concerned with operational effectiveness and organizational profitability will likely include dunning procedures.

6.3.8 Other Configuration Tips

The previous suggestions are the most critical from an audit and control perspective. Depending on your organization and business processes, the following ideas may also help enhance your internal control environment and allow better risk management. As with all other suggestions, the relevance of each of these to audit success is tied to your business risks:

▶ Alternate Payment Currencies — When alternate payment currencies may be used, configure SAP to maintain automatic account assignments, including clearing accounts, for payment differences that may arise as a result of payment currency.

▶ Duplicate Business Partners — Enable SAP functionality for detecting potential duplicates when customers or vendors are being entered. Duplicate business partners within SAP ERP Financials Financial Accounting can lead to duplicate payments, extending too much credit, and other undesired issues. SAP will create a warning message if the address entered is the same as the one in the system, and present the user with a list of potential duplicates that he can review before completing processing.

6.4 Additional Procedures and Considerations

As we have discussed earlier in this book, configuring SAP the "right" way is often not enough. User interaction with the SAP system plays a large part in the effectiveness of business processes managed by SAP. This section highlights additional procedures and considerations that can help you further strengthen your order-to-cash processes and withstand audit scrutiny.

6.4.1 Implement Order Entry Completeness and Timeliness Procedures

Failure to enter sales orders completely or in a timely fashion can result in lost business, delayed payment receipts, and other unintended consequences. For organizations that accept manual orders through fax, postal mail, or even email, processes can be even more challenging. Implement procedures to ensure that all orders get entered into SAP in a timely manner. This may involve logging all incoming fax orders, mail orders, and other order receipts and periodically reconciling this log to what has been entered into SAP. An auditor is likely to compare the date that an order was received to the date it was entered into the system, so mechanisms to ensure that order entries are expedited can be valuable. Care should also be taken when processing these orders to prevent duplicate entries, because customers might send multiple faxes or fax orders that have also been sent in the mail.

6.4.2 Provide Order Confirmations

Mistakes happen during order entry. Transposing numbers or other typos during order entry (or even on customer order submission) can cause products or quantities to differ from intent. Processing orders where such mistakes have been made can add significant cost to the business — requiring returns processing, customer credits, and a myriad of other activities that detract from normal operations. Order confirmations can help ensure that the customer has the chance to correct any mistakes (either on the part of order entry or due to customer error). These days, email confirmations can occur in real-time, and problems can be corrected often before goods are shipped.

6.4.3 Eliminate Duplicates from the Material Master and Customer Master

Despite best intentions, duplicate records can periodically creep up in master data records. Within the material master, duplicate records could eventually lead to different pricing for the same product. Duplicate customers could cause your organization to over-extend credit to a customer, process duplicate orders, or misapply customer payments resulting in time-consuming reconciliation procedures. Regardless of the cause, periodically review customer and master data records for potential duplicates, and correct any issues found.

> **Querying for Duplicate Master Records**
>
> Standard transactions and reports within SAP typically don't have the flexibility to compare the full complement of fields that could indicate potential duplicate records. As such, use of SAP query or custom ABAP reports are common, as are queries within SAP NetWeaver Business Warehouse (SAP NetWeaver BW) (where master data is available in the warehouse). Many auditors choose an offline approach, downloading key tables from SAP and use specialized audit tools such as ACL or IDEA to query for duplicates. These tools contain "sounds like" and other specialized functions to identify hard-to-detect duplicates. If your internal auditors use such a tool, you may be able to leverage software already in house. Typically, table MARA is sufficient for finding duplicates in the material master, and KNA1 is sufficient for duplicates within the Customer Master. Whichever technique you use, working with your auditors to develop effective search criteria can help ensure that you find problems before your auditor does.

When searching for duplicate records, consider creative queries that may indicate possible duplication. Because SAP has functionality to prevent the most obvious duplicates from being entered, when duplicates do appear, they are often due to typos or other conditions that may be missed by SAP checks.

Creative conditions for finding duplicates within the material master include:

▶ Same name or description
▶ Similar name with same supply area and plant
▶ Same dimensions and weight
▶ Same bill of material details

Creative conditions for finding duplicates within the customer master include:

▶ Similar names
▶ Same phone number, fax line, or similar communication match
▶ Same numeric portion of the address (postal code + street number)

If during such a review duplicate entries are discovered, additional research may be warranted to determine if any undesired conditions have been created as a result.

6.4.4 Establish Procedures for Verifying Pricing Conditions

Given the complexity of establishing and maintaining appropriate pricing strategies within SAP, particularly in industries where price changes are common, ensure that internal procedures effectively validate the pricing within SAP. Typical audit tests for pricing include:

▶ Verifying that pricing conditions configured in SAP comply with the organization's pricing policy

▶ Assessing procedures that management uses to verify pricing

▶ Selecting a sample of sales orders, recalculating pricing outside of SAP based on the organization's pricing policy, and comparing to what the customer was charged

▶ Reviewing customer pricing complaints for trends or other issues that may indicate processes are not working as intended

Periodically Verify Pricing Conditions

For many organizations, having a quality assurance process over pricing procedures is not only important but critical to business operations. Often, this QA process occurs as part of any pricing change. Procedures may be manual or facilitated through SAP; however, because pricing will be a key portion of many order-to-cash audits, ensure that whatever techniques you use to verify pricing conditions are effective.

Pricing: The Difference Between Financial and Operational Auditing

In Chapter 1, we discussed the variety of different types of audits and how success in one type of audit has limited bearing on success in another. Nowhere is this more apparent than when it comes to audit treatment of pricing. In a financial statement audit (including audits for Sarbanes-Oxley compliance), the focus is on accurate financial reporting. What we charge customers and whether we make money is irrelevant as long as we record and report on the relevant transactions accurately and fairly. From a financial statement auditing perspective, pricing is only relevant to the extent that customer receivables (assets) and related prepayments or overpayments (liabilities) are accurate based on whatever price the customer was contracted to pay. Of course, poor pricing does not make a sustainable business model, so an operational audit may likely focus a lot of attention on pricing policies, procedures, and controls. In this type of audit, how we price is highly relevant. As mentioned in Chapter 1, understanding the type of audit you will be undergoing is vital to audit success.

Sample Sales Orders and Verify Correct Pricing Calculation

When verifying the accuracy of pricing, an auditor will commonly select a sample of sales orders and confirm the price charged to customers on the order to the organization's pricing policy. This approach gives additional assurance above and beyond validating pricing conditions within SAP, because it focuses on the desired outcome — a correctly charged price. Sometimes, when reviewing price conditions, you may find that the information appears to be accurate and complete, but the way that the conditions are actually applied to a customer order (defined by configured pricing procedures) may differ from expectations. Thus, what appeared to be valid pricing leads to an invalid outcome. Periodically selecting a sample of sales orders across a variety of customers, distribution channels, and sales organizations, and verifying that the price charged on these orders is appropriate, can provide you with additional assurance that pricing conditions have been set up accurately. The frequency of this review will depend on how often prices change in your organization, and the risks associated with inaccurate pricing. Of course, any discrepancies should be investigated and resolved immediately. Because your auditor will likely perform this type of test, self-auditing using the same procedures can give you a leg up.

> **Maintaining Evidence of Self-Auditing Procedures**
>
> When you are conducting your own self-audits, remember the concept of evidence that we discussed in Chapter 1. Self-auditing is a great way to identify improvements to your own internal processes, but if you want your procedures to also count toward reducing the effort of any auditors who may be reviewing your SAP system, maintain sufficient proof of your review.

Review Customer Pricing Complaints

Sometimes, customer pricing complaints may be one-off situations. In other cases, they may point to a larger system or process problem that should be investigated and resolved. As part of a periodic review of customer complaints, examine pricing-related complaints to look for trends or other issues that should be resolved. From an internal control perspective, fixing the specific issue alone is not sufficient — identify and resolve the root cause to ensure that similar problems don't happen in the future. The auditor should be able to see that you have taken action as part of your review process.

6.4.5 Review One-Time Customer Usage

In many organizations, controls defined for one-time customers are less stringent than those for standard customers fully entered into SAP. If this is the case in your organization, periodically monitor one-time customer usage to ensure processing is as intended (low dollar amounts, and low transactions). One-time customers can be selected from the customer list, report RFDKVZ00, and then further investigated.

6.4.6 Monitor Customer Payments and Payment Application

In addition to having strong controls in the sales order, pricing, delivery, and billing components of SAP, procedures should also ensure that funds are actually received and applied appropriately to customer accounts. In addition to the standard controls provided by SAP, also:

▶ Reconcile bank accounts used to collect customer payments and ensure all reconciling items are resolved in a timely basis

▶ Review accounts receivable aging reports and investigate amounts that have been outstanding for an unacceptable period of time

Your auditor will likely perform these procedures as well, so maintaining documentation of your review and follow-up will help expedite this portion of the audit.

6.5   Management Monitoring: SAP Report Highlights

Monitoring procedures are a core part of an effective internal control structure. SAP contains numerous reports that you can use to identify and monitor potential risks within the order-to-cash cycle. Diligent review of these reports and investigation of suspicious items complements the configured controls within SAP, and rounds out your ability to survive an order-to-cash audit. This section highlights a few examples.

6.5.1   Reports Identifying Changed Data

SAP reports that monitor changes to sensitive data are valuable for ensuring that all changes (including initial creation) have been authorized and entered accurately. These reports provide valuable information, because they show both the old values and the new values that replaced them. The frequency that these reports should be reviewed will depend on the risk that inappropriate changes to the relevant data elements could pose to your operations. Data change reports should be reviewed by someone other than employees who can make changes to data.

Each review should, at a minimum, cover the period since the last review, which you can select using the date selection criteria in the reports below. Limiting "Changed By" selections (where available on the reports) to individual employees or small groups of employees can draw attention to suspicious activity. But, when filtering selections using additional criteria, ensure that by the end of the review process that you have covered every change made during the review period.

Pricing Condition Changes

Review the Changed Documents for Conditions report RV16ACHD to display changes to pricing conditions. As an additional selection option, you can also display conditions that have been deleted. This report can also be accessed through menu path

Logistics • Sales and Distribution • Master Data • Conditions • Select Using Condition Type • Display or through Transaction VK13, although both of these paths require an additional step. Upon entering a relevant pricing condition, select from the menu: Environment • Changes • Change Report (The pricing condition you entered on the initial screen will not carry to this selection screen).

Customer Changes

Review the Display Changes to Customers report RFDABL00 to display changes to customer records. Reviews can be filtered by company code and sales area data, if desired. Although this report can be large, once data has been returned, you can filter on field values most relevant from an internal control perspective (such as company name, address, or shipping condition). This report can be found under menu Logistics • Sales and Distribution • Master Data • Business Partner • Customer • Display Changes, or accessed directly through Transactions OV51 or S_ALR_87012182.

> **Using Other Reports for Customer Change Monitoring**
>
> Other reports for monitoring customer changes exist, such as those accessed through Transactions VD04 or XD04; however, they should not be the only reports that you review. These reports are customer specific, and require that you enter a customer to see what has changed. The intent of a review such as this is to make sure that all changes are appropriate, including those of which you may not be aware (and thus do not know the relevant customer number). These reports are useful if you are investigating changes to a specific customer but should not be your sole source for customer change monitoring.

Customer Credit Changes

Review the Display Changes to Credit Management report RFDKLIAB to display changes to credit management data, including changes to credit limits and removal of customer credit blocks. Reviews can be filtered by credit control area, if desired. This report can be found under menu Accounts Receivable • Credit Management • Credit Management Info System, or accessed directly through Transaction S_ALR_87012215.

6.5.2 Incomplete Information or Processing

Some SAP reports highlight situations where data is missing or processing is not fully complete. In some cases, missing data may indicate processing problems, and in other cases, missing data could result in transactions that do not have enough information to be fully processed through Sales and Distribution. Document blocks can also prevent transactions from being fully completed. The frequency that these reports should be reviewed will depend on the risk that having incomplete data could pose to your operations.

Missing Customer Data

Run the Customer Master Data Comparison report RFDKAG00 (Transaction F.2D) to identify customer records that have been created in SD but not in SAP ERP Financials Financial Accounting (or vice versa). Identification of customers who have not been maintained in SAP ERP Financials Financial Accounting could indicate processing problems, and SAP ERP Financials Financial Accounting customers not in SD could be indicative of fraud.

Missing Credit Data

Run the Customers with Missing Credit Data program RFDKLI10 (or Transaction F.32) to identify customer records with incomplete credit management information.

Incomplete Sales Orders

Run the Incomplete SD Documents report RVAUFERR (or Transaction V.00) to identify sales or delivery documents with incomplete information. The frequency at which you review this report should be heavily based on the risks associated with each transaction type. For example, you may determine that reviewing for incomplete billing documents should occur more frequently than reviewing for incomplete quotations because of your business functions. Items returned from this query are automatically sorted oldest to newest.

A common audit test involves aging of incomplete documents. Aging refers to a process whereby results are grouped into categories based on how long they have been incomplete. An auditor performs a different analysis on documents created more than 30 days ago that are still incomplete, for example, than documents that were created yesterday. While the standard report does not facilitate an aging-style summary, you can create your own aging-style analysis by selecting "Change Layout" and choosing the Filter tab, as shown in Figure 6.12: Filtering Incomplete SD Documents. Add the "Created On" field to the Filter Criteria, and then set an appropriate date range for the list. When reviewing reports filtered by different aging categories, pay particular attention to patterns within the "Created By" field. Certain employees appear with much more frequency than others — this may lead to additional training or coaching opportunities.

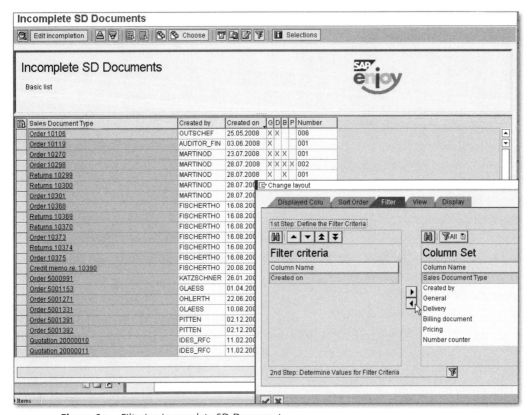

Figure 6.12 Filtering Incomplete SD Documents

Outstanding Invoices

Periodically review outstanding orders that have not yet been invoiced and verify that sufficient justification exists. At period-end in particular, these items can impact revenue recognition, so care should be taken that all items that can be cleared are resolved. You can use program SDBILLDL, or Transaction VF04, to access the Maintain Billing Due List screen. Results are shown by expected billing date, from earliest to latest. You can also filter results for more effective monitoring.

Outstanding Goods Shipment

SAP contains numerous reports for monitoring the status of sales documents as they move through the delivery cycle. These reports should be reviewed frequently (at least weekly, and potentially more frequently depending on the sensitivity that your customers may have to timely shipment) and older items should be investigated and resolved. Examples include:

- Backorders: Program RVAUFRUE, Transaction V.15
- Outbound Deliveries to be Posted: Transaction VL06, program WS_DELIVERY_ MONITOR.

You can also view sales order wordlists by shipping point, and select a delivery creation date in the past to view old, outstanding orders. This can be accomplished through Transaction VL04, program RV50SBT1.

Billings Awaiting Posting to the General Ledger

If you are using both SD and SAP ERP Financials Financial Accounting, invoices posted through SD are typically automatically posted to the SAP ERP Financials Financial Accounting General Ledger system. Various conditions can cause the invoices not to be posted to the accounting component, and thus you should periodically review for billing documents that have not yet posted to SAP ERP Financials Financial Accounting. Review and resolution of these items is critical around key accounting periods (such as period-end) to ensure that accounting transactions have been posted appropriately.

You can access this information though Transaction VF03, or program SAPMV60A. From the Display Billing Document screen, click on the Selection icon to the right of the Billing Document field to allow selection of documents still to be passed to accounting. Using the Posting Status field (as shown in Figure 6.13: Billing Documents Not Posted to the General Ledger), you can filter by specific reasons why these documents have not been posted. Provide an explanation to your auditor for all items on this report, and show what you have done to ensure that accounting records are accurate.

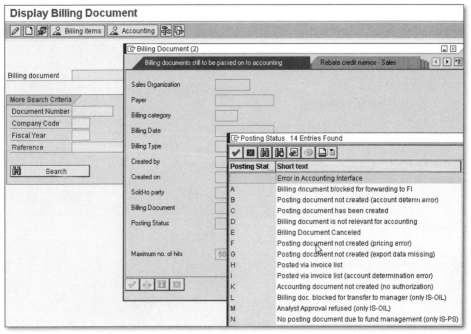

Figure 6.13 Billing Documents Not Posted to the General Ledger

Transaction XFX3 provides another way to review incomplete billing documents. Ensuring that all issues have been resolved by the end of each month is important, because your auditor will likely review these reports as well.

6.5.3 Customers Exceeding Credit Limits

Someone independent of the sales function should periodically review customers exceeding their credit limits and verify assumptions related to recoverability. Using the Credit Overview screen, program RFDKLI40, select customers in excess of a defined threshold above (or below, if desired), their credit limits. By entering a percentage in the "Credit Limit Used" field, as shown in Figure 6.14: Customers Exceeding Credit Limits, SAP lists all customers exceeding their credit limits by the defined percentages — in this case, 110% of the credit limit to 999% of the credit limit. Instead of using percentages, you can also enter a specific amount by which a customer is exceeding his credit limit, by using the "Excess Amount" field.

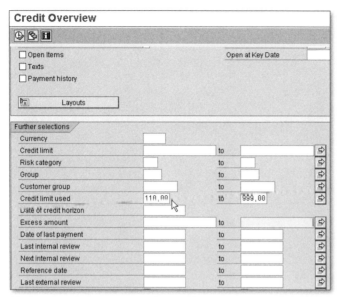

Figure 6.14 Customers Exceeding Credit Limits

6.5.4 Potential Issues

Certain SAP reports highlight potential issues that should be investigated. These issues could result from processing problems, fraud, or errors. One example includes Invoice Numbers Allocated Twice (Transaction S_ALR_87012341). Review reports such as these periodically (at least once per period), to investigate issues and determine and resolve root causes.

6.6 Summary

In this chapter, we reviewed risks within the SAP order-to-cash cycle. To mitigate those risks, we highlighted a series of controls across four main categories. Related to security and master data, we explored segregation of duties, critical transactions and important authorization objects. We then highlighted a series of configurable SAP controls that may be reviewed during an SAP audit. We reviewed a series of process-based controls and procedures that can strengthen risk management of order-to-cash processing, and closed with an overview of key SAP reports.

In the next chapter, we look at the purchase-to-pay process and examine similar control categories related to the SAP MM component.

"Price is what you pay. Value is what you get." — *Warren Buffett*

7   Purchase-to-Pay Cycle

To an auditor, reviewing the purchase-to-pay cycle is a chance to get management's attention, and to demonstrate the value that an audit can provide. In many other areas of the business, measuring the value of audit findings and recommendations can be very subjective. Opportunities for improving efficiency, reducing general business risk, or enhancing management insight are certainly important, but quantifying the impact that those improvements have on the business can be challenging. In the purchase-to-pay cycle, as with other areas of the business where cash is leaving the company, findings and recommendations can often be measured in tangible (and recoverable) dollars. And it's because of this reality that audits covering the purchase-to-pay cycle can be both frequent and thorough.

Beyond just providing a better foundation for audit success, however, controls over the purchase-to-pay cycle can have a dramatic impact on the profitability and success of your company. Being able to stay competitive in today's markets necessitates acquiring the goods and services required to run your organization at a fair price. Depending on your industry, the speed at which you can acquire goods and services may directly impact your ability to fulfill customer needs, and thus make the difference between a sale and a lost opportunity. Negotiating contracts and pricing, managing the timing and receipt of goods, and taking advantage of payment discounts are all part of a well-run purchase-to-payment cycle. Your diligence in configuring SAP and designing effective processes to mitigate purchase-to-payment risks is not only important for the audit but for your ongoing business success as well.

In this chapter, we explore the SAP purchase-to-pay process, supported by the Materials Management in SAP ERP component (part of the SAP ERP Operations Suite). Within Materials Management in SAP ERP, we address purchase requisitions and orders, goods receipts, invoice management and payment, and dispute resolution. Similar to the approach used for the financial reporting cycle in Chapter 5, and the order-to-cash cycle in Chapter 6, we review the risks inherent in the process and a sampling of SAP configurable controls commonly reviewed during an SAP purchase-to-pay audit. We also highlight a series of processes and procedures that, if applied consistently, can mitigate a number of risks within this cycle and put you in a better position for an audit.

> **Note**
>
> If you have read Chapters 5 and 6, you will see some overlap between the controls recommended for the financial reporting and order-to-cash cycles, and those recommended for purchase to pay. Vendor master data management is similar to customer management and there are many processing similarities resulting in similar control recommendations. Additionally, not all Materials Management in SAP ERP customers use the SAP ERP Financials Financial Accounting component for accounts payable, and thus, payables-related information is also included here to ensure complete coverage of the purchase-to-pay process.

7.1   Risks

Because the purchase-to-pay process ultimately results in cash leaving your organization, the cycle is ripe for fraud and abuse. Similar to the order-to-cash process discussed in Chapter 6, purchase-to-pay *risks* can also have a significant operational impact. Improvements in the purchasing cycle can directly increase your organization's bottom line, and inefficiencies, conversely, can add unnecessary costs. Compliance risks are also present, because regulations such as the Foreign Corrupt Practices Act (FCPA) dictate how the purchasing process works in certain situations. Even the number of employees involved in the purchase-to-pay cycle can be significant, because organizations implement more self-service purchasing options such as corporate procurement cards.

In Chapter 1, we discussed the concept of risk and how internal controls are designed to mitigate specific business risks. When preparing for an SAP audit covering the purchase-to-pay process, think through some of the things that could go wrong in the purchase-to-pay process that could adversely affect your organization. A few of these risks include:

▶ Duplicate payments — SAP can warn users if payments appear to be duplicates, and the three-way match process (invoice > receipt > PO) ensures that payments do not exceed what was ordered and what was received; however, not all payments go through this process and duplicate payment checking is rudimentary. Additionally, organizations running multiple instances of SAP may find standard functionality inadequate to prevent duplicate payments if care is not taken to establish effective monitoring procedures.

▶ Overpayments — On the surface, the risk of overpayment can seem miniscule. In reality, however, overpayments are a common occurrence in many organizations.

Whether due to complex rebate or discounting agreements, mistakes when updating PO pricing, or multiple and inconsistent contract agreements across disparate geographic regions, the reasons for overpayments are many. Given that an entire service industry focused on payment recovery has emerged, the existence of overpayments is anything but abnormal.

A Curious Phenomenon
The way that your vendors and other business partners communicate with your organization through the purchase-to-pay process provides a great indicator of their integrity and own internal control processes. When late making a payment, you likely hear from your vendor quickly and repeatedly. After making an overpayment or duplicate payment, however, you may find a surprising number of vendors remain silent. Some vendors may go as far as to dispute a duplicate or overpayment claim. Because of this all-too-real phenomenon, strong controls over the purchase-to-pay cycle are absolutely critical.

▶ Discounts not taken — Many contracts allow discounts for early invoice payment. Discount terms can be complex, however, and employees may not always select the appropriate terms on initial contract entry. Additionally, failure to enter information into SAP in a timely fashion can result in discounts being missed, as can documents blocked for posting that are not cleared quickly. While often the dollar impact for any given invoice is small, when multiplied across all of the purchases that your organization makes, missed discounts can have a real impact on your bottom line.

▶ Inability to reconcile invoices to purchase orders (POs) or receipts — SAP contains strong matching functionality; however, ineffective purchasing or receiving procedures can make it difficult to tie payments to the orders to which they apply, particularly if partial receipts become a factor. As a result, available discounts may not be fully recognized, payables balance based on vendor liabilities can become questionable, and supplier relationships can become damaged.

▶ Payment made for damaged shipments — SAP controls that govern invoice payment require that all relevant data be entered into the system in a timely manner. In some organizations, the quantity and/or quality of goods is not verified upon receipt resulting in payment that, while often recoverable, could have been prevented.

▶ Liability not recognized when incurred — While this risk primarily affects the financial reporting cycle discussed in Chapter 5, unrecognized liabilities can be the direct result of ineffective processes in the purchase-to-pay cycle. SAP records accounting entries on shipment of goods; however, these entries do not affect liabilities until the payment document is created, and blocked receiving or payment documents among other conditions can prevent creation of the appropriate accounting entries. Not only can failure to recognize liabilities impact financial reporting, it can also influence management decision making.

▶ PO changes not subject to scrutiny — SAP can be configured through the release strategy to require specific control procedures before a PO can be processed; however, PO changes after initial approval may not go through the same level of scrutiny if SAP is not configured appropriately.

▶ Inaccurate vendor activity reporting — In the age of business intelligence, management decisions around product pricing, vendor utilization, purchasing policies, and corporate expenditures is dependent on the accuracy of information. Data quality issues such as duplicate vendors can skew reporting and decision making. SAP contains numerous controls to help maintain data quality; however, many of these need to be configured appropriately to be relevant to your organization.

▶ Fraudulent transactions — The Association of Certified Fraud Examiners estimates that corporations, on average, lose 7% of revenue to fraud. Whether associated with contract manipulation, vendor kickbacks, fictitious vendors, or even diversion of otherwise legitimate payments, the existence of fraud in the purchase-to-pay process can have a noticeable impact on profitability.

Of course, each of these risk categories is broad. As mentioned in Chapter 3 on the discussion of designing appropriate controls during an implementation, effectively managing risks requires understanding specific situations for which controls can then be applied. For example, we mentioned above how management decision making can be adversely affected by duplicate vendors. Duplicate vendors can be the result of numerous issues, all of which should be addressed through internal controls. A duplicate could result from the user entering the vendor and ignoring a warning message that a duplicate already exists. It could result from decentralized vendor management and no process to validate vendors across vendor management functions, or across SAP instances. Vendors who move or change names could be entered multiple times in the system. And, of course, a duplicate could be the result of intent to commit fraud. For each of the risks that you identify in your environment, it's important to understand how they could come about and how you have addressed them in your SAP implementation or surrounding processes.

Later in this chapter, we provide suggestions for SAP configurable controls that can help mitigate some of the risks inherent in the purchase-to-pay process, and highlight important business processes that can also strengthen control. Before that, however, we'll discuss SAP master data and security issues critical to the integrity of the purchase-to-pay cycle.

7.2 Security and Master Data

SAP security can provide a powerful level of control by limiting abilities to only a small group of authorized users. Master data controls are also critical due to the effect that master data has on business transactions. When preparing for an audit, ensuring that strong *security and master data* processes are in place is a good first step toward audit success.

7.2.1 Preventing Segregation of Duties Conflicts

A segregation of duties review is a core component of most types of SAP audits. In Chapter 4, we discussed *segregation of duties* in the context of general computer controls (GCCs) and the IT function, which helps support controls within each SAP-enabled business process. Appropriate segregation of duties is also important within the purchase-to-pay process. Insufficient segregation of duties could lead to unauthorized purchases, undetected errors, or even outright fraud.

Table 7.1: SD Segregation of Duties Highlights illustrates some of the abilities that should be segregated within the Materials Management in SAP ERP component. This is by no means a complete list, because complete rule sets within security management tools like SAP BusinessObjects Access Control can have hundreds of rules for Materials Management in SAP ERP alone. To survive an SAP audit where purchase-to-pay is part of the review, however, you should at least prevent violations such as these.

The Ability To:	Should Not Be Combined with the Ability To:
Create/maintain POs	Maintain vendor master data
Create/maintain POs	Approve POs
Approve POs	Receive goods against those POs
Maintain vendor master data	Reconcile reconciliation accounts
Maintain vendor master data	Create/maintain vendor payments
Process goods receipts	Create/maintain vendor payments
Process goods receipts	Create/maintain POs
Process goods receipts	Maintain vendor master data
Process goods receipts	Maintain material master data
Create/maintain vendor payments	Approve purchasing documents

Table 7.1 SD Segregation of Duties Highlights

Dealing with Small Teams

The best way to deal with segregation of duties is to prevent potential conflicts using SAP security. In some situations, however, traditional security-enabled segregation may not be possible. Perhaps a single employee manages a group of functions in a remote location, and as a result his duties cannot be effectively segregated. Many auditors understand such business realities. However, if this describes your situation, have monitoring and review procedures in place (and working) to mitigate the risks of insufficient security.

7.2.2 Restricting Transactions to Functional Purchasing Organizations

Within many organizations, the purchasing function can be highly complex, with regulations that must be adhered to by specific geography. Purchasing teams may be organized by product, vendor industry, or by geographic region. Depending on industry, purchasing organizations can deal with thousands of vendors. Managing this volume of information can be complex.

Whether managing vendors or managing POs, segregating the ability to create and maintain data can help reduce the potential for errors and abuse. Most organizations *restrict purchasing* by purchasing entity, purchasing group, and plant, using entity values EKORG, EKGRP, and WERKS, respectively within the authorization objects M_BEST_WRK, M_BANF_WRK, M_BEST_BSA, and M_BANF_BSA. Purchasing activities are also often also restricted by document type using entity values BSART, and by release codes through authorization objects M_BANF_FRG and M_EINK_FRG.

Guilty Until Proven Innocent?

In addition to reviewing how you have leveraged SAP security to control Materials Management in SAP ERP master data and sales transactions, your auditor will also likely question those techniques that you did NOT use. For example, if you restrict purchasing transactions postings by purchasing entity and purchasing group, your auditor will likely ask why you have not further restricted postings by plant. Be prepared to discuss this issue in terms of how you have managed business risk and what factors in your environment lead you to believe that current security settings are appropriate.

7.2.3 Limiting Access to Powerful Transactions

When assigning security privileges, ensure that powerful SAP transactions and abilities within the Materials Management in SAP ERP component have been *limited* to a small number of personnel. Even if these functions are rarely used, the ability of a user to perform them poses risk to the organization and thus creates audit concern. A few of these transactions include:

- The ability to perform mass maintenance on purchasing info records (MEMASSIN)
- The ability to perform mass maintenance on POs (MEMASSPO)
- The ability to confirm vendor changes (FK09)
- The ability to delete archived purchasing records (RM06ID47)
- The ability to perform mass vendor maintenance (XK99)
- The ability to delete vendor master data (MK06)
- The ability to unblock business partners (MK05)
- The ability to process blocked invoices (MR02)
- The ability to enter credit notes (MRHG)
- The ability to delete logs for mass changes (MSL2)
- The ability to utilize movement types typically designed for new implementations (movement types 561, 562, 563, 564, 565, and 566)

In addition to limiting access to these abilities through security, you can further strengthen controls by monitoring their usage. This monitoring should be independent of the group able to perform these transactions. Being able to show an auditor that the use of powerful transactions is both limited and effectively monitored is ideal.

> **Raising the Bar: Better Control over Powerful Transactions**
>
> Organizations looking to overachieve and virtually eliminate the risks of powerful transactions should consider removing these abilities from all users, and only assigning them at time of need (particularly in the case of mass-maintenance transactions). Once the relevant process has been completed and verified, access can once again be removed.

7.2.4 Establishing Controls and Security over Master Data

Master data tables drive SAP transaction processing. Strong *controls* over master data, whether it be creation, modification, or deletion, are necessary for audit success. As it relates to master data in the purchase-to-pay process, the auditor will generally look to ensure that:

- The ability to change master data is limited to a core group of employees (for each type of master data)
- Employees who make changes to master data have sufficient knowledge and training on organizational policies and SAP usage to understand the issues and implications
- Procedures exist to verify the integrity of sensitive master data fields, such as bank account numbers and alternate payees

- ▶ Procedures exist for authorizing changes to master data that can affect the purchase-to-pay cycle (typically in advance of the change)
- ▶ Independent quality assurance processes validate master data changes
- ▶ Master data is periodically reviewed for relevance (e.g., unused vendors are inactivated)

Organizations may choose to manage certain purchase-to-pay master data, such as vendor data, centrally or locally. Auditors often view centralized maintenance as providing stronger control with more consistency; however, business circumstances will dictate which is right for you.

Restricting Changes to Business Partners

SAP provides a variety of mechanisms to restrict changes to business partner master records. Security permissions can be set to restrict changes by specific field values (e.g., names beginning with A to D), to specific fields within the business partner record, on authorization groups, by business partner role, on relationship category, or by relationship field groups. Due to the impact the quality of business partner data can have across the organization, tighter restrictions are generally preferable to more open security models. In general, restrict the ability to create, change, delete, and in some cases, even view specific business partner data to only a small handful of trained employees, and only within their defined area of responsibility. Some of the key authorization objects for doing this are shown in Table 7.2: Business Partner Authorization Objects.

Auth. Object	Name	Purpose
B_BUPA_ATT	Business Partner: Authorization Types	Restrict modifications to specific business partners based on the value of any business partner field
B_BUPA_FDG	Business Partner: Field Groups:	Restrict modifications to fields within business partner maintenance, or viewing of those fields
B_BUPA_GRP	Business Partner: Authorization Groups	Restrict modifications to business partners by authorization group
B_BUPA_RLT	Business Partner: Roles	Restrict modifications to business partner roles
B_BUPA_BZT	Business Partner Relationships: Relationship Categories	Restrict modifications to business partner relationship categories
B_BUPA_FDG	Business Partner Relationships: Relationship Field Groups	Restrict modifications to specific fields within business partner relationships

Table 7.2 Business Partner Authorization Objects

Restricting Changes to Vendor Accounting-Related Master Records

Similar to customer records, vendor master records also contain important SAP ERP Financials Financial Accounting–related data. Specific information such as vendor reconciliation accounts and bank data can be important for general internal control as well as fraud prevention. As such, maintenance over certain vendor master data fields is important to financial reporting.

If you are using SAP purchasing, vendor master data is generally managed centrally through the purchasing component, with specific permissions related to accounting details. Vendor data can also be managed directly within SAP ERP Financials Financial Accounting. From a segregation of duties perspective, the entry and maintenance of accounting related vendor details should be segregated from the purchasing function. SAP provides a variety of mechanisms to restrict changes to vendor master records, including account, application, company code, account group, or specific fields within the vendor master. Some of the key authorization objects for doing this are shown in Table 7.3: Vendor Master Authorization Objects.

Auth. Object	Vendor	Purpose
F_LFA1_BEK	Accounts Authorization	Restrict modifications to vendor master data by vendor account range
F_LFA1_APP	Application Authorization	Restrict the ability to modify vendor data to purchasing data (PUR) or financial accounting data (SAP ERP Financials Financial Accounting)
F_LFA1_BUK	Authorization for Company Codes	Restrict the ability to change the vendor by company code
F_LFA1_GRP	Accounts Group Authorization	Restrict the ability to change the vendor based upon account group
F_LFA1_AEN	Change Authorization for Certain Fields	Restrict modifications to vendor master data by defined fields

Table 7.3 Vendor Master Authorization Objects

Restricting Changes to Material Master Records

The material master is affected through the purchase-to-pay cycle, and includes accounting data, purchasing information, and other details relevant to the purchasing cycle. While the material master also affects production and inventory management, not within the scope of this book, the effect on the purchase-to-pay cycle should be addressed through security. From a segregation of duties perspective, the entry and maintenance of accounting-related material details should be segregated from the inventory function.

SAP provides a variety of mechanisms to restrict changes to material master records, including company code, plant, and material type. Some of the key authorization objects for doing this are shown in Table 7.4: Material Master Authorization Objects.

Auth. Object	Material Master	Purpose
M_MATE_BUK	Company Codes	Restrict modifications to material master data by company code
M_MATE_WRK	Plants	Restrict modifications to material master data by plant
M_MATE_MAR	Material Types	Restrict the ability to change the material master data by material type

Table 7.4 Material Master Authorization Objects

Restricting Changes to Goods Receipts

SAP provides a variety of mechanisms to restrict changes to goods receipts, including plant and movement type. Key authorization objects for this are shown in Table 7.5: Goods Receipt Authorization Objects.

Auth. Object	Goods Receipt for PO	Purpose
M_MSEG_BWE	Movement Type	Restrict modifications to goods receipt by movement type
M_MSEG_WWE	Plant	Restrict modifications to goods receipt by plant

Table 7.5 Goods Receipt Authorization Objects

Restricting Changes to Banking Master Records

The ability to change banking data should also be tightly restricted, as bank account information can be highly susceptible to fraud. SAP provides a variety of mechanisms to restrict changes to banking master records. Security permissions can be set to restrict changes based account, credit control area, and specific fields within credit management. Some of the key authorization objects for doing this are shown in Table 7.6: Banking Authorization Objects.

Auth. Object	Banks	Purpose
F_BNKA_BUK	Authorization for Company Codes	Restrict modifications house banks and bank accounts company code
F_BNKA_MAN	General Maintenance Authorization	Restrict the general ability to maintain bank master data

Table 7.6 Banking Authorization Objects

7.3 SAP Configurable Control Considerations

In Chapter 2, we reviewed the typical process for auditing SAP and introduce a series of audit assurance "layers" upon which an auditor will typically build his confidence in SAP processing. In this section, we explore the Component-Specific Technical Settings layer related to Materials Management in SAP ERP. Specifically, we introduce a number of *SAP configuration suggestions and considerations* that can enhance processes over the SAP purchase-to-pay cycle.

This list is by no means exhaustive, and we fully expect that you will utilize many more configurable SAP controls than are mentioned herein. This section highlights some of the control features within SAP that, in our experience, could be more comprehensively used by organizations running SAP applications. Regardless of whether you agree with the control technique, consider the risks addressed by these recommendations and ensure that, where appropriate, you have addressed these risks within your organization.

Assess Your Own Risks

The recommendations provided here are suggestions only, and should be reviewed in the context of your own business risks and anticipated value. You may find some of these suggestions unreasonable for your business environment, and you may choose to address the underlying risks in different ways, perhaps even outside of SAP. Effective SAP control is not a one-size-fits-all situation.

7.3.1 Configure SAP Data Quality Checks

Data quality problems affect many organizations. While SAP supports strong data integrity checks, many of these need to be turned on and configured for your business. Failure to take advantage of these capabilities places reliance on user diligence during document entry, and after-the-fact reviews to detect any errors or abuse. Many auditors now use specific tools to detect potential data problems in both master and transactional data, so utilizing these techniques on your most important data elements can help prevent audit embarrassment.

Define Important Fields as "Required Entry"

By default, the fields that SAP requires for transaction processing or master data entry may not be all the fields that you need to fully process business transactions in your environment. Configuring SAP to flag situations where additional information may be required can help ensure a high level of data integrity.

For example, you may choose to require a phone number for every vendor so that you have enough information to contact them if questions arise. You may require a payment address, ensuring that whenever a purchase is made, sufficient information exists to provide payment upon receipt. You may also choose to require a reconciliation account for all vendors, making it easier to reconcile customer payments to orders. Special consideration should also be given to required data for sensitive accounts such as one-time vendors (many audit texts suggest requiring the "Authorization" field within the Control section of General Data).

Figure 7.1: Maintain Field Status Groups shows an example where a company requires entry of the bill-to address, including street and postal code. This particular setting is available in the IMG under FINANCIAL ACCOUNTING • ACCOUNTS RECEIVABLE AND ACCOUNTS PAYABLE • VENDOR ACCOUNTS • MASTER DATA • PREPARATIONS FOR CREATING MASTER DATA • DEFINE ACCOUNT GROUPS WITH SCREEN LAYOUT (VENDORS).

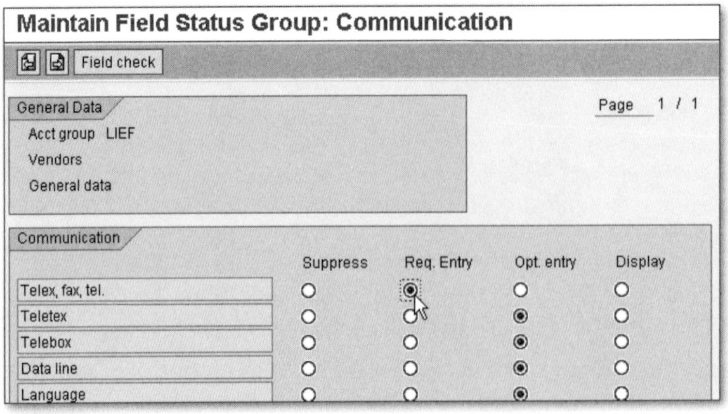

Figure 7.1 Maintain Field Status Groups

Field status groups within SAP enable additional data handling procedures over individual fields and field groups based on the type of transaction (e.g., create, change, display). For controlling key data, the field status groups that you'll most likely use are "Required Entry" and "Display." Use "Required Entry" to specify those fields that must contain data, and "Display" for those fields that you wish the user to see but not have the ability to change. Change any fields that are not used to "Suppress" or "Hide" (depending on the screen) to prevent user confusion.

Configure General Payment Tolerances

At times, the vendor invoice may be different from the calculated invoice price based on PO amount and receiving quantity. This may be due to estimated pricing that has changed from original estimates, surcharges, or other fees added to the invoice, or other conditions. Depending on your business preferences, you may choose to write off small differences rather than invest time and energy in resolving small-dollar discrepancies. SAP allows you to establish payment tolerances, based on specific conditions (defined within tolerance keys), establishing controls over invoice entry and payment. Using tolerances also ensures that employees do not write pay more than acceptable per company policy, and is thus a control over both entry errors and intentional policy circumvention.

Depending on the type of tolerance key being used, you can set upper bounds, which prevent overpayment, and lower bounds, which prevent underpayment, as shown in Figure 7.2: Defining Tolerance Limits by Tolerance Key provides an example of this. In this case, the price variance tolerance key has been set with both absolute and percentage limits. When both absolute and percentage limits are defined, SAP will use the lower value of the two.

Within SAP, you can define these tolerances at the company code level within defined tolerance keys. By default, these tolerance keys include:

▶ AN – Amount for Item Without Order Reference — For invoices without order reference, this tolerance compares every line item against the defined absolute upper limit.

▶ AP – Amount for Item with Order Reference — If activated, this tolerance checks line items referenced to orders against the defined tolerances.

▶ BD – Form Small Differences Automatically — SAP compares the balance of the invoice against the defined upper limit, and posts the difference, if it's less than the absolute upper limit, to Expense/Income from Small Differences. This results in a zero balance and allows the document to post.

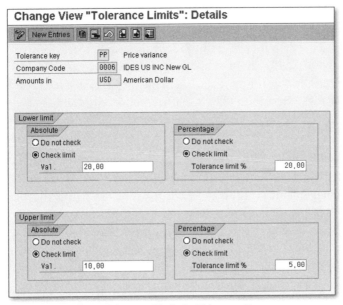

Figure 7.2 Defining Tolerance Limits by Tolerance Key

- ▶ BR – Percentage OPUn Variance (IR before GR) — This tolerance uses a complex calculation to basically compare what was invoiced to what was ordered, and block payments where the variance exceeds a defined threshold. The OPUn (order price unit) is often used when the units of measure between order quantity and order price differ (e.g., order in pieces but priced by weight).

- ▶ BW – Percentage OPUn variance (GR before IR) — This tolerance uses a complex calculation to basically compare what was invoiced to what was received, and block payments where the variance exceeds a defined threshold, based on order price unit as described above.

- ▶ DQ – Exceed Amount Quantity Variance — The variance is calculated based on multiplying the order price and the difference between what was invoiced and what was received (if goods receipt has taken place), or what was invoiced vs. what was ordered (if goods have not been received). Because this variance is compared to an absolute upper and/or lower limit, it allows for smaller quantity variances for higher-priced items, and greater quantity variances for lower-priced items.

- ▶ DW – Quantity Variance when GR Qty = Zero — This tolerance applies to situations where goods receipt is specified for an order but has not yet been posted.

- ▶ KW – Var. from Condition Value — SAP takes the ratio of planned delivery costs to planned quantity, and multiplies this result by the quantity invoiced before comparing to the absolute or percentage variance.

Importance of Checking Conditions

Several large publicized frauds have occurred over the last few years where vendors have manipulated freight charges, taxes, and other purchase add-ons to circumvent typical three-way-match controls. In these cases, the quantity and price invoiced matched what was ordered and received (enough to allow a payment in unsophisticated systems), but the vendor fraudulently marked up additional charges. In one publicized case, a set of twins charged the U.S. government almost $900,000 in shipping charges for two 19 cent washers. Tolerance key KW, by checking planned delivery costs to actual costs, can help eliminate this type of problem. Analytics, which compare freight costs to total order value, can also highlight conditions where this type of fraud scheme may occur.

- ▶ LA – Amount of Blanket PO — SAP calculates the variance between what has already been invoiced on the PO (aggregating what has already been invoiced with the current invoice) and the PO value limit, and compares to the absolute or percentage tolerances defined.

- ▶ LD – Blanket PO Time Limit Exceeded — SAP blocks payment for invoices exceeding the number of days defined, either by invoicing preceding the start of the PO validity period, or received after the end of the validity period.

- ▶ PP – Price Variance — SAP determines the difference between invoice price and order price for each item and compares this variance to the absolute and percentage limits defined.

- ▶ PS – Price Variance: Estimated Price — For order items marked as estimated price, SAP determines the difference between invoice value and (quantity invoiced X order price) compares this variance to the absolute and percentage limits defined.

- ▶ ST – Date Variance (Value X Days) — This variance takes the difference between scheduled delivery date and invoice entry date, and multiplies by the item amount. Similar to condition DQ, this tolerance key allows a higher date variance for small amounts and a lower variance for larger amounts.

- ▶ VP – Moving Average Price Variance — SAP calculates the ration of the moving average price resulting from the invoice to the old price, and compares this to the defined tolerance.

Invoices that exceed the defined tolerance amounts are automatically blocked for payment. Payment differences are automatically posted to appropriate SAP General Ledger accounts, if open item clearing is used. Tolerances are defined through the IMG using: MATERIALS MANAGEMENT • LOGISTICS INVOICE VERIFICATION • INVOICE BLOCK • SET TOLERANCE LIMITS, or Transaction OMR6. Amount checks must also be activated within Transactions OMRH and OMRI.

7.3.2 Establish Dual Control over Sensitive Fields

Certain data fields can be particularly sensitive — either because entry errors can cause significant harm, or because they are particularly susceptible to fraud. Vendor bank accounts, alternative payees, or payment terms, for example, could be manipulated for fraudulent purposes. To protect against inappropriate changes to sensitive fields, SAP provides a *dual control* setting that places a block on payment transactions whenever a field defined as being sensitive is changed. The block can only be removed by someone with a user ID other than the ID that changed the data. While such a control will not mitigate collusion, it does ensure that at least two individuals agree with the change.

You establish dual control by defining sensitive fields in the IMG using FINANCIAL ACCOUNTING • ACCOUNTS RECEIVABLE AND ACCOUNTS PAYABLE • VENDOR ACCOUNTS • MASTER DATA • PREPARATIONS FOR CREATING VENDOR MASTER DATA • DEFINE SENSITIVE FIELDS FOR DUAL CONTROL (VENDORS). Figure 7.3: Dual Control over Vendor Fields illustrates the simple process used to set the fields that will have this additional checking in place. Over 200 fields within the vendor record are available for dual control; however, many would not normally be considered sensitive. Configure the most critical and sensitive fields for dual control, but be careful not to go overboard.

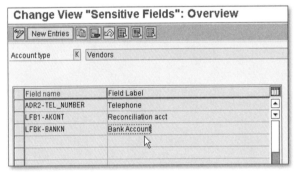

Figure 7.3   Dual Control over Vendor Fields

7.3.3 Ensure Robust Release Strategy Configuration

Release strategies allow SAP to ensure appropriate authorization and control across the purchasing cycle, and are an extremely powerful method of control. With this power comes complexity, however, and with complexity comes the risk of error. For any SAP audit where purchasing is in scope, you are practically guaranteed an audit assessment of SAP's *configured release strategy*. When defining your release strategy, as shown in Figure 7.4: Configuring the Release Strategy, ensure that you have established criteria for all relevant combinations of material groups, plants, purchasing groups, and other similar categories based on your corporate purchasing policy, or else the auditor may find a gap in the release strategy.

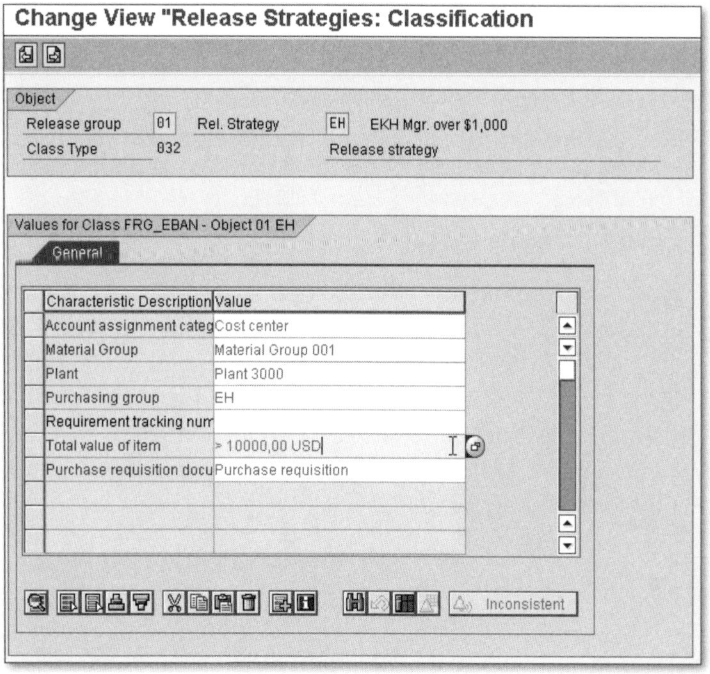

Change View "Release Strategies: Classification

Object
Release group   01   Rel. Strategy   EH   EKH Mgr. over $1,000
Class Type   032   Release strategy

Values for Class FRG_EBAN - Object 01 EH
General

Characteristic Description	Value
Account assignment categ	Cost center
Material Group	Material Group 001
Plant	Plant 3000
Purchasing group	EH
Requirement tracking num	
Total value of item	> 10000,00 USD
Purchase requisition docu	Purchase requisition

Inconsistent

Figure 7.4 Configuring the Release Strategy

The release strategy is configured in the IMG at MATERIALS MANAGEMENT • PURCHASING • [PURCHASE REQUISITION/PURCHASE ORDER] • RELEASE PROCEDURE. Release procedures can be established with your without classification, although because "with classification" allows approval for individual line items, it provides for a more powerful level of control. Release procedures can also be implemented for purchase requisitions, for POs, or for both.

Do I Need Both?

Organizations that work with both purchase requisitions and POs sometimes wonder if they need to implement robust release strategies for both, or whether one will suffice. Defining release strategies at the requisition level allows some problems to be detected early in the purchasing cycle; however, if POs can be created without reference to a purchase requisition, then risks mitigated through the purchase requisition release strategy can be effectively bypassed. The right answer depends on your specific business circumstances and risks; however, the use of both provides the greatest level of risk mitigation.

In general, the procedures for authorizing and validating changes to purchase requisitions or POs should be the same as that for new requisitions or POs. If the change authorization process is less robust than that for new orders, organizations can find the change order process used to circumvent intended controls.

7.3.4 Require Purchase Requisition Reference

If purchase requisitions are a key part of the purchase-to-pay control process within your organization, configure SAP to *require reference to the purchase requisition* whenever a PO is created or modified.

7.3.5 Strengthen Controls over Blanket POs

From an internal control perspective, the use of *blanket POs* creates more risk than standard purchasing processes that utilize specific POs and required goods/service receipts before payment. The use of blanket POs should be restricted to limited situations, and limits should be assigned to any blanket PO so that the amounts are not totally open ended. Tolerance key LA within the release strategy defines how SAP treats invoices, which, when aggregated against other invoices already applied to a blanket PO, exceed the PO limit.

7.3.6 Use Source Determination When Possible

As part of the purchasing process, organizations develop relationships and favorable pricing and servicing arrangements with suppliers. If purchases are made outside of this preferred vendor pool, however, an organization may find that employees are purchasing items at a higher cost than what can be realized through existing pricing agreements, or that the organization is receiving a lower quality of service than other arrangements allow. As such, procedures that ensure that purchases are make to preferred supplies helps minimize the risks of both unfavorable pricing and poor quality. *Source determination* (configured in the IMG at MATERIALS MANAGEMENT • PURCHASING • SOURCE DETERMINATION) should be configured to ensure that vendors providing the best level of price and service are selected during purchasing. While not every material will be appropriate for source determination, you can review assigned source lists through Transaction ME06.

7.3.7 Prevent Reversal of Goods Receipt after Invoice Processing

If you are using SAP's goods receipt–based invoice verification process, configure SAP to *prevent the reversal of goods receipt after invoice processing*. This setting can be controlled through Transaction OMJJ, as shown in Figure 7.5: Preventing Goods Receipt

Reversal After Invoice Processing. For movement type 102, Reversal of GR, uncheck the default setting that allows reversal of goods receipt despite invoice receipt.

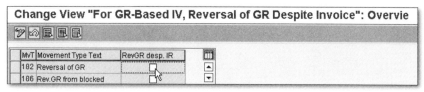

Figure 7.5 Preventing Goods Receipt Reversal After Invoice Processing

7.3.8 Define Appropriate Payment Different Reason Codes

Define *reason codes* that make sense for your business and allow for effective monitoring and decision making. When payments differ from SAP calculated amounts, payment codes effectively track causes and deal with recurring purchasing or vendor situations that should be resolved. Because of this, reason codes serve as a control over recurring issues, which consume business resources to resolve.

7.3.9 Configure Mandatory Goods Receipt for Relevant Items

Certain purchases should always be followed by a goods receipt, because goods receipt mitigates the risk of purchasing fraud as well as overpayment for goods not received. Define goods receipt as mandatory, and also configure SAP to prevent this indicator from being changed on subsequent purchasing documents. Figure 7.6: Configuring Mandatory Goods Receipt shows where this setting is configured. Select the relevant account assignment through configuration in the IMG at MATERIALS MANAGEMENT • PURCHASING • ACCOUNT ASSIGNMENT • MAINTAIN ACCOUNT ASSIGNMENT CATEGORIES, and in the Detailed Information section, ensure that both Goods Receipt and GR Ind. Firm are checked for all relevant account assignment categories. Requiring an invoice receipt may also be appropriate, and ensure that this field cannot be changed as well.

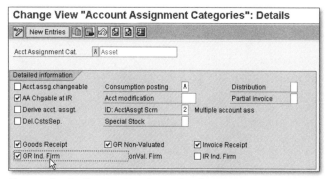

Figure 7.6 Configuring Mandatory Goods Receipt

7.3.10 Remove Unlimited Overdelivery Capabilities

By default, SAP has a purchasing value key that allows for *unlimited overdelivery* of goods. This effectively negates controls in the release strategy, because PO quantity becomes irrelevant, and thus this setting can be used to perpetuate fraud. Figure 7.7: Removing Unlimited Overdelivery shows where this setting is configured, accessed through the IMG at MATERIALS MANAGEMENT • PURCHASING • MATERIAL MASTER • DEFINE PURCHASING VALUE KEYS.

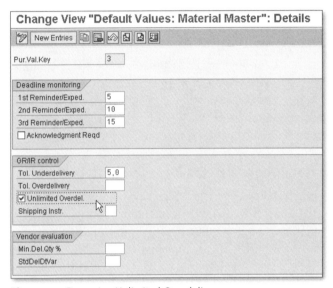

Figure 7.7 Removing Unlimited Overdelivery

7.3.11 Configure Stochastic Invoice Blocking

SAP's stochastic blocking functionality can provide an additional level of control over outgoing payments. Tolerance keys provide a good level of control; however, because these keys define specific limits beyond which SAP will place payment blocks, the intent of this control can be bypassed if employees or vendors learn of key thresholds and process transactions just below these thresholds. *Stochastic blocking* allows for an additional random check, and also applies to invoices that may not be subject to any other blocking reason.

You configure stochastic blocking settings in the IMG through MATERIALS MANAGEMENT • LOGISTICS INVOICE VERIFICATION • INVOICE BLOCK • STOCHASTIC BLOCK. First, activate the stochastic block for each company code, and then set the stochastic block values. On the *Change View "Stochastic Block: Values": Overview* screen, set both the threshold value and the percentage for each company code. The percentage defines how often an invoice above the set threshold value will be blocked with the stochastic block. Any invoice over the threshold value is blocked at exactly the percentage input. Invoices below the threshold are blocked in direct relation to their percentage of the threshold level using the following formula: (invoice amount / threshold value) × percentage.

Reviewing Figure 7.8: Stochastic Blocking, company code 0006 has a threshold value set at $10,000 USD, with a percentage of 20%. An invoice of $15,000 would have a 20% change of being blocked. An invoice amount of $6,000 would have a 12% chance of being blocked (6,000/10,000 × 20%). Conversely, that same $6,000 invoice for company code 0008 would be blocked 50% of the time given the established configuration.

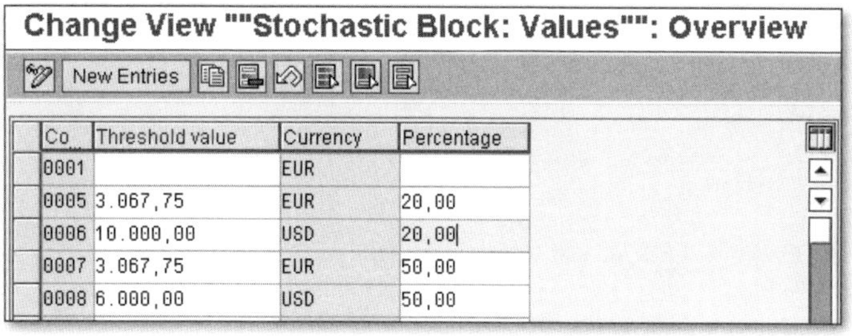

Co...	Threshold value	Currency	Percentage
0001		EUR	
0005	3.067,75	EUR	20,00
0006	10.000,00	USD	20,00
0007	3.067,75	EUR	50,00
0008	6.000,00	USD	50,00

Figure 7.8 Stochastic Blocking

The threshold values and tolerances that you configure will depend on your level of business risk and the extent of other controls that you have over the purchase-to-pay process. Because any invoice can be selected for additional evaluation, stochastic blocking provides a great additional control and can detect situations where policies are intentionally circumvented.

7.3.12 Other Configuration Tips

The suggestions above tend to be the most critical from an audit and control perspective. Depending on your organization and business processes, the following ideas may also enhance your internal control environment and allow better risk management. As with all other suggestions, the relevance of each of these to audit success is tied to your business risks:

- Alternate Payment Currencies — When alternate payment currencies may be used, configure SAP to maintain automatic account assignments, including clearing accounts, for payment differences that may arise as a result of payment currency.

- Duplicate invoice check — SAP duplicate invoice checking is not enabled by default. Configuring this setting can reduce, but likely not eliminate, the processing of duplicate invoices.

- Alternative Payee — If your business does not require the periodic use of alternative payees, which should be controlled through SAP's dual control over sensitive fields function discussed in this section, then this field should be suppressed on all relevant documents. Abuse of the alternative payee is a common fraud technique, and removing this ability can eliminate this as a possibility.

- Duplicate Business Partners — Enable SAP functionality for detecting potential duplicates when vendors are being entered, based on address (through function module ADDR_ENABLE_DUPLICATE_CHECK). Duplicate business partners within SAP ERP Financials Financial Accounting can lead to duplicate payments, lack of visibility into purchasing activity, and other undesired issues. SAP will create a warning message if the address entered is the same as the one in the system, and present the user with a list of potential that duplicates he can review before completing processing. Users should be trained on appropriate investigation and the procedures to follow when SAP flags a potential duplicate match.

7.4   Additional Procedures and Considerations

As we have discussed earlier in this book, configuring SAP the "right" way is often not enough. User interaction with the SAP system plays a large part in the effectiveness of business processes managed by SAP. This section highlights *additional procedures and considerations* that can help you further strengthen your purchase-to-pay processes and withstand audit scrutiny.

7.4.1   Implement Invoice Payment Completeness and Timeliness Procedures

Failure to process invoices completely or in a timely fashion can result in lost discounts, upset supplier, and other unintended consequences. For organizations that accept invoices through fax, postal mail, or even email, processes can be even more challenging. *Implement procedures* to ensure that all invoices get entered into SAP in a timely manner. This may involve logging all incoming fax orders, mail orders, and other order receipts and periodically reconciling this log to what has been entered into SAP. An auditor is likely to compare the date that an invoice was received to the date it was entered into the system, so mechanisms to ensure that entries that are expedited can be valuable. Care should also be taken when processing to prevent duplicate entries, because vendors might send multiple faxes or fax orders that have also been sent in the mail.

7.4.2 Eliminate Duplicates from the Vendor Master and Material Master

Despite best intentions, *duplicate records* can periodically creep up in master data records. Within the vendor master, duplicate records could result in price negotiations based on an incomplete picture of purchasing activity. Duplicate material master records could result in duplicate purchases. Regardless of the cause, periodically review vendor and material master data records for potential duplicates, and correct any issues found.

Querying for Duplicate Master Records

Standard transactions and reports within SAP typically don't have the flexibility to compare the full complement of fields that could indicate potential duplicate records. As such, use of SAP query or custom ABAP reports are common, as are queries within SAP NetWeaver Business Warehouse (SAP NetWeaver BW) (where master data is available in the warehouse). Many auditors choose an offline approach, downloading key tables from SAP and use specialized audit tools such as ACL or IDEA to query for duplicates. These tools contain "sounds like" and other specialized functions to identify hard-to-detect duplicates. If your internal auditors use such a tool, you may be able to leverage software already in house. Typically, table MARA is sufficient for finding duplicates in the material master, and LFA1 is sufficient for duplicates within the Vendor Master. Whichever technique you use, working with your auditors to develop effective search criteria can help ensure that you find problems before your auditor does.

When searching for duplicate records, consider creative queries that may indicate possible duplication. Because SAP has functionality to prevent the most obvious duplicates from being entered, when duplicates do appear, they are often due to typos or other conditions that may be missed by SAP checks.

Creative conditions for finding duplicates within the vendor master include:

- Similar names
- Same bank account number
- Same tax ID number
- Same phone number, fax line, or similar communication match
- Same numeric portion of the address (postal code + street number)

Creative conditions for finding duplicates within the material master include:

- Same name or description
- Similar name with same supply area and plant
- Same dimensions and weight
- Same bill of material details

If during such a review duplicate entries are discovered, additional research may be warranted to determine if any undesired conditions have been created as a result.

7.4.3 Confirm Vendor Payables Balances

When auditing accounts payable balances in the SAP General Ledger, many auditors send out what are known as *confirmation letters* to independently verify the balances of vendor payables accounts. Confirmation letters help the auditor independently validate the value of the account balance, ensuring that there are no disputed or missing items included in the total. Confirmation letters cannot always identify unrecorded liabilities (particularly if associated with vendors not yet within SAP); however, they can be effective at validating balances for vendors who are frequently used.

Because auditors are likely to confirm balances anyway, a good practice is to use standard SAP functionality to confirm your own vendor balances in advance of the audit. Depending on the process used, the information that you receive back may even allow the auditor to reduce his testing. Transaction F.18 generates vendor confirmation letters. This function can also be accessed through menu path ACCOUNTING • FINANCIAL ACCOUNTING • ACCOUNTS PAYABLE • PERIODIC PROCESSING • PRINT CORRESPONDENCE • BALANCE CONFIRMATION • PRINT LETTERS. You can select vendors who meet certain criteria (e.g., one-time vendors, those with balances between specified amounts, those with recent postings, etc.) or even take a random sample.

When using confirmations, one of the most important settings is the Confirmation Procedure, under the Output Control section of the form, as shown in Figure 7.9: Confirmations. SAP allows three different types of confirmations to be generated:

- Balance Notifications
- Balance Requests
- Balance Confirmations

The strongest confirmation procedure is the Balance Request, because it requests that the vendor responds with the balance shown in his system without influencing him with what you show within SAP. A more common and still strong confirmation procedure is the Balance Confirmation, commonly known as the positive confirmation or positive inquiry. The Balance Confirmation requests that the vendor responds to the confirmation letter, indicating that he either agrees with a balance or shows a different balance (included in the response). Balance Notifications are not usually effective confirmation procedures. The Balance Notification requests a response only if the balance differs from vendor records, thus making the potentially incorrect assumption that non-receipt of a response indicates agreement with the balance (in reality, it could also indicate that the letter was never received, or the recipient has not had time to respond).

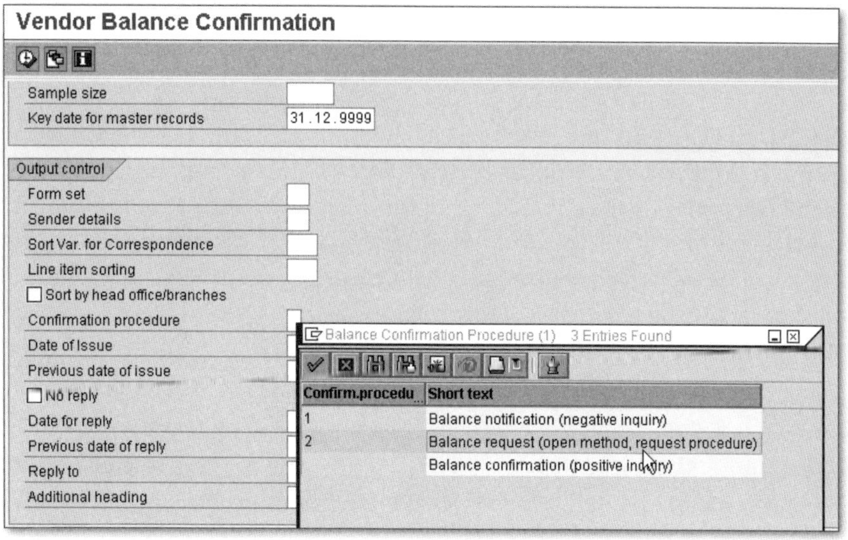

Figure 7.9 Confirmations

7.4.4 Standardize Naming Conventions

Standards governing naming conventions and address entry can go a long way to minimizing duplicate entry. Many common duplicate detection procedures rely on a level of consistency with data entry, and the effectiveness of these procedures can be greatly increased if *standard naming conventions* and data entry specifications are used consistently across your organization.

7.4.5 Review One-Time Vendor Usage

In many organizations, controls defined for *one-time vendors* are less stringent than those for standard vendors fully entered into SAP. One-time vendor functionality typically bypasses standard controls over vendor approval, payment terms, and vendor tolerances. Periodically monitor one-time vendor usage to ensure that processing is as intended (low dollar amounts and low transactions). One-time vendors can be selected from the *Vendor List*, report RFKKVZ00, and then further investigated. Payments to one-time vendors can be further investigated using report RFKEPL00, or Transaction S_ALR_87012103. Situations where one-time vendor functionality is being overused should be investigated and resolved before the audit, and transactions to these one-time vendors (where functionality has been abused), should be reviewed for validity.

7.4.6 Closely Monitor Evaluated Receipts Activity

For companies with many regular purchases with proven vendors, SAP *Evaluated Receipt Settlement* (ERS) functionality can provide significant efficiency gains. For vendors established as ERS vendors, SAP automatically generates an invoice document (to be paid given relevant payment terms) upon entry of goods receipt. Because the PO establishes the items ordered, the quantity ordered, and the agreed-on price, while the goods receipt establishes how many of those items were actually received, SAP has enough information to process payment without needing a vendor invoice.

Use of ERS has risks, however. The three-way-match allowed by checking a vendor-created invoice against the related PO and goods receipt allows entry mistakes to be detected. When relying on ERS, mistakes made when you enter PO or receiving details directly into SAP carry through directly to the SAP-generated invoice and ultimately the payment. As such, ERS vendor activity should be monitored closely. At a minimum, this typically includes periodic monitoring of vendors established as ERS vendors to ensure that they are appropriate and continue to meet the quality standards established by your organization.

> **Monitoring ERS Changes**
>
> When working with ERS vendors, certain types of changes can pose serious risks to the integrity of vendor payments. For example, if a PO price change is mis-keyed (a situation that causes problems in multiple organizations), inaccurate payment would occur. Depending on the size of the mistake, this inaccuracy could cause millions of dollars to leave the organization without authorization (a situation that we've also encountered during prior reviews). While these funds can often be recovered, the resources spent resolving the issue and the interest lost until any overpayments have been recovered pose unnecessary costs to your organization. Monitoring can mitigate this type of risk (such as reviewing changes exceeding a specified threshold); however, these procedures should be in place and periodically tested for effectiveness.

7.4.7 Periodically Review Authorization Limits

Have an organizational policy for approval *authorization limits*. Most organizations set these limits by role; however, no matter how your organization has defined authorization limits, ensure that they are implemented accurately in SAP. The auditor will compare your organizational policy to SAP configuration, so any discrepancies should be resolved before the audit. Additionally, periodically review these authorization limits to ensure that they are still appropriate based on your business. As business conditions change, these limits typically should follow — what was appropriate years ago may no longer be appropriate in today's environment.

7.4.8 Monitor Effectiveness of Receiving Procedures

Goods receipt provides an important control over the purchase-to-pay cycle. *Receiving procedures* should ensure that your organization only pays for the quantity of items actually received, and does not pay for damaged or poor quality materials. Sometimes, receiving processes can be rushed, however, and goods are received without effective counting or quality control procedures. This process increases the risk that your organization pays for goods that it cannot use, and after time cannot dispute. Establish processes for receiving goods and services into SAP, including policies for over/under receipts, quality assessment, and timing of SAP input. As with all policies, periodically self-audit your own performance to identify and correct process deviations.

7.4.9 Monitor Vendor Payments and Payment Application

In addition to having strong controls in the PO, receiving, and payment components of SAP, procedures should also ensure that funds are actually applied appropriately to *vendor accounts*. In addition to the standard controls provided by SAP, also:

► Reconcile bank accounts used to pay vendors and ensure that all reconciling items are resolved in a timely basis

► Review accounts payable aging reports and investigate amounts, including those resulting from disputes, that have been outstanding for an unacceptable period of time

Your auditor will likely perform these procedures as well, so maintaining documentation of both your review and follow-up will expedite this portion of the audit.

7.4.10 Limit, if not Prohibit, Manual Payments

Manual payments, by nature, effectively bypass traditional purchase-to-pay controls build in SAP. As a result, the use of manual payments should be severely limited, if not completely prohibited. If used, manual payments should follow organizational authorization limit guidelines, which for manual payments, should be at least as strict as those payments configured in SAP, if not even more strict. Your auditor will likely review manual payments as a specific audit step, and question any payments or payment amounts that should have been processed directly in SAP.

7.5   Management Monitoring: SAP Report Highlights

Monitoring procedures are a core part of an effective internal control structure. SAP contains numerous reports that you can use to identify and monitor potential risks within the purchase-to-pay cycle. Diligent review of these reports and investigation of suspicious items complements the configured controls within SAP, and rounds out your ability to survive a purchase-to-pay audit. This section highlights a few examples.

7.5.1   Reports Identifying Changed Data

SAP reports that monitor changes to sensitive data are valuable for ensuring that all changes (including initial creation) have been authorized and entered accurately. These reports provide valuable information, because they show both old values and the new values that replaced them. The frequency that these reports should be reviewed will depend on the risk that inappropriate changes to the relevant data elements could pose to your operations. *Data change reports* should be reviewed by someone other than employees who can make changes to data.

Each review should, at a minimum, cover the period since the last review, which you can select using the date selection criteria in the reports below. Limiting "Changed By" selections (where available on the reports) to individual employees or small groups of employees can help to draw attention to suspicious activity. But, when filtering selections using additional criteria, ensure that by the end of the review process that you have covered every change made during the review period.

Vendor Changes

Review the *Display Changes to Vendors* report RFKABL00 to display changes to vendor records. Reviews can be filtered by company code and purchasing organization data, if desired. Although this report can be large, once data has been returned, you can filter on field values that are most relevant from an internal control perspective (such as address, alternate payee, or bank details). This report can be found under menu INFORMATION SYSTEMS • GENERAL REPORT SELECTION • FINANCIAL ACCOUNTING • REPORTS FOR ACCOUNTS PAYABLE ACCOUNTING • MASTER DATA • DISPLAY CHANGES TO VENDORS, or accessed directly through Transaction S_ALR_87012089.

Source List Changes

Review the *Changes to Source List* report via Transaction ME04 to display changes to defined source lists. Information is sorted by material number, and can be filtered by any number of criteria, if desired. Although this report can be large, once data has been returned, you can filter on field values that are most relevant from an internal control perspective.

> **Using Other Reports for Vendor Change Monitoring**
>
> Other reports for monitoring vendor changes exist, such as those accessed through Transactions MK04 or XK04; however, they should not be the only reports that you review. These reports are vendor specific, and require that you enter a vendor to see what has changed. The intent of a review such as this is to make sure that all changes are appropriate, including those of which you may not be aware (and thus do not know the relevant vendor number). These reports are useful if you are investigating changes to a specific vendor but should not be your sole source for vendor change monitoring.

7.5.2 Incomplete Information or Processing

Some SAP reports highlight situations where data is missing or processing is not fully complete. In some cases, missing data may indicate processing problems, and in other cases missing data could result in transactions that do not have enough information to be fully processed through Materials Management in SAP ERP. Document blocks can also prevent transactions from being fully completed. The frequency that these reports should be reviewed will depend on the risk of what having *incomplete data* could pose to your operations.

Missing Vendor Data

If you use both Materials Management in SAP ERP and SAP ERP Financials Financial Accounting, run the *Vendor Master Data Comparison* report RFKKAG00 to identify vendor records that have been created in Materials Management in SAP ERP but not in SAP ERP Financials Financial Accounting (or vice versa). Identification of vendors that have not been maintained in SAP ERP Financials Financial Accounting could indicate processing problems, and SAP ERP Financials Financial Accounting vendors not in Materials Management in SAP ERP could be indicative of fraud.

Financial Accounting Differences

If using both Materials Management in SAP ERP and SAP ERP Financials Financial Accounting, run the SAP ERP Financials Financial Accounting Comparative Analysis report, program SAPF190, to identify differences between debit and credit transaction figures from vendor accounts and posted documents. This report also compares debit and credit figures from vendor accounts with application indexes, used for open item managed accounts.

GR/IR Clearing

Periodically, goods are received without a corresponding invoice, or invoices are received without a corresponding goods receipt. These issues must be cleared to ensure accuracy of inventory and accounting records, and facilitate management reporting based on complete and accurate information. GR/IR clearing accounts can be access through Transaction F.19. GR/IR discrepancies for specific POs can be viewed with Transaction MB5S. At a minimum, this information should be reviewed and cleared as possible for period end; however, the quantity of GR/IR discrepancies at many organizations may necessitate a more frequent review.

Outstanding POs

Periodically review and investigate outstanding orders that have not yet been received and invoiced. Because overdue POs can affect the ability to meet customer demands and satisfy business needs, care should be taken that all items that can be cleared are resolved. You can use program RM06EM00, or Transaction VL10B to access the POs, Fast Display screen. You can filter results for more effective monitoring.

7.5.3   Potential Issues

Certain SAP reports highlight *potential issues* that should be investigated. These issues could result from processing problems, fraud, or errors. One example includes Invoice Numbers Allocated Twice (Transaction S_ALR_87101127, program RFB-NUM10). Review reports such as these periodically (at least once per period), to investigate issues and determine and resolve root causes.

7.6   Summary

In this chapter, we reviewed risks within the SAP purchase-to-pay cycle. To mitigate those risks, we highlighted a series of controls across four main categories. Related to security and master data, we explored segregation of duties, critical transactions, and important authorization objects. We then highlighted a series of configurable SAP controls that may be reviewed during an SAP audit. We reviewed a series of process-based controls and procedures that can strengthen risk management of purchase-to-pay processing, and closed with an overview of key SAP reports.

"The secret to creativity is knowing how to hide your sources."
— *Albert Einstein*

8 SAP Audit Tricks and Tools

Sometimes, no matter how hard you prepare for an audit, your auditor still finds problems where you didn't even know they existed. Perhaps a setting in SAP appears to be configured correctly, but a custom transaction that you developed for a completely different purpose seems to bypass the normal SAP controls. Maybe you are convinced that your processes work 99% of the time, and your auditor just happened to catch the single exception during the year. Or perhaps you feel your auditor has psychic powers, and calls you the day after a key system setting changes. If you have ever wondered how your auditor works such magic, then this chapter is for you.

In this chapter, we share a few of the secrets that auditors use to find potential problems with SAP. We describe the Audit Information System (AIS) — powerful functionality readily available within every SAP system. We share information about increasingly popular Computer Assisted Audit Techniques (CAATs) and the inexpensive tools that auditors typically use to perform this type of analysis and generate impressive results. We also introduce the SAP BusinessObjects portfolio of governance, risk, and compliance (GRC) products, and the concept of continuous auditing and continuous monitoring that these tools support. The techniques that we describe range from the simple to the complex, and you can begin using many of them yourself once you understand the basics.

By the end of this chapter, you will understand specific tools and techniques that you can implement in your environment to better identify, track, and monitor potential internal control problems. You will walk away with specific testing techniques that can find potential problems where none were anticipated. You will also understand the situations that may warrant additional tools and the benefits that these can provide. In short, by the end of this chapter, you will have the facilities to move beyond simply surviving an SAP audit to also testing and monitoring like an auditor to stay ahead of potential problems.

8.1　The Audit Information System (AIS)

One of the best-kept secrets within SAP systems is the Audit Information System (AIS). Delivered as a standard part of SAP, AIS is essentially a portal, providing a centralized set of SAP-related audit information and reports for by SAP system audits and financial statement-oriented audits. Because it groups and collects audit-relevant information into a single area, AIS provides a good starting point for many SAP audits.

An Old, Yet Relatively Unused Tool

AIS functionality has been a part of the SAP Basis system for decades. We have been told that AIS was developed by SAP in response to requests from external auditing firms for a tool able to easily find, evaluate, and download information from the SAP system. While AIS allowed for some direct reporting out of SAP, it was primarily used for downloading data into flat files for analysis with specialized audit tools.

For many years after first being introduced, AIS seemed to be a tool used primarily by the large public accounting firms — many organizations did not even know that it was already part of their SAP systems. In the last few years, AIS has undergone a fairly significant overhaul. In the early days, AIS required specific configuration to use it effectively. SAP recently introduced a set of audit-centric security profiles that provide access to AIS functions through the user menu. Some of the reports have been cleaned up, and the new audit roles allow data access to be restricted in a way that more closely aligns with auditor responsibilities. While improvements can still be made, the current AIS system has taken shape as a key audit tool.

8.1.1　Accessing the AIS

In older versions of SAP, you used Transaction SECR to access AIS. Because AIS has been overhauled, you can now grant AIS functionality through a series of predefined roles with the SAP system, by adding these roles to a user through Transaction SU01. You can easily find these roles by searching on the string "*AUDITOR*". A composite security role, SAP_AUDITOR, can be used to grant access to all AIS functionality, or several dozen single roles that allow you to segregate AIS functionality at a more granular level. Figure 8.1: AIS Roles shows a selection of these AIS-specific roles.

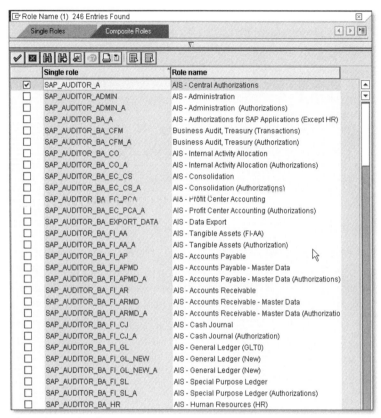

Figure 8.1 AIS Roles

Significant Improvement in Auditor Security

The introduction of audit-specific roles in SAP version 4.6c is a significant step forward to being able to grant appropriate auditor access to SAP. In earlier versions of SAP, security administrators often found themselves individually defining 'display only' access auditor profiles — a time-consuming and nearly impossible exercise.

Many organizations find it beneficial to copy the SAP-delivered audit security roles and edit these roles to more closely match their business and security needs, typically using a Z_SAP_AUDITOR_* naming convention. Remember when assigning AIS access that, depending on your security policies and type of auditor being granted access, you may want to restrict the role to the defined period for the audit. For internal auditors who are part of your organization and may need to access the AIS system frequently, you can typically make the role assignment valid for an indefinite period, as shown in Figure 8.2: Assigning AIS Roles.

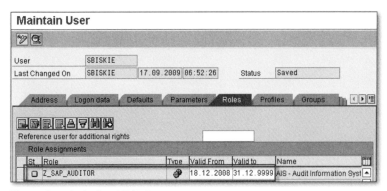

Figure 8.2 Assigning AIS Roles

8.1.2 Navigating the AIS

Fundamentally, AIS segregates audit information into two primary categories: a system audit and business audit. The system audit deals primarily with SAP basis configuration, security, and other details traditionally associated with an IT audit. The business audit sections are primarily geared toward settings and reports relevant to a financial statement audit. Many audit departments have historically segregated technical IT audits from financial or operational audits, although these days it's not uncommon to have an integrated audit, performed by an individual auditor or a team, which covers all aspects.

Once a user has been assigned an appropriate AIS role, he can begin navigating the AIS system through their user menu, as shown in Figure 8.3: AIS User Menu. In this example, the auditor has access to the entire AIS through composite role SAP_AUDITOR. If a single role had been granted rather than the composite role, such as SAP_AUDITOR_BA_EC_CS, then the auditor would only be allowed to see relevant portions of the menu.

AIS does not really provide any new functionality to an auditor. Each of the programs, transactions, and reports available in AIS are generally accessible through other areas of the system through standard user menus. The advantage of AIS is that it consolidates these functions in a single place that the auditor can access, without navigating through a complex set of standard reporting trees.

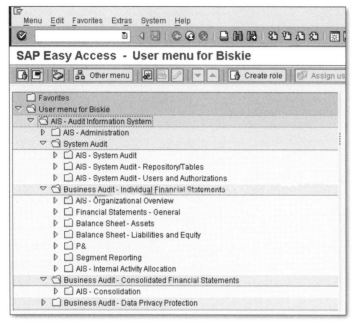

Figure 8.3 AIS User Menu

8.1.3 Using AIS to Prepare for your Audit

If your auditor will be using AIS for all or a portion of your audit, you have practically been given the questions on which you will be tested. In addition to the guidance already presented in this book, reviewing each item in AIS with your newfound knowledge of how to think like an auditor will put you in a good position for the audit.

Be Cautious of Assigning AIS Roles to Non-Auditors

While we recommend mapping AIS transactions and programs to your business processes to ensure someone in your organization is periodically looking at the same information that your auditor will review, we do not recommend granting AIS roles to individual employees unless they have been thoroughly vetted. Auditors by nature of their role have the authority to view information across the organization, and often have access to sensitive data that standard employees should not be able to see. If you do assign AIS privileges to non-auditors in your organization, perform a thorough review of the role definition and ensure that it does not conflict with your information security policies. If not, you are apt to find yourself in the ironic situation of being written up on an audit because of your use of auditor roles.

Because AIS is merely a collection of information already within SAP, ensure that for every report and transaction within AIS, an appropriate person in your organization has been assigned to review and monitor the information. While that should generally be a given, upon mapping AIS information to the reports and transactions that your personnel routinely access, you can sometimes find gaps where employees are either unaware, or have gotten lax in their review procedures.

While AIS has been significantly enhanced over the last several years, there is still room for additional improvement. The current focus remains on SAP Basis and financial reporting. Aside from the accounting impact of transactions created in the SAP ERP Operations Suite, AIS is silent as to the integrity of business activities for SD, Materials Management in SAP ERP, and similar components. Certain analysis, such as audits pertaining to SAP authorizations, are fairly rudimentary and do not provide the level of assurance the tools such as SAP BusinessObjects Access Control provides. Despite its weaknesses, however, AIS is still a powerful tool and a great starting point for an SAP audit. If your auditor uses the AIS system, sit down with them and jointly walk through the areas that they rely upon most, so you can better your own operations.

8.2 Computer Assisted Audit Techniques (CAATs)

Less than two decades ago, auditors performed the vast majority of their audit work manually, referencing paper documentation. A typical purchase-to-pay audit involved matching hardcopy POs to paper receiving documents to physical invoices. The advance of ERP systems, like SAP, fundamentally changed the audit world. Today, more transactions are performed electronically, and traditional paper trails are practically non-existent.

As technology has changed, the traditional audit process has changed as well. Audit techniques that leverage the processing power of computers and the volumes of data now available in business applications have emerged. These techniques are commonly called Computer Assisted Audit Techniques (CAATs), audit analytics, or audit data analysis. While many auditors still use traditional procedures, those who have adopted CAATs have seen tremendous benefit in both the quality of their findings as well as audit efficiencies. Even if your auditor is not currently using CAATs, applying similar testing procedures to your SAP environment can yield tremendous benefit.

You might think of CAATs as a form of data mining, geared specifically toward providing audit insight. Typical CAAT-related testing would query SAP data to look for situations where the data does not conform to expected business rules. For example, if company policy states that every vendor must have a defined credit limit, CAATs interrogate SAP credit management records to see if any active vendor has missing credit limit data, or an unreasonably large credit limit (thus circumventing the intent of the control).

"The Truth is in the Transactions"

One of the leading providers of audit analytic software, ACL Services, has a saying that "the truth is in the transactions." This saying goes to the fundamental premise of CAATs — that no matter how your system is configured or what your employees are telling you is happening, the data ultimately sheds light on reality.

By evaluating the transactional data stored in SAP, you can see potential problems that might otherwise be hidden. For example, a traditional segregation of duties analysis, which ties users to the SAP roles/profiles to which they have been assigned and subsequently the transactions and authorization objects associated with these roles/profiles, can be complex and time consuming. By directly querying SAP master data and transaction tables, however, you can quickly spot potential SOD violations where the same user created a vendor and posted invoices to that same vendor. This analysis can be accomplished purely based on the user ID that SAP records with each of these transactions, with no need to review SAP security settings.

This same analytic test would also catch situations that would not be detected through traditional SOD analysis. For example, imagine a situation where the user was legitimately part of the vendor master data creation team, and subsequently transferred to accounts payable (where they legitimately had the ability to process vendor invoices). Direct data analysis using CAATs would identify this potential conflict, as the "created by" or "modified by" ID recorded in the vendor master record would be the same as the ID that processed invoices against that vendor. If the user did not have the ability to maintain vendor master data at the same time that he had the ability to process invoices, however, (the user roles/profiles were appropriately changed when they transferred departments) this type of exception would not be discovered by directly examining SAP security settings. Thus, the use of CAATs in this situation can find potential issues where it may not initially seem that a problem exists.

Just an Indicator

Results returned from CAATs generally do not provide conclusive evidence that a problem has occurred, but rather highlight situations where indicators exist that might point to a problem. Each potential exception needs to be examined to determine if a problem has actually occurred.

8.2.1 Benefit of CAATs

When compared to traditional audit techniques, often based on rotational audit scheduling (for example, evaluating a specific business process every two years) and sampling procedures (examining a subset of items and drawing a correlation between observations and what may be expected in the entire population), CAATs provide a number of significant advantages:

▶ 100% testing — by going directly against SAP data, CAATs can test every transaction instead of just a sampling of transactions. For example, rather than taking a sample of POs and determining whether the approver was within his authorization limits, CAATs can examine every single PO approval for compliance. This ensures more reliable testing results.

▶ Improved testing frequency — Because CAATs are essentially a set of computerized queries against business data, once designed they can be easily automated and set to run on a schedule basis. For example, whereas a traditional payroll audit may occur once every several years, CAAT testing against payroll data could be set to run along with every payroll run. This helps problems be detected quickly so the underlying issues can be resolved before resulting in a snowball effect.

Think Your SAP System and Data is Clean? Think Again!

Some of the success of CAATs as an audit technique is driven by the mistaken belief that many people have that if their systems are configured to prevent problems, then the opportunities for issues are few. In reality, a wide variety of situations could result in an auditor finding problems through CAATs:

▶ Other systems — Other systems feeding data to SAP may not be as well controlled or as properly configured as your SAP system.

▶ Improvements in SAP — If your SAP system configuration has matured over time, the control configuration you use today may have been different in the past — possibly impacting the integrity of older transactions or master data.

▶ Business changes — The configuration settings and parameters/tolerance levels you currently use may have been appropriate at the time they were configured, but giving changing business conditions may no longer be relevant to your environment.

▶ Warning messages — Users may ignore warning messages and process duplicate transactions or post erroneous data, either intentionally or through neglect.

▶ Ineffective monitoring — If appropriate personnel are not effectively reviewing SAP exception reports and key information, then problems that should normally be caught through the normal course of business may go undetected.

For these issues and more, the use of direct data interrogation as an audit technique can provide value to your business.

▶ Data correlation — Most CAAT software tools can read data from any source — an important feature when analyzing business data for audit and control purposes. Despite having highly integrated systems like SAP in most organizations today, rarely does an organization find itself relying exclusively on a single system, and as a result, organizations often lack the ability to effectively correlate insight gain from one system with data contained in another. For example, a useful audit test would be to compare the daily time recorded by hourly employees in SAP to the information contained in the organization's physical security system, where employees use badge scanners to enter and exit the building. Such insight can lead to interesting audit findings, but rarely is all of this information stored centrally in SAP.

Because of these benefits, CAATs allow auditors to provide more timely, more reliable, and better overall insight into current business conditions.

8.2.2 Examples of CAATs in Common Business Cycles

Audit testing using CAATs can provide beneficial results in any business cycle, and in fact is valid for any type of process where electronic data is available.

Within the financial reporting cycle, possible tests might highlight transactions where:

▶ High-dollar journal entries are posted near period-end (possibly in an attempt to manipulate financial reporting)

▶ Direct general ledger postings occur at odd times, such as at night or during holidays (possibly in an attempt to hide these postings)

▶ Duplicate journal entries may have been posted (likely the result of error)

▶ Clerks with a high number of reversing entries (could be a training issue, or an attempt to hide fraud)

▶ A general ledger posting hits an account that has not been used in a very long time (possibly the result of error or fraud)

▶ An SAP general ledger posting not associated with a typical allocation (for example, with allocating IT costs across departments) is split among a large number of accounts (potentially in a fraudulent attempt to minimize the likelihood that it's found during an account review)

Within the order-to-cash cycle, similar tests can be created to highlight potential problems within this business process. For example:

- Sales order cancellations near period-end (may indicate an attempt by sales personnel to manipulate sales numbers)
- Dormant customer accounts posting a large sale near period-end (may indicate another technique for fraudulently manipulating sales)
- A customer credit increase, followed shortly by a sale to that customer and subsequently followed by a credit limit decrease (potentially highlighting an attempt to manipulate credit limits)
- Customer credit memos in excess of recent customer purchases (may be the result of error or fraud)

Similarly, the purchase-to-pay cycle can have a number of valuable analytics for highlighting potential problems:

- Vendors with an address, phone number, or bank account similar to an employee address, phone, or bank (may be an indicator of fraud)
- Split purchases, where the aggregate amount of POs or invoices exceeds the employee's individual authorization limit (perhaps an attempt to circumvent authorization limits by creating multiple purchases)
- Multiple vendors with the same address, phone, or bank account (a good indicator of possible duplicate vendor)
- Invoice numbers from the same vendor, occurring on a near-unbroken sequence (possible indicator of fraud)

As you can see, the possibilities for CAATs are nearly endless. For almost any problem that you can identify, analytic testing procedures can be developed to identify the situation and investigate appropriately.

The Secret to Designing Effective CAATs

Auditors are not the only people who can benefit from the use of CAATs. By developing your own CAAT-type testing, you can proactively identify potential problems and resolve them well before your auditors come on-site. The secret to developing this type of testing is to first think of an internal control (or conversely a risk) that you are looking to gain assurance on. Next, ask yourself two related questions:

- If this control were to fail, how might it look in our data?
- If this control were operating as intended, is there anything in our data that would help indicate this fact?

If either of these questions can be answered, then you have the basis for designing your own CAATs.

8.2.3   Using CAATs in an SAP Environment

On a fairly simplistic level, you can perform some basic CAATs against your own SAP data using a variety of SAP tools. Provided you have appropriate access through SAP security, you can use SAQ Query (transaction SQ01) to execute some simple CAATs. Within the QuickViewer, for example, you can query an SAP table to look for potential indicators of problems like those we have just described. For example, Figure 8.4: Building a Query through QuickViewer shows an example of where the user is building a query against table T000 (the table containing information about SAP clients), to look for recent changes to SAP client settings. In this case, the query could be set to prompt the user for a "Last Changed by" user ID, allowing the detection of changes to the client table by unexpected users, or the "Date of Last Change" field to identify changes that to client settings that might have occurred since the last "approved" set of changes.

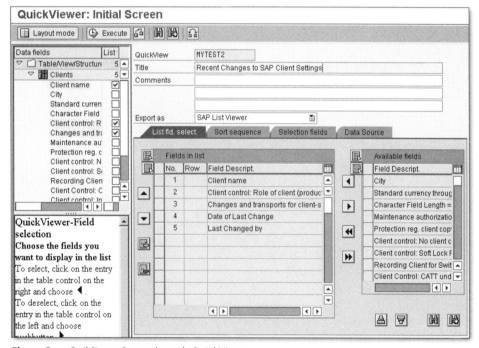

Figure 8.4   Building a Query through QuickViewer

For slightly more complex analysis, you could use the Infoset Query option, also within Transaction SQ01. Of course, because these queries run against your production SAP instance, care must be taken to ensure that they are optimized and will not have a production impact — and as a result, many organizations tightly control access to develop ad-hoc queries through SAP Query.

Using SAP Business Warehouse

If your organization uses the SAP NetWeaver Business Warehouse (SAP NetWeaver BW), you may be able to write queries within this application to also mimic the functionality of simple CAATs. Because many organizations replicate only a subset of their SAP data within SAP NetWeaver BW, first, confirm that the warehouse contains the type of data you need to build the analysis, and that data is refreshed in a sufficiently timely manner to meet your needs, before investing much time.

While you can likely generate simplistic CAATs through user queries, more complex analysis involving data correlation or complicated table joins may be best performed through custom ABAP programs. Of course, ABAP development generally follows your organization's SAP change control process, and likely involves scheduling and prioritizing development along with other changes that your organization may need — thus the frequency at which you can develop new analyses is likely low.

8.2.4 Specialized CAAT Tools

Most likely, if your auditor is testing using CAATs, he is not using direct SAP functionality. The sophisticated analysis that many auditors require can be difficult to develop directly in SAP. As such, most auditors use third-party programs, such as ACL or IDEA, for developing and running audit analytics against SAP data.

Compatibility with SAP

The more popular third-party audit analytic tools are directly compatible with SAP. ACL Direct Link, for example, is certified for SAP NetWeaver® and provides direct and seamless access to SAP ERP data, while still restricting the user to the access associated with his SAP user ID.

In addition to allowing the auditor to perform his own analysis with limited reliance on technical SAP resources, specialized CAAT tools have several other advantages. These tools contain audit-specific functionality not found in most other query tools. For example, the auditor can identify suspicious patterns in numbers, based purely on the frequency of digits, using a function based on Benford's Law. Auditors can perform sophisticated duplicates testing with "sounds like" functionality to flag records even if they are not spelled the same. And when sampling is warranted (such as when the auditor needs to verify inventory), these applications provide statistically valid sampling functions.

Specialized software tools for CAATs typically have the ability to read data from practically any source, allowing correlation between not only information in SAP but also information in your organization's other systems or in third-party system. The later point can be an advantage when, for example, you are matching your vendor list to a list of prohibited vendors posted on relevant government websites. Analysis such as this can serve as additional checks on top of controls that you may configure directly in SAP.

Because these tools are extremely powerful, auditor friendly, and inexpensive to implement, they are popular in the audit community. The increase in auditor comfort with technology has also facilitated the increasing adoption of CAATs for even complex audits like an SAP audit. Because both ACL and IDEA dominate the marketplace, you will very likely find that your auditor uses one of these tools. This can be a significant advantage if you choose to leverage one of these tools for your own testing purposes — being able to leverage tests that your auditor has already created can provide you with immediate results, requiring limited additional development.

8.3   SAP BusinessObjects GRC Solutions

In the last several years, SAP has invested heavily in solutions for GRC. SAP now provides a suite of solutions that, if implemented correctly, can facilitate your ability to not only survive an audit but also stay on top of the ever-changing risks in your organization. Highlights include:

▶ SAP BusinessObjects Access Control — Specific to security and segregation of duties, this tool is a must-have to survive an SAP security audit. In our experience, the complexity of SAP security is such that it's nearly impossible to address all potential audit concerns using standard functionality. SAP BusinessObjects Access Control makes ongoing management of segregation of duties, privileged user access, and powerful transactions a breeze.

> **More Than a Handful of Security Issues**
>
> When first implementing SAP BusinessObjects Access Control, many organizations find that they have thousands of potential security problems. Prioritizing and remediating these issues becomes a priority — your auditor will be pleased that you are monitoring security issues but will want to see continued improvement on addressing these findings. Focus your attention on the areas of highest risk, and put in place and monitor compensating controls on those problems that you have identified but have not yet had a chance to resolve.

- ▶ SAP BusinessObjects Process Control — Providing the ability to automatically monitor configuration settings and transactions, this tool is gaining popularity within the SAP GRC portfolio. Early versions of this tool provided basic functionality but failed to be comprehensive, but from what we have seen, SAP has made significant progress building out functionality and enhancing the value of SAP BusinessObjects Process Control. This is a tool to watch, because the direction that SAP has chosen for the product will both support audit success and, more importantly, enhance your ability to proactively manage your business risks.

- ▶ SAP BusinessObjects Risk Management — Supporting risk-related strategic planning, SAP Risk Management allows organizations to identify, monitor, and react to critical risk information. This tool allows both quantitative and qualitative analysis, as well as dashboard-style reporting. As we described in Chapter 1, internal controls are a response to business risk, and SAP Risk Management provides the platform by which you can make your most important risk-related decisions.

- ▶ SAP BusinessObjects Global Trade Services — Facilitating efficiency and compliance related to international trade, this solution is ideal for organizations with complex trade agreements or cross-border issues.

- ▶ SAP BusinessObjects Environment, Health, and Safety Management — This solution helps organizations manage health and safety risks, as well as the emerging area of environmental risks.

Much can be said about the SAP BusinessObjects GRC solutions, and their ability to facilitate audit success. If you are interested in learning more about this emerging suite from SAP, read the book *SAP Governance, Risk, and Compliance* by Sabine Scholer and Olaf Zink. You can also read more about specific solutions within this portfolio with the books *Cross-Enterprise Integration with SAP GRC Access Control*, and *Implementing SAP BusinessObjects Global Trade Services*.

8.4 Continuous Auditing and Continuous Monitoring

While not new, the concepts of *continuous auditing* (CA) and *continuous monitoring* (CM) gained significant momentum in the audit and GRC disciplines over the last few years. While the end-user audience is fundamentally different (continuous auditing is focused on optimizing audit processes, while continuous monitoring is typically implemented by functional business areas), the premise of these techniques are the same. Both support the use of technology to monitor risks and internal controls on a near real-time basis. Think of CA/CM as the evolution of CAATs we discussed in Section 8.2, Computer Assisted Audit Techniques (CAATs) — putting these techniques on steroids by scheduling and automating tests to run with minimal manual interaction.

Continuous auditing and continuous monitoring have the potential to provide significant business benefit by offering:

- Improved effectiveness of risk/control assessments
- Timely determination if internal controls are operating effectively
- Rapid identification of specific deficiencies and anomalies
- Reduction in errors and fraud
- Increased monitoring consistency
- Reduction in costs and revenue leakage
- Documented evidence for internal and external auditors
- Reduction in ongoing compliance costs

Potentially, the largest benefit, however, is the ability to identify potential problems before they escalate, and allow management to resolve the underlying issues before they cause significant and sustained harm to the organization.

Because testing routines are run on a continuous basis, organizations must put processes in place to ensure that the results identified are being regularly investigated and resolved. Continuous monitoring software generally includes the ability to track and manage issues, escalate exceptions (for example, route exceptions to higher levels of management if not resolved within defined thresholds), and adjust parameters to exclude false positives.

SAP BusinessObjects Process Control provides continuous auditing and continuous monitoring capabilities. Other third-party tools exist as well, including those from the CAAT auditing software vendors. Continuous auditing and monitoring has the potential for providing significant business benefit, and should be strongly considered by any organization seriously looking to monitor and manage their business risks and controls.

8.5   Summary

In this chapter, we shared three common tools used by auditors to find problems in your SAP system and data, and also shared information about an emerging trend toward continuous auditing and monitoring. We discussed the Audit Information System, a free utility available to all SAP customers that you can leverage to identify potential problems in advance of an audit. We shared the popular audit technique,

Computer Assisted Audit Techniques (CAATs), and provided a variety of examples about the types of problems CAATs can identify. We demonstrated how basic CAATs can be performed using tools readily available within SAP, and highlighted the specialized software applications available for more advanced analysis. We also walked through the SAP BusinessObjects GRC solutions suite, and indicated where you can go for more information. Finally, we discussed the trends in continuous auditing and monitoring, and described how these techniques can provide sustained business benefits.

In the next and final chapter, we share a few final preparatory steps that you can take in advance of an audit to be better prepared.

"By failing to prepare, you are preparing to fail." — *Ben Franklin*

9   Final Audit Preparations

If you've followed the advice set forth in this book, applying not just the tactical recommendations but also the principles behind this advice, you are fundamentally ready for an SAP audit. As you get closer to the date of your upcoming SAP audit, a little extra time spent preparing in advance will pay dividends once the audit begins. Advance preparation can shorten the overall audit cycle, reduce the time that the auditor needs from you and your team, and sets the stage for a positive, productive audit. While it's possible to "pass" your audit without these additional steps, spending sufficient time preparing should increase your likelihood of success.

In this chapter, we share a final set of simple steps that you can implement to prepare for an SAP audit, and make the process as smooth as possible. We walk through information to gather in advance, and give examples of how this can be effectively presented to the auditor to minimize internal time required to explain procedures and practices. We discuss the benefits of management testing in advance of the audits, and highlight special considerations around data privacy and security of auditor data, training the auditor, and requests for direct SAP access. We also share advice from a group of experts — people who have been both auditors and auditees — and provide tips based on decades of experience.

If you are about to go through an SAP audit, this chapter is a must read. By the end of this chapter, you'll have a checklist of information and supporting documents to make available to your auditor. You'll understand ways to prepare your audit team for the upcoming audit process, and you'll have a specific plan for preparing for your next SAP audit.

9.1   Overview

By following the recommendations and considerations outlined in this book, you have set the foundation for a relatively painless SAP audit (at least, as much as any audit can be painless). While you are fundamentally ready for your next audit, some additional advance preparation can make the audit process flow more smoothly, and reduce the time commitment required by you and your team.

Once you have learned of an upcoming SAP audit, spend additional time before the audit in preparation mode, in what we'll term the *audit preparation phase*. While no hard-and-fast rule applies, many will tell you that an hour spent preparing in advance for the audit can save two to four hours during the actual audit, so it's time well spent. In general, your audit preparation steps will focus on three key areas:

- Documentation
- Systems
- Employees

You'll want to prepare a set of important documentation for the auditor, giving him a faster start and reducing the time that you and your staff spend responding to basic inquiries. You'll prepare SAP and other relevant systems for the audit — ensuring that audit IDs and other setup processes are ready for the auditor to be on-site. You'll also prepare your employees to address audit questions and understand their roles in the audit process. We discuss each of these categories throughout this chapter.

> **Preparation Goal**
>
> When making final preparations for the SAP audit, the key is to take your information, your processes, and your employees, and prepare them for your auditor's assessment. A subtle shift in focus from the way that you operate to the way that your auditor can most efficiently review how you operate can cut down on audit time significantly.

These preparation steps are less about adding new internal controls to your organization and more about validating and communicating the controls that you have in a manner designed to streamline the audit process. While you can still add additional controls and improve existing controls prior the start of an audit, to a large extent, it's too late to make significant improvements. The best strategy at this point is to honestly assess where you are, have documentation that supports current reality (not where you would like to be), and be in a position to discuss with your auditor both known problems and potential areas of concern.

9.2 Pre-Planning

In Chapter 1, we discuss how every audit can vary based on audit objectives, and your experience with one SAP audit may drastically differ from the next. As such, as soon as you first learn about the audit, set up a meeting with your auditor to discuss the process and begin making arrangements for having the auditor on-site. The sooner that you can have this meeting, the better you'll be able to adapt your audit preparation steps to the specific audit that you'll be encountering.

Take the Communication Initiative

While many auditors, as part of the normal audit process, will send an announcement letter and set up a pre-audit planning meeting in advance of the audit, don't sit around waiting to hear from your auditor. As soon as you learn that your SAP system may be under review, take the lead by contacting your auditor and setting up a time to discuss the upcoming review. Being proactive can't hurt, and in many cases, this first interaction can help to set a positive tone for the remainder of the audit.

Certain questions are important to have answered by your auditor sooner rather than later. These questions relate to the planned scope, duration, and timing of the audit, and include:

▶ When is the audit tentatively slated to start, and how long is it expected to last?

▶ What specific areas of SAP will be under review? If this audit has been conducted in the past, will there be any changes in focus from prior reviews?

▶ What time period is being covered by the audit?

▶ What information can we provide to you (the auditor) in advance so you can be best prepared once you come on-site?

The Audit Period

The historic period of time over which the auditor will be interested in evaluating SAP settings and related processes is called the audit period. An SAP audit could be a point-in-time (e.g., as of December 31) or over a period of time (e.g., January 1 to December 31). Knowing that the audit period is important will directly influence your preparation effort. If an audit covers a period of time, then every setting, transaction, and manual activity during that period could be under audit scrutiny. Thus, in your preparation, provide the auditor with information on any significant changes (positive or negative) to settings, policies, or procedures during this period.

The answers to these four questions will tell you how much time you have to prepare, and where to focus your attention. As such, getting to these answers quickly is important. Also useful, but not as time sensitive as the previous three core questions, are answers to the following questions:

▶ What is triggering this audit?

▶ Who will be receiving the audit report?

▶ What type of time commitment do you expect from our team, and are there certain individuals that you'll need to spend more time with than others?

▶ If multiple auditors will be involved, who is responsible for what parts of the audit, and how much time is each expected to be involved?

▶ How much will each auditor know about our systems and processes before coming on-site and interacting with the team?

▶ What level of SAP experience and understanding will each auditor possess, and what gaps would you expect that our team needs to fill?

Influencing Audit Team Composition

For recurring audits, where you may be involved with the same audit group on a yearly or otherwise rotational basis, you often develop familiarity with various auditors. If you have had a great audit experience from a particular auditor, feel free to request him again. Conversely, if you had any challenges with a particular auditor in the past (perhaps the result of personality conflicts or issues raised that were not thoroughly investigated and ultimately inaccurate), ask about having the auditor replaced with someone who will work better with your team. You may not always be able to influence the audit team composition, but you may be surprised how flexible the audit group can be if you work politely with them early on.

The answers from these questions will help you direct your activities in the period leading up to the audit. We discuss these activities in the remaining sections of this chapter.

9.3   Documentation: Preparing an Audit Binder

The concept of an *audit binder* is simple — to gather a core set of information relevant to an audit in a single, easy-to-reference location. Preparing an audit binder, to be provided to your auditor in advance or at the start of an audit, is one of the easiest things that you can do to reduce overall audit time. The audit binder minimizes team disruption by anticipating, as much as possible, the type of information that the auditor will need to see and provide it to the auditor at the start of the audit. This approach reduces unnecessary inquiries of you and your team, and also ensures that the auditor has the most accurate information. Having information available in advance of the audit can help avoid scrambling at the last minute to gather requested details, and also reduce the risk that outdated or inaccurate information is provided to the auditor by employees rushing to get something out quickly.

Some information can be easily anticipated in advance and included in the audit binder. As discussed in Chapter 1, during the audit planning phase, your auditor typically gathers information that will define the audit scope and test program, as well as prepare himself with relevant questions pertaining to your audit. Additionally, the auditor is likely to review a certain set of documentation as part of the audit. Information that describes your SAP system and details supporting processes falls into these categories, and thus it's important to populate it into the audit binder.

Using Electronic Content Management Systems

While in this chapter we discuss the audit binder in terms of a paper-based hardcopy document, you can apply the audit binder concept electronically as well. Many organizations already use electronic content management systems for managing policies, procedures, and other corporate documents. Some content management systems also facilitate control self-assessments and manage audit-related documentation. Elements of SAP BusinessObjects Process Control can store and manage some of this information as well. The key emphasis in this section is less about the format that you provide the information in, and more about the information that you make available to the auditor at the start of the audit process.

The contents of the audit binder can generally be divided into the following sections:

▶ SAP system information

▶ SAP support team organization details

▶ Policies and procedures (including approved exceptions)

▶ Self-assessment procedures and results

▶ Known weaknesses and mitigation procedures

Each of these sections would then contain the most current information related to these topics. Because much of this information changes over time, once you have created the audit binder, at the start of every audit you would typically update the information to the most current details. We discuss each of these sections next.

9.3.1 SAP System Information

For a technical SAP audit, your auditor will need to know details about your current *SAP system* and supporting infrastructure. At a minimum, this information would include the following:

▶ SAP version(s) and release number(s) for each instance of SAP

▶ Clients in each SAP instance

▶ Active company codes in the production client

▶ Installed components, including:

▶ When installed

▶ Any problems or workarounds

▶ Scheduled upgrades and/or other changes

▶ Customization details, if any

▶ Database(s) and version(s)

▶ Server specifications for application server, database server, and other servers supporting SAP

▶ Network diagram covering SAP and interfaces to/from SAP

This information gives your auditor a good picture of your environment, and will help him plan a better audit and avoid asking questions that could have been addressed in advance. Gather much of this information yourself, although some of the latter bulleted items may require the assistance of your organization's information technology department.

SAP Version(s) and Release Number(s) for Each Instance of SAP

Each version of SAP has differences that can affect audit procedures performed. Releases do not dramatically impact audit procedures but can impact recommendations. SAP version and release numbers can be accessed from the menu bar using SYSTEM • STATUS, as shown in Figure 9.1: Determining Your SAP Release Number. You'll need this for each instance of SAP that you are running in your organization.

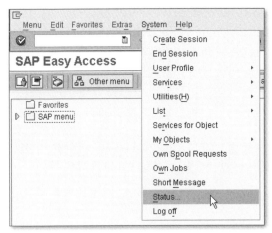

Figure 9.1 Determining Your SAP Release Number

Clients in Each SAP Instance

Clients in SAP can be productive or be used as part of the development and testing cycle. Knowing which clients contain production information (some organizations have several) and which are used for testing and development is important from an audit planning perspective. Each active SAP client will be important as the auditor reviews general computer controls (GCCs), as discussed in Chapter 4, and separate audit procedures may need to be performed on each productive client. A diagram depicting how changes flow between clients during the SAP transport process (e.g., DEV > QAS > UAT > PRD), is helpful — create one if you do not already maintain one in your organization.

Active Company Codes in the Production Client

Company code information is also vital for the auditor, because certain control settings that we have described in this book are company code dependent. Quickly understanding what company codes are relevant to the audit will help your auditor plan and test more effectively. You can list out company codes yourself, or provide company code information directly from SAP by providing the contents of table T000, through Transactions SE16 or SE16n (as shown in Figure 9.2: Providing Company Code Details). The latter method is preferable because it ensures that you don't miss anything or accidentally transpose numbers, causing the audit to question the accuracy of all the information in the audit binder.

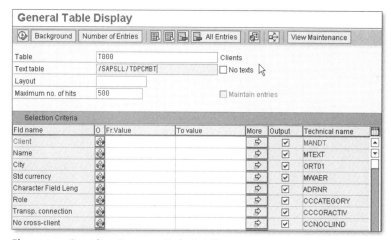

Figure 9.2 Providing Company Code Details

Installed components

As for SAP components, both installation and customization details are important. The original installation date will tell the auditor how long you have used that particular component, and different audit tests are applicable for new implementations vs. more mature installations. If you have had any specific problems where you had to develop manual or programmatic workarounds, a brief discussion of these will also help the auditor determine scope and testing procedures. Areas like this where you may not be using standard SAP functionality, or using it in a way other than intended, are critical to communicate early. Failure to disclose this information could result in the auditor spending a lot of time in areas that are not relevant to your environment, or with processes that have a purpose but may not be common to what the auditor has typically seen. Additionally, if any upgrades or other system changes have been scheduled, making these changes known is also important. For many types of audits, if the system is about to change, it may make sense to defer the start of the audit.

Customization Details

Understanding any custom ABAP programs that you have developed will help the auditor determine the risks associated with each of these changes and whether any specific audit consideration should be given to customizations. Some customizations could result in new transactions that should be included in testing procedures. Others may create reports that should be assessed for integrity. The auditor may also examine security settings associated with the custom programs. When developing your list of customizations, be inclusive — if the auditor later determines that customizations have been made beyond what you have detailed, it may cause him to question the integrity of other information that you've provided and necessitate more thorough audit testing procedures.

Database(s) and Version(s)

As part of the GCC review discussed in Chapter 4, your auditor will likely also examine controls at the database and network layers. As discussed in that chapter, controls within SAP are only reliable for transactions and other changes flowing through the SAP interface — changes made outside of SAP effectively bypass these controls. Your auditor will likely look at database-level controls, including restrictive use of privileged users, database maintenance procedures, monitoring of direct database changes, and other similar processes. Understanding the database version and patch level can help the auditor assess inherent risks at the database layer, and plan the audit appropriately.

Server Specifications for Application Server, Database Server, and Other Servers Supporting SAP

Also as part of the GCCs review, the auditor will likely review controls at the network and server level. This would generally be a fairly technical review, looking for gaps in security, problems in patch levels, and other general administrative issues. Not all auditors will need (or ask) for this information, but because it can sometimes take time to pull together with IT, gather this information and have it ready in advance.

Network Diagram Covering SAP and Interfaces to/from SAP

In Chapter 4, we also discussed the issue of interfaces and the impact that these can have on SAP. SAP processing can be complete and accurate, but if SAP receives incomplete or inaccurate information, these problems ultimately end up in SAP. A comprehensive SAP audit will typically look at controls over interfaces, and in some cases, may go all the way into the originating and receiving systems as well. Having a current diagram showing these interfaces and connections will greatly assist the auditor and prevent numerous questions.

> **Added Benefit**
>
> Surprisingly, few organizations, in our experience, maintain network diagrams (in addition to much of the information proposed for this section of the audit binder). Failure to maintain such information raises an audit red flag — maintaining systems can be tough as personnel change if good documentation and other communication vehicles fail to exist.

9.3.2 SAP Support Team Organization Details

During your SAP audit, your auditor will be doing more than just looking at SAP configuration and system documentation. You auditor will also need to speak with the people who support SAP and use the system in various capacities. In this section of your audit binder, put information such as:

- The organization chart for the group that supports and manages SAP
- Contact list for key SAP support personnel, including:
  - Project manager
  - Head of development
  - Head of QA
  - Security administrator
  - SAP Basis administrator
  - Employees comprising the SAP steering committee
- SAP experience and training profile for key support personnel
- Calendar of upcoming vacations and key events

As part of your pre-planning conversation with your auditor, also discuss communication channels for the audit. For example, some organizations choose to have a primary point-of-contact through which the auditor can arrange all appointments and meetings (making sure the auditor is speaking with the right people for his inquiry). Others prefer that the auditor contacts relevant employees directly. Regardless of your chosen protocols, the information in this section of the binder will help the auditor understand who he will need to contact at various points during the audit process, how long he has worked with SAP, and when he is available.

The Organization Chart for the Group That Supports and Manages SAP

A good organization chart is one of the first places an auditor will want to look to understand the SAP support process. If your SAP support function is large, your org chart does not need to include every single employee within the support group. Ideally, however, include the major functions along with the people who lead those functions. Your org chart might extend into the business areas as well, if functional team leads or other crossover-type personnel are not technically within the support function but involved with support SAP nonetheless.

Contact List for Key SAP Support Personnel

Even if you'll be centrally arranging meetings between your auditor and other key personnel, your auditor needs a way of contacting employees directly. Failure to provide the auditor with a direct contact method could be interpreted as an attempt to influence or obstruct the audit process. If this information is already maintained within an employee directory or other similar reference, don't recreate it; however, ensure that the auditor has appropriate access and has been provided instructions for finding employees on the organization chart.

SAP Experience and Training Profile for Key Support Personnel

Most audits assess the competency of personnel involved. Showing the auditor that SAP support personnel have the appropriate background and training for their roles will help in that process. The personnel profile does not need to be an entire resume, but it should include information about their education, relevant work experience, prior experience with SAP, and additional SAP training they have received since joining your organization. Competency assessments are difficult for an auditor to perform, but in addition to the skills and experience you document on paper, the auditor will additionally evaluate key employees as he works with them during the audit. The section on preparing your team for the audit later in this chapter will help with that aspect of the assessment.

Calendar of Upcoming Vacations and Key Events

While it sounds simple, this item is an extremely important component of the audit binder. Auditors often juggle multiple schedules, and delays due to unanticipated vacations or other events can cause the audit to drag out longer than desired. In addition to vacations, key events to communicate include:

- ▶ Recurring meetings (where employees may be occupied or where you wish the auditor to attend)
- ▶ Scheduled training, conferences, or other off-site events
- ▶ Anticipated dates where team members may be unavailable (e.g., key times during a maintenance cycle)

By getting this information to the auditor in advance, you are better able to ensure that the time you and your team spend with the auditor occurs when you have the most flexibility and can accommodate audit demands.

9.3.3 Policies and Procedures

The next section of the audit binder typically includes a current set of *policies and procedures*. If your organization uses an intranet site or other electronic means to store policies and procedures, you don't need to recreate this information — simply point the auditor to that location (after ensuring he has access). At a minimum, provide policies and procedures related to:

- ▶ Information security
- ▶ Change management and development
- ▶ System operations and monitoring

These procedures should include any corporate-wide details, as well as information that may be specific to SAP. Additionally, include any procedures related to how users interact with SAP. As mentioned in Chapter 4, your auditor will want to ensure that your everyday SAP activities are consistent with your organization's defined policies and procedures.

Policies and Procedures Best Practices

If you can influence the content of your policies and procedures, ensure that they contain the following elements:

- ▶ Effective date
- ▶ Version number and date last updated
- ▶ Change history
- ▶ Audience (locations and departments to which the policy applies)
- ▶ Related policies and procedures

If you have been granted any policy exceptions for SAP configuration or operations, also include the details of these exceptions in the audit binder. Because the auditor will likely compare your processes to these defined policies and procedures, failure to include details on policy exceptions will result in unnecessary audit effort.

9.3.4 Self-Assessment Procedures and Results

Throughout this book, we have recommended a variety of *self-assessment procedures*. One of the best things that you can do to survive an SAP audit is to honestly evaluate and assess your own performance. This process is typically known as a *self-assessment*. You may be surprised after your first self-assessment as to how much you find out about your own operations.

The term "self" in self-assessment can be a bit of a misnomer. While a self-assessment can include an individual's evaluation of his own performance, in audit terminology, the term also more broadly refers to an organization's or department's evaluation of their own performance (not necessarily by the individual performing the task being evaluated).

> **Self-Assessment Side Benefits**
>
> In addition to helping you better understand your own operations and state of preparedness for an audit, a self-assessment can provide an additional benefit. Depending on the type of audit and how well you have performed and documented your self-assessment procedures, your auditor may actually be able to place some reliance on your self-assessment process and reduce audit testing as a result.
>
> To receive this type of benefit, talk to your auditor about what he would need to reduce his testing procedures. Small adjustments to procedures that you may be performing already can potentially reduce audit effort. However, if your auditor indicates that he might be able to use some of your self-assessment procedures, then he will have to do some testing on your self-assessment process. If your auditor finds that the results from his independent testing differs from your self-assessment, not only can he not place any reliance on the self-assessment, but he will likely increase overall audit testing because he is now forced to question the integrity of all the information that you provide. Don't cheat on self-assessments — the ramifications can be harsh.

Self-assessment, sometimes referred to as *Control Self-Assessment* (CSA), has been recognized by the audit community for decades. In the United States, self-assessment procedures have become increasingly popular in the last few years as the Securities and Exchange Commission (SEC) has recognized the validity of self-assessment procedures for certain types of lower-risk control testing related to the Sarbanes-Oxley Act. Whether officially termed "self-assessment," or part of general management monitoring procedures, in specific scenarios auditors can and do reduce their work as a result of self-assessment procedures.

As it relates to the audit binder, include information about self-assessments that you have performed during the audit period. You should include:

- An overview of your self-assessment process
- Qualifications of individual assessors (if using a peer-review process)
- Results and follow-up actions

Including this information in the audit binder will help the auditor determine to what extent, if any, he can rely on your procedures. Even if the auditor will be unable to reduce audit work as a result of your self-assessment, including this level of detail is likely to generate a favorable audit impression due to your overall organization (increasing the likelihood that if you are organized in this regard, you are organized related to other areas for which you are responsible) and preparedness.

An Overview of Your Self-Assessment Process

Documenting your self-assessment process is important, because procedures can vary widely from organization to organization. Be as detailed as possible related to these procedures. For example, if there are specific questions or tests you perform, include those in this section. If your self-assessment follows a structured, schedule process, then describe that process in detail. Flowcharts and timelines can be helpful as well.

Qualifications of Individual Assessors

In conjunction with a self-assessment of an employee's own performance and compliance with procedures, many organizations also perform a periodic peer review — someone independent of the process being evaluated performs the evaluation and provides feedback and recommendations. For a self-assessment process to be effective, the individuals performing the evaluation need to be competent and qualified. If you perform a periodic review of your SAP security processes, for example, but that review is conducted by someone with no background in SAP security, then the results may be questionable.

By highlighting the qualifications of the individual assessors (and in particular, qualifications related to the areas that they are assessing), you provide the auditor with important details that may influence whether your work can also be relied on for the audit. If you have done any training related to your self-assessment process, those details are valuable as well. Pulling together this documentation also helps you assess how much reliance you may be able to place on the results for your own internal evaluations.

Results and Follow-up Actions

The quality of your self-assessment process is measured in part by the findings you uncover and the follow-up actions you take as a result of the process. By showing the auditor that your self-assessment process does result in valuable information that you use to improve the business, you increase the auditor's confidence in your processes. As you determine follow-up actions related to your self-assessment, also follow-through to resolution and complete these action steps.

9.3.5 Known Weaknesses and Mitigation Procedures

The most non-productive thing that can happen during an audit is that your auditor spends time testing, investigating, and reporting on concerns of which you are both *aware*, and have either already addressed through *mitigating procedures* or have plans to address. This wastes your auditor's time, it wastes your time, it wastes your team's time, and it wastes management time. In this section of the binder, document issues where:

▶ Segregation of duties issues exist

▶ SAP configured control settings are less than ideal

▶ Processes for supporting SAP could be strengthened

Beyond just documenting known issues, however, also indicate what you have done to mitigate the risks associated with these issues. This allows the auditor to determine what level of additional testing, if any, may be required.

No Such Thing as a Free Pass

Don't be surprised if an issue or concern that you disclosed to your auditor in the audit binder later appears in the final audit report. Remember from Chapter 1 that auditors have an obligation to ensure that recipients of the audit report understand the relevant risks related to the audit objective. If something you have disclosed relates to a type of risk that must be reported, and your auditor does not feel that risk has been effectively mitigated, then the auditor is obligated to make mention of it in the audit report. Don't use this as an excuse to not disclose issues or concerns, however. The benefit that you'll receive through full disclosure will far outweigh problems caused by items on an audit report — particularly if the auditor is also able to disclose that verifiable plans are underway to address the issue.

Segregation of Duties Issues Exist

Companies running SAP commonly find themselves in situations where, for various reasons, ideal segregation of duties does not exist at the time of an audit. Perhaps a small division does not have enough employees to effectively segregate key duties.

Maybe turnover has created a gap that has not yet been filled. You might have inherited an SAP system with numerous security problems, and you have not yet been able to fix them all.

If in your SAP system you already know that certain people have roles or profiles that violate traditional segregation of duties requirements, document these for your auditor. We have discussed in earlier chapters the importance of SAP security as a control, and how a segregation of duties analysis will be part of any SAP audit. By communicating known issues up-front, you may be able to save on audit investigation time. Of course, given the risks that segregation of duties issues can pose, also describe additional controls that you have put into place to mitigate this risk. Perhaps you have put workflow in place to route transactions from these employees for a secondary review. Maybe you have established a special monitoring process over these employees. Whatever the case, ensure that these mitigating procedures are also included in your documentation so that your auditor has the ability to assess their adequacies.

SAP Configured Control Settings Are Less Than Ideal

As you have read through this book, you may have identified additional SAP configurable controls that you are not using, or not using to their fullest. Documenting these in advance saves the time that it would take your auditor to discover and document these for you. And by including your mitigation procedures, you also demonstrate to your auditor that you are already taking action to address these issues.

For example, assume that you have not configured payment tolerances into SAP. This increases the risk that errors or attempted abuse could result in an erroneous payment. You could mitigate this risk by having a more thorough review of payment transactions. Including this information in the audit binder could result in the auditor not spending any time assessing configured SAP payment tolerances because you have already indicated they are not currently in use. The auditor would then focus his time on the integrity of your payment review process.

Processes for Supporting SAP Could be Strengthened

We spent considerable time in Chapter 4 describing the portions of an SAP audit dedicated to supporting SAP. If, during your daily management activities, or part of your self-assessment work, you determined that support procedures need improvement, document these in the known issues section of the audit binder as well. Perhaps user testing procedures over SAP changes are insufficient, or delayed communication of employee changes from HR is causing security gaps. Like you did for SAP configuration changes, document not only known process problems but also the steps that you have taken or will take to address these.

9.4   Systems: Preparing for the Auditor

In addition to preparing documentation for your auditor, during the audit preparation phase, you should also be preparing your SAP system for the review. Hopefully, by now you have appropriately configured available control settings in SAP, as we have discussed in previous chapters. When *preparing SAP for your auditor*, you typically:

▸ Create and test auditor IDs

▸ Reconcile to a non-production test environment

▸ Ensure resolution of prior audit issues

Each of these items facilitates the auditor's review, and doing these in advance will save time once the audit starts.

9.4.1   Creating and Testing Auditor IDs

If you recall from Chapter 1, your auditor may be an *internal auditor* or an *external auditor*. If an internal auditor is conducting your audit, most likely he is already part of your organization and already has an appropriate SAP ID (although depending on the review, you may need to temporarily grant access to information that he does not typically have as part of his normal setup). If your auditor is an external auditor, you'll typically either provide him with a temporary SAP ID with display-only access to portions of SAP that he needs for the review, or choose to not grant him direct access (and have him work with your staff to get the information that he needs).

> **Gotcha!**
>
> When establishing SAP access for your auditors, follow your corporate guidelines and do not give too much access. An audit concern could be raised regarding the SAP security administration process if the auditor can process transactions in production, see confidential information that he should not have access to, or update IMG settings. For auditors who are not part of your organization, also disable his access upon completion of the review or risk a concern related to termination of unused access.

In Chapter 8, we discussed the Audit Information System (AIS) within SAP, along with some of the pre-defined auditor profiles that are currently delivered with SAP. These profiles can be a good starting point for creating IDs for your auditors.

9.4.2   Reconciling to a Non-Production Test Environment

While not always the case, certain types of audit tests may require entering transactions into SAP and viewing how the system reacts (e.g., entering an amount over the established threshold and ensuring that SAP blocks the transaction). Don't allow anyone to enter fictitious transactions into your production system, even if you are convinced that SAP will block the transaction. As such, this type of audit testing is typically performed in a testing client. Because your audit is most likely over your production SAP client(s), however, the auditor needs a way to ensure that what he is seeing in the test is consistent with the behavior in production. As such, *reconcile* your test system to production and show any changes to either system since the last refresh of your test environment. Ideally, if you are able to refresh your test environment shortly before the audit, you can minimize reconciliation issues.

9.4.3   Ensuring Resolution of Prior Audit Issues

The final step in preparing your SAP system for the audit is to ensure that any prior audit issues have been *resolved*. Hopefully, these issues were resolved shortly after the last audit, and this is merely a secondary check to make sure something hasn't changed. Your auditor will definitely review each prior audit finding as part of the SAP audit. Findings that appear on consecutive audit reports raise a huge audit red flag (particularly if an agreed-on change was determined as a result of the prior audit), and will very likely result in more audit scrutiny across the entire review than if every issue was effectively addressed.

> **Investigate Root Causes**
>
> If you double-check prior audit findings that had been addressed, and find that something has come undone, investigate and be comfortable with what happened. During your root-cause analysis, you may find that someone in the organization is manipulating SAP against management's intent, and it's much better for you to find such an issue before your auditor does.

While this step may seem basic, it's surprising how many organizations have repeat audit findings. Double-check everything at this point. Even where problems were fixed, changes in personnel, errors in transports, processes degrading over time, or any number of factors can cause these fixes to come undone. A little extra time spent double-checking can prevent a large headache during the audit.

9.5 Employees: Preparing Your Team

The third and final component of your audit preparation is focused on your *employees*. Your documentation may be top notch, your SAP system may be appropriately configured and ready for the audit, but if your team is not ready, you are setting yourself up for problems. Prior to your SAP audit, spend time getting your team ready for the audit experience. A few considerations include:

- Explain the audit process
- Establish audit ground rules
- Backfill responsibilities
- Perform a readiness review
- Designate a facilitator

These additional steps will help ensure that your team is in sync and ready to do their part during the audit.

9.5.1 Explain the Audit Process

Many employees struggle during an audit because they simply do not understand the process. Spend time with your team, either individually or as part of a larger group session, *explaining* the audit process and what they can expect during the upcoming SAP review. Sharing the first several chapters of this book is a good start, and will help the discussion. Employees who understand the audit process, including why your auditor is posing the questions he is asking, are likely to be better auditees and support a more efficient and effective audit.

9.5.2 Establish Audit Ground Rules

Once your team understands the audit process, also establish (and communicate) a common set of *ground rules* for how your team will work with your auditor during the audit. In addition to the suggestions provided throughout this book, consider tips such as:

- Don't withhold information from the auditor
- Direct the auditor to someone who may know the answer if you do not
- Don't make jokes
- Clarify if you don't understand the auditor's question
- Don't assume that the auditor understands how SAP works

► Talk to your manager if you think the auditor's request is inappropriate

► Don't be adversarial

These tips may seem like common sense, but from our own audit experience, employees often don't understand the basics.

9.5.3 Backfill Responsibilities

Your auditor may need to spend a lot of time with certain employees, depending on his role. This can cause a lot of stress, particularly for key employees who may already work extended hours. If, based on the nature of the audit, you feel that certain employees may require a sizeable amount of time with your auditor, consider backfilling their daily responsibilities. This allows them to work with the auditor in an unrushed manner, getting your auditor the results that they need quickly, while ensuring that your key employees have sufficient time to answer questions and explain responses without feeling rushed and possibly leading the auditor down the wrong path. Without guidance, sometimes auditors may spend more time researching issues than need be, and a knowledgeable helping hand can help speed up the process and get the auditor out of your hair as quickly as possible.

9.5.4 Perform a Readiness Review

Sometimes, the best way to prepare for something is to practice, and an audit is not different. If you have never been through an SAP audit before, having an independent party perform a *readiness review* can provide tremendous value. Not only can you identify problems of which you might otherwise been unaware, you can also identify potential flags that your team may be creating based on how they interact with the reviewer. A readiness review does not need to replicate an entire audit to be valuable, and can often be performed for a fraction of the time. Typically, you bring in someone with audit experience, either from within your organization or through and external organization, to make an assessment and provide preliminary recommendations. The goal is to find potential problems early, and address any potential issues before the audit starts.

9.6 Expert Advice

Surviving an SAP audit can be a daunting feat, but as you have learned in this book it does not need to be. To help round out our advice, we sought *expert advice* from a cross-section of experts, including internal and external auditors, business manages, and consultants — some of whom have been on both the giving and receiving ends of audits. Their advice is consistent with what we have shared in this book, and falls into a number of key themes:

- Having the right perspective
- Incorporating audit thinking into your everyday work
- Preparing in advance
- Being organized
- Participating in the process, and staying in control

Take what they have to say to heart. These people are some of the best and the brightest, and each has useful advice to share.

9.6.1 Having the Right Perspective

Sometimes, audit success is all about attitude, and a number of our experts see this as one of the most critical success factors.

The Auditor as a Resource

David T. Flynn
18 years of governance, risk, and compliance experience
Managing Director, Detroit Resources Global Professionals

> *One of the best ways to survive an audit is to view the auditor as a project re-source rather than an obstruction or opponent. A project leader who is open to hearing about issues and takes them seriously will typically be treated fairly by the auditor. The best auditors will respect a project leader like this, and will not waste that person's time with insignificant findings.*

> *Whenever I have reviewed a major implementation, there are three things that almost always show up: weak security, inadequate documentation, and insufficient training. These issues are often the result of a well-intentioned project team that is trying to go-live on schedule. Security is put in loosely to ensure that no one is inadvertently locked out during the critical early days and weeks of a new system. Documentation and training may be wasted if significant changes to the system occur late in the project, so they are pushed back. In the long run, these issues can have serious impacts on the success of the implementation and serve as a source of audit issues well into the future.*

Check Your Attitude

Porter Broyles, ACDA

6 years of audit experience

Expert with ACL and continuous auditing

Continuous Controls Analyst

> *Audit's job is to help you succeed. The best audit engagements are the ones wherein the auditor and auditee work together. The auditor's job is to provide independent observations, but this does not mean it has to be adversarial. When the auditor comes to you, embrace the opportunity to improve your processes; don't see them as the enemy. Similarly, if an auditor approaches you from an adversarial position, work with him to see the possible win-win scenarios available by working together.*

> *Don't hide your concerns/problems; if audit stumbles across an issue, they will wonder what else is management hiding from them. If you are open about your concerns, audit might be able to validate your concern or find a solution that you've over looked. It also saves them from wasting their time and yours tracking down known issues.*

Advantage of a Positive Working Relationship

Jenny Banker

15+ years of business management experience

Distinguished HR Director

> *Ensuring that you have the right checks and balances in your processes allows you not to worry when you are about to have an audit. Also, getting prepared before they arrive is also crucial. I have gone through a variety of audits in my career and most have been quite positive. You need to be confident that you and your staff are doing the right things all along. The audit then merely confirms that your team and company have set up systems and processes well.*

> *Looking at auditors as part of your team instead of as the "enemy" also creates a much more positive outcome. Work with them, not against them. I have seen other departments not be responsive and antagonistic and it creates more "audit issues" than when you have an environment based on a positive working relationship.*

Just Another Business Event...

Joe Herr

40 years of experience helping organizations achieve leadership, excellence, and business sustainability

"The Horse Whisperer for Business"

Global Director for international consultancy

> *Never treat an audit any different than you would any normal everyday event in your business life. If you are forced to treat audits different than the way you perform your normal business activities, there are likely gaps in your normal business processes.*

9.6.2   Having an Audit Mindset

As we discussed in the first several chapters of this book, learning to think like an auditor and applying this type of thinking to your daily activities will help ensure a sustainable process for insulating you from audit-related concerns.

Apply Audit-Type Critical Thinking Skills Daily

Damon Rosenthal, CISA

18+ years of audit and IT security

Risk & Security Management at a large global financial institution

> *Prepare, plan, and execute by applying audit skills/thinking in your operations and building this mindset into your work all year. Consult audit if and when necessary. Conduct regular self assessments on your processes and procedures. Have a process in place to act on and remediate audit concerns promptly. Use this to get ahead of audits and stay ahead of trends. Conduct a post mortem audit process with your top people to discuss what was reviewed and comments made. Build processes to spot trends and factor them into your annual objectives and budgets for further remediation or enhancement work to stay ahead of audit expectations. Overall, you are doing your organization good by being proactive. Just think of the benefits of removing your management audit worries and impressing audit with your operations.*
>
> *If all else fails...hire the auditor! (look for audit experience when hiring)*

More than Survival, It's a Business Necessity

Kevin C. Carlson

Former VP of an international internal auditing firm

First of all, an organization's guiding control environment "goal" should be higher than "survival" of an outside audit. The primary benefit to an organization of strong controls is the financial, operational efficiency, and effective risk management. These benefits can be earned every day, regardless of whether an audit is occurring.

The key to audit "survival," in any case is pro-actively incorporating the control environment, policies, procedures, and the on-going measurement, and supervision to ensure that any outside audit findings are merely a confirmation that the control environment is sound. Depending on the aggressiveness and attitude of the outside auditor (it may be impossible to satisfy some), an on-going, pro-active best practice control effort, with clear plans, and expectations of strong controls, is the best defense. An organization can benefit from an outside opinion, even if the outside opinion is "OK."

Do it Right the First Time

Kevin C. Christ
IT Executive Consultant and Coach
Multiple Acting CIO roles
Former IT Consulting Partner with Deloitte

Process design, completed properly, provides an immediate leg up on future audit documentation. Process design, not completed properly, is destined to be repeated.

The business case for SAP or any ERP often contains a healthy estimate for reduction of work. Using the concepts of lean, best-practice, and re-engineering a generation ago, process engineers focus on removing all of the inefficiencies from the new streamlined, cross-functional processes. Often, the focus is on removing all activities that do not provide directly identifiable value to the end customer. With good intent, these teams then march forward and remove all of the "inefficient" control activities from the process; "controls don't add customer value" and tend to bog down the business processes. The thinking is, "Why do things like review and approve when you can just get it right the first time?"

However, neither the SEC nor the Audit Committee of the board quite see controls as unnecessary overhead. As a result, late in the implementation or immediately following, the controls have to be added or re-added to the processes and documented. Likewise, security is often a late entrant into the implementation and becomes a scramble to wrap-up around a relatively completed configuration.

My advice would be to understand the controls and security requirements early during process design, and to design and document correctly the first time. Consult with Internal Audit early and often in the requirements and configuration activities, and include them as an essential approval at key milestones.

9.6.3 Preparing in Advance

As we have also shared in this book, the time you spend preparing for an audit contributes to audit success.

Prepare and Self-Assess

Norman Comstock, CIA CGEIT CISA CISSP QSA
Over 15 years experience of internal audit/IT audit/GRC
Managing Director at UHY Advisors

To survive an SAP audit — proactively prepare for the audit. Audit pain is inversely relative to the degree of preparation. This anecdotal theorem can have an exponential effect in an SAP environment. Spot checking and regularly monitoring is good management practice to curb the potential for audit surprises. This is true for a newly deployed environment or a mature, "stable" environment. The age-old adage "know thyself" isn't just for philosophers and theologians. An annual risk assessment coupled with earnest self-assessments scattered over the course of the year in key SAP areas like security, customizations, change control, operations, and training can quickly indicate areas that need attention or may lead to future systemic failures. Think of the self-assessment as a diagnostic, surprise quiz that is administered weeks ahead of the big exam. You're not happy with the quiz or the timing, but it helped you prepare for the final exam.

Designing SAP specific self-assessment questionnaires can be pivotal in helping triage current or emerging issues quickly. An SAP specific self-assessment can also bring daylight to the obscure issues, risks, and mitigation alternatives. The self-assessment taker responds quickly to those items that they are sure about and investigate the items less familiar. A learning moment? An investment in better audits? Yes, because you groom the organization to be better-prepared auditees. Of course, self-assessments aren't bulletproof. Chalk it up to bravado, overconfidence, or themes more nefarious; sometimes, the responses provided are misleading. You end up with what the respondent wants you to believe instead of the real condition. "It's fine. We're still working on it but no one has complained. Our group has a growing set of competing priorities. Why does this matter?"

Contrasting the assessment results with metrics like emergency changes, open help-desk tickets, and number of new user requests, role changes, and terminations can be a compass to find the fuzzy semblance of truth. These metrics are the leading and lagging indicators of manual control fatigue, incomplete testing, inadequate training, unauthorized change, or business process evolution. The true state of the environment lies between how the users feel about the fidelity of the SAP environment and how IT is aligned with the business users' objectives. Cooler heads prevail when they take time to navigate the SAP landscape and plan for the audit hotspot. The "devil" of the audit is getting the auditees to understand the details that they are responsible for.

Don't Assume — Verify

Derek Warburton

SME (Retired) — Internal controls and corporate fraud detection

In my experience in working with many F1000 companies who have deployed SAP, there is often a general sense in senior management and often within the internal audit department that SAP, being a sophisticated and comprehensive system, will prevent many common internal control breaches.

The fact is that to some degree, deploying an ERP like SAP can indeed help shore up internal controls across an enterprise. But it doesn't occur simply by deploying the software. SAP has to be "told" or configured to best enable internal controls, because each organization has different processes.

The key message I tried to convey to organizations using SAP was not to assume that all controls and SOD are working effectively, and rather, be sure to test those controls with the same vigor as you would before you deployed SAP. In many cases, organizations found that not only were internal controls not working as effectively as they had hoped, but in some cases, the internal controls were less effective than what they previously had. That's not a reason to panic, but it's an eye opener for many organizations. The good news is that they can remedy the situation through fine tuning their SAP configurations, and continue to validate effectiveness of controls through on-going testing.

Don't assume that SAP or any other ERP is foolproof, especially early on in its deployment. Be vigilant with testing, and assume the worst is possible. If you've performed extensive testing for SOD and internal controls, and found little to be concerned about, then that's good news. But don't be surprised if you find many issues that need addressing or rectifying. Also don't underestimate the ability for someone or perhaps a couple of people working in concert (combining their abilities within SAP to perform specific tasks) to work around the internal controls. It may even be a well-intended workaround to expedite what is perceived as an urgent business process. The problem is that a control that can be breached for good reasons can also be breached for the wrong reasons.

To make this case more tangible, let me share a true story. I used to run a sales division for a company that produced audit analysis software. One of our customers (the internal audit department of a F1000 company) decided to purchase an add-on software component that facilitated easier data access and extraction of data from within SAP, for comprehensive audit testing. The customer was concerned about the effectiveness of internal controls with their SAP deployment. Our company did provide a price quotation to the customer. A couple of weeks later, our Accounting department notified me that we received a check from this company. The interesting aspect of this is that the company had never raised a P.O., and our company had never issued an invoice. Someone, well intended as they were, had indeed worked around the controls. And the total amount of money was for only a few thousand dollars. The irony of a control being breached in the process of acquiring technology specifically to test these types of controls is extraordinary. Imagine though if this person, or others who became aware of this control vulnerability, took advantage of this control weakness for unscrupulous and more costly outcomes.

SAP and other ERPs can provide tremendous value and can facilitate effective internal controls, but you must confirm these controls are working, just as you would if you didn't use SAP. Don't assume anything, other than the worst case. In fact, assume that until the configuration of SAP is fine tuned and tested, that some of your internal controls could be more vulnerable than they were with older systems in place.

Plan from Inception

Harvey Berger, CPA, CFE, CISSP, CISA, MCSE
16+ years of international experience in assessing and remediating internal controls over financial reporting
Specialist in forensic analysis, SAP compliance, and ERP GRC

Surviving a SAP audit is made much simpler if it's properly planned from inception; it's indeed all about planning! Although this sounds rudimentary, it's often overlooked and not given enough attention; however, it's vital for project success.

Audit planning must be prioritized along with senior management's commitment and tone that auditing is necessary, required, and value added. Lessons learned have proved that good business practices are consistently maintained with proper planning and senior management's continued support of the audit function.

Keys to a successful SAP audit:
SAP audit planning should start early, as early as in the requirement phase of the initial SAP implementation. It needs to be incorporated into the design of the SAP production environment to bring risk-based solutions along with key information to management and to auditors. This information has to be available, complete, and accurate. Each SAP project must take into account the business function along with the related audit requirements.

SAP audit planning should be performed by a competent risk-based person with extensive knowledge of risks, mitigating controls along with project management expertise.

The execution of these two key steps will drive audit success, and as a result, when the yearly audit work is to be performed, there is an established robust foundation build within SAP so that management and auditors can select their samples and obtain the information online and follow-up with minimal disruption.

Seek Advice and Coaching

Karen Kronauge, CIA
15+ years of financial management, audit, and compliance experience expert in policy management and compliance optimization
GRC consultant and former VP Finance

Whenever trying to do something well, it helps to seek guidance from a professional coach. An audit can be a scary endeavor, and the ramifications of an unflattering audit report can affect your reputation and potentially even your career. Be proactive and take steps to ensure that you are truly ready for an audit. Many organizations find it useful to bring in an expert audit facilitator and coach to help ready people, processes, and systems for audit scrutiny. A good coach can help you quickly identify potential problem areas, and address these long before an audit starts.

When seeking assistance, look for someone who has been an auditor, ideally with both internal and external audit experience. Your best defense against an audit is sometimes having an auditor on your team. You may be surprised to learn the frequency at which auditors incorrectly cite rules or requirements to try and emphasize their points of view — whether intentionally or the result of ignorance.

A good coach will know when your auditor is being unreasonable, and help you push back when necessary. He can be your advocate when working through potential issues, ensuring your case is presented in the best light. A good coach will help facilitate tough conversations, and help you develop reasonable plans to mitigate risk in a way that doesn't overburden your organization with inefficient control processes. By working with an outside audit coach, you get the advantage of expert advice when you need it most, without the cost of staffing and managing this role full time.

9.6.4 Being Organized

In addition to advance preparation, spending time internally to organize and ready your team and your processes will pay off when the auditors come in.

Use an Accepted Framework

Vance J. Sanders, CPA CISA CITP
15+ years of audit and financial accounting experience
Controller for a financial services firm

Prior to initiating any audit, general computer controls, application controls, or otherwise, it's essential to properly determine the desired purpose and extent of the examination. Once the purpose and extent have been agreed on, the next step is to identify the risk universe to be assessed. A prudent information system auditor will build the assessment using a generally accepted information technology risk framework. There are several strong IT risk frameworks available to utilize. The two that I have most often worked are: CobiT "Control Objectives for Information and related Technology" and Val IT. Both of these frameworks were created by the Information Systems Audit and Control Association (ISACA). I have found that developing an IT risk assessment within a proven risk framework has strengthened the IT assessments and produced much stronger and more valuable audit findings.

Maintaining Ongoing IT and User Alignment

Bob Mellgren, PMP, Six Sigma Green Belt
20 years of accounting, internal audit, IT operations management
Process improvement and ERP implementation expert
Manager at an international consultancy

One of the critical success factors for surviving an SAP audit, no matter the scope and level of audit, is making sure that you have 'seamless' coordination between the user community and your technical SAP support personnel. When internal audit conducts walkthroughs and interviews separately between the user community and technical SAP resources, unnecessary 'red flags' can occur when getting different answers from both constituents for the same questions. This can occur when coordination between the groups during periodic security audits (including review of segregation of duties 'collisions') and development cycles has not been as close as it should be.

To facilitate coordination, a 'best practice' would be to continue to maintain an SAP steering committee, including user and technical leads, even though major development of SAP may not be occurring during the present time. This can facilitate better SAP development and related understanding between all groups, which will lead to internal audit work that is not spent chasing 'false positives' (issues that may not exist but be the result of misunderstandings). In summary, a 'gapless' bridge between stakeholders can lead to audits that focus on real and 'value-add' observations as opposed to recommendations that don't match anyone's understanding of the system.

Use the Right Tool for the Job

Gary Reck
Vice President and Global Managing Director
The Hackett Group

Systems, not people, are the audit solution of the future. The technology is there, and if your firm is still relying on spreadsheets, security logs, and manual signoffs for input access to financial ERP data and a multitude of feeder systems, you may want to re-think your strategy.

While various software vendors also offer direct SAP audit tools to uncover fraud and the purposeful misuse of the data secured in the actual ERP environment itself, the Enterprise Performance Management (EPM) vendors offer the umbrella protection needed to cover the numerous feeder systems and links, both automated and manual, which are necessary to ensure that data integrity survives the auditor's most thorough investigations.

EPM was introduced to the financial marketplace in the mid- to late 1990s, and it has been used heavily since the inception of the Sarbanes-Oxley Act of 2002. Technology solutions such as EPM provide credible, auditable controls that can surround SAP (or any other ERP system). These solutions are clearly here to stay, as noted by the changing landscape over the last five years, which saw almost all of the EPM vendors being gobbled up by the ERP vendors (like Hyperion [Oracle], Cartesis, Business Objects, SRC and Outlooksoft [SAP], and Cognos [IBM]).

Finally, while there are many SAP partners out there, may I suggest that you keep an open mind and look for the best solution for your organization.

9.6.5 Participating in the Process, and Staying in Control

It has been said that you control your own destiny, and this additional advice involves actively participating in the audit process and staying in touch and in control. No one is a victim.

Take the Communication Reins

Todd McGowan, CPA, CISA
20 years of internal and financial audit experience
Emphasis on managing information technology risks
Former Deloitte Partner

When working with your auditor, take control of the communication process and don't be left in the dark:

1. *Request an upfront planning meeting to discuss the scope and timing of the auditor's fieldwork*

2. *Based on the scope, identify key individuals who the auditors will likely want to meet with first (e.g., SAP Security manager, Application change control manager, etc.).*

3. *Inform the key contacts who will be interacting with the auditors to make whatever time available they need and to be timely with responding to their questions or requests.*

4. *Request periodic (weekly) status meetings with the lead auditor to understand if there are any interim findings to discuss or to understand what the status of the audit work is.*

5. *Request a closeout meeting to discuss any findings and to make sure that the facts of the findings are clearly understood.*

Ultimately, it comes down to communication. If you haven't heard much from the auditor, don't be afraid to pick up the phone to call him or drop him an email to set up a time to discuss the progress of the audit or the findings.

Educate the Auditors

Daniel B. Langer, CPA, CIA, CCSA
25+ years in audit, accounting/finance, and business leadership roles
Experience working in a diversity of industries in over 25 world markets

As an auditee, it's important to be aware of what auditors typically do in planning and preparing for an audit. A good auditor will invest as much as 15% to 20% of the audit time in the pre-planning and planning phase of the audit. The remaining time will be devoted to the field work (65% to 70%) and developing the audit report and closing out the audit (the remaining 10% to 20% of the time).

It's not uncommon for the pre-planning and planning phases of the audit to be conducted primarily by the individuals designated with audit team leadership. These individuals tend to have more advanced experience, including more in-depth exposure to a range of both functional audit areas and potentially various industries. Often, these individuals have been trained in professional services, which would have provided them with experience in examining books, records, processes, and systems for a diversity of client companies. Although they will commonly have a team of individuals, potentially having less experience assigned to the fieldwork phase of the audit, the team leaders commonly perform much of the audit planning and preparatory work, along with the reporting and audit closing procedures.

You can expect the planning effort to include a review of a range of financial information, product literature, client service reports, backorder and sales pipeline reports, listings detailing key customers and related sales volumes, receivable aging schedules, history of writeoffs, key vendors and related summary disbursements, related cash management information and organization charts. It's helpful to understand historical trends so the some of the planning information obtained may be for an extended period of time, such as profit and loss, balance sheet, sales, and/or disbursement extending for the most recent 12- to 18-month period, looking for trends/shifts in financial performance.

Often, an analytical review of this information will be performed in parallel with introductory planning calls with key personnel expected to function in an audit liaison role. Conversations with these individuals help educate that the auditors about the business, key risks and challenges, recent changes, strengths, and areas for development.

The philosophy in working with the audit community should be one of openness and honesty. Although there are always opportunities for improvement, openness, and honesty about the area to be audited, including highlighting changes, challenges, and any anticipated hurdles in operating the function are important to disclose upfront.

Push Back When Necessary

Scott Dickinson

More than a decade of experience in governance, risk, and compliance
Former external auditor and internal audit consultant

> *No matter how much your auditors kick and scream — claiming they need more access to your SAP system to perform their testing — never, ever give them SAP_ ALL or similar privileged access to SAP. This will come back to haunt you for sure. Auditors don't get a 'pass' on your own internal control procedures just because they are audit.*

Know Your Rights

Lambert Lam

15+ years of risk management, internal audit, and technology experience in both consulting and corporate environments
Operational Risk Management Director for a financial services firm

> *You probably already know some basics about preparing for an audit, and making sure you manage that project and relationship professionally. But did you know that there are International Standards for the Professional Practice of Internal Auditing? Most audit departments will try to follow these standards even though they do not read them to you before the audit. And knowing a few key standards may help you prepare for an audit, and respond during an audit. If you feel that the audit is not meeting some of these standards, feel free to ask about gaps in a professional manner.*
>
> *Before the audit begins, consider the criteria that you have to determine whether management objectives and goals are accomplished. If you feel that they are adequate, document them to the extent possible and ensure that the audit leverages that information. Internal auditors must use this criteria in their evaluation of controls, if management criteria is adequate. Definitely ask for an explanation if the auditors do not feel that your criteria is sufficient. Asking for explanations leads to our next key standard.*
>
> *Audit communications must be accurate, objective, clear, concise, constructive, complete, and timely. If you feel the communication is unclear or timely, once again ask your audit team about it — professionally.*

Lastly, your auditors must possess the knowledge, skills, and other competencies needed to perform the audit. Be very careful about questioning whether this standard is met. But if you feel the team does not have the proper skill set, carefully discuss your concerns with audit management.

If you want to impress, or possibly astonish, your auditors, then you can mention the standards by number. Engagement objectives is covered under standard 2210 (and 2210.A3 for the example I used). Communication is covered under standard 2420. And tread lightly if you question whether they meet the Standard 1210, which covers proficiency.

9.7 Summary

In this chapter, we have shared specific steps to employ as you prepare for an upcoming audit. We have described documentation to provide the auditor in advance, steps for readying your systems for audit analysis, and techniques for preparing your team for the audit process. We have also shared a wealth of real-world audit advice for getting through an audit as painlessly as possible.

At this point in the book, you have learned about the audit process, you have received specific tips and advice for configuring SAP and designing your SAP-enabled business processes, and you have read about ways to prepare yourself for your next audit. Your success is now up to you. While we have shared a lot of advice, the breadth of SAP is such that there is plenty left unsaid. Hopefully, by now you understand the principles behind an audit and recognize the type of thinking to apply throughout all of your processes to be better prepared. By reading this book, you have already taken the first step toward surviving an SAP audit. Apply what you have learned, begin to apply audit-type thinking in your decision-making processes, and don't hesitate to seek additional advice and support.

The Author

 **Steve Biskie** is the founder of ERP Audit Solutions, a consultancy focused on helping companies manage the SAP audit process through custom training, coaching, and consulting solutions. He is also a Director at ACL Services Ltd, a worldwide provider of audit analytics software. He has been involved in the audit of SAP systems and implementation of GRC processes in SAP environments since 1993 as an external auditor, internal auditor, consultant, and project team member. Steve was a part of the SAP Influence Council for the first version of SAP's Management of Internal Control solution, has chaired SAP Steering Committees, and ran an internal controls compliance initiative for a multi-billion dollar organization. Steve is a nationally-recognized expert on SAP audit and control, and speaks frequently on the subject at various international conferences. Holding an MBA in Accounting with a concentration in Accounting Information Systems from Michigan State University, Steve is a Certified Information Systems Auditor (CISA), Certified Information Technology Professional (CITP), and a non-practicing Certified Public Accountant (CPA). He can be contacted at *steve@erpauditsolutions.com*.

Index

C

Teaches how to design, configure, and implement the FSCM Collections, Dispute, Credit, and Biller Direct components

Provides proven guidance and real case studies for extending an ERP Financials infrastructure with FSCM

Includes coverage of advanced topics including extensions, re-porting with NetWeaver BI, and workflow design

Sreedhar Narahari

Receivables and Collections Automation with SAP FSCM

The primary purpose of the book is to provide finance team members, implementation project managers, and consultants with a comprehensive, practical guide to the FSCM applications available for automating the receivables and collections management functions. Focusing primarily on the core functions of the Biller Direct, Credit Management, Collections Management, and Dispute Management applications, the book offers readers a roadmap for implementation, integration, and customization.

approx. 450 pp., 79,95 Euro / US$ 79.95
ISBN 978-1-59229-245-5, March 2010

>> www.sap-press.com

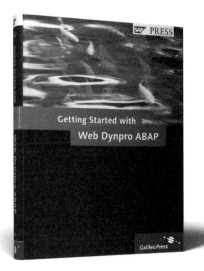

Covers all Finance-related processes, from purchasing and production to distribution

Teaches how to integrate Financial Accounting and Controlling with MM, PP, and SD

Details financial statement preparation and reporting

Andrea Hölzlwimmer

Optimizing Value Flows with SAP ERP

This book is written to teach financial consultants, IT managers, and integration consultants how value flows can be enhanced across an organization's entire finance and logistics chain. The book takes a process-oriented approach to the problems presented by non-integrated value flows in an organization and explains the solutions available in the SAP system. With this book you'll understand integrated value flows and learn about the important integration concepts, such as management of master data. You'll explore the central processes of purchasing, production, distribution accounting, and reporting, and you'll understand the impact of system settings and integration points as they relate to the overall process.

approx. 350 pp., 79,95 Euro / US$ 79.95
ISBN 978-1-59229-298-1, Dec 2009

>> www.sap-press.com

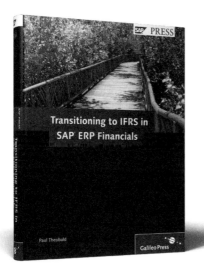

Provides a detailed overview for transitioning SAP ERP Financials to IFRS

Features practical coverage of the complete conversion project, including a case study

Includes the US GAAP/IFRS deltas and their mapping to SAP ERP components

Paul Theobald

Transitioning to IFRS in SAP ERP Financials

This book will provide conversion project teams with a roadmap for preparing their SAP ERP Financials systems for conversion to IFRS. It will include detailed coverage of the transition process, an overview of the US GAAP/IFRS deltas and how they are mapped in ERP Financials, and real-world advice from an IFRS conversion project at a large petrochemical company. Its primary purpose is to gives finance professionals, executives, technical staff, project managers, and consultants a concise guide to jump-starting their IFRS projects in upgrade or non-upgrade scenarios.

approx. 320 pp., 79,95 Euro / US$ 79.95
ISBN 978-1-59229-319-3, Dec 2009

>> www.sap-press.com

Provides a comprehensive guide to using the key SAP Geneeral Ledger functions effectively

Includes detailed coverage of SAP General Ledger processes, design, and customization options

Features extended sections on integration with subledgers, customization with BAPIs, and fast-close optimization

Shivesh Sharma

Maximizing SAP General Ledger

Successful integration of the SAP General Ledger into an existing infrastructure can make a significant impact on the ROI of an ERP Financials upgrade. Many users, however, lack the guidance necessary to sort through the integration and customization options available, particularly as consulting budgets are being slashed around the world. This book provides implementation teams, functional and technical teams, and end-users with a roadmap for the maximum utilization of the SAP General Ledger. This book focuses using the General Ledger in real-world situations and details how to customize and optimize it for specific business processes, and it teaches how to and integrate it with other SAP components. It will also help readers develop knowledge and strategies for enhancing the SAP General Ledger and integrating it with other SAP services and components.

approx. 500 pp., 79,95 Euro / US$ 79.95, ISBN 978-1-59229-306-3, Dec 2009

>> **www.sap-press.com**

Interested in reading more?

Please visit our Web site for all
new book releases from SAP PRESS.

www.sap-press.com